AUG -- 2021

AMERICANON

AMERICANON

An Unexpected U.S. History in

Thirteen Bestselling Books

JESS McHUGH

DUTTON

DUTTON

An imprint of Penguin Random House LLC
penguinrandomhouse.com

LIBRARY OF CONGRESS CATALOGING-IN-PUBLICATION DATA
Names: McHugh, Jess, author.
Title: Americanon: an unexpected US history in thirteen bestselling
books / Jess McHugh.
Other titles: Unexpected US history in thirteen bestselling books
Description: [New York] : Dutton, [2021] | Includes bibliographical
references and index.
Identifiers: LCCN 2020055756 (print) | LCCN 2020055757 (ebook) |
ISBN 9781524746636 (hardcover) | ISBN 9781524746650 (ebook)
Subjects: LCSH: National characteristics, American. | Books and
reading—United States—History. | Social values—United
States—Miscellanea. | United States—Social life and
customs—Miscellanea.
Classification: LCC E169 .M454 2021 (print) |
LCC E169 (ebook) | DDC 973—dc23
LC record available at https://lccn.loc.gov/2020055756
LC ebook record available at https://lccn.loc.gov/2020055757

Printed in the United States of America
1st Printing

BOOK DESIGN BY KATY RIEGEL

For John J. Schortmann Jr.—a talented storyteller,

an avid reader, and an American in

the best sense of the word

That which we do is what we are. That which we remember is, more often than not, that which we would like to have been; or that which we hope to be. Thus our memory and our identity are ever at odds; our history ever a tall tale told by inattentive idealists. RALPH ELLISON[1]

Contents

AMERICANON

Introduction

Nothing seemed to dampen the din of Noah Webster's home in the early nineteenth century. With his seven children running through the house, peals of laughter and shrieks of play punctuated his workdays. The sound of water boiling for tea or his wife preparing lunch—there was never silence. Try as he might, Webster could never find the peace required to concentrate. One day, a solution finally dawned on him: a material that could dull even the boom of a crashing ocean. He filled the walls of his study with sand.[1]

Finally free to think in silence, he turned to his life's work: writing the American dictionary. Noise would be only one of Webster's innumerable foes throughout his decades-long project. He feared regional division, foreign cultures, and variations in accent. His plans for the dictionary—and for the United States at large—extended far beyond the task of lexicography. Webster longed to codify national identity, to create a single, galvanizing definition of "American." His critics decried his project as "perfectly absurd,"[2] "vulgar,"[3] and "subtle poison."[4] But Webster's dictionary would succeed in becoming one of the perennial bestsellers in U.S. history, defining much more than words for generations of Americans. In writing a dictionary that many Americans now refer to as simply *the* dictionary, he hoped to give them a blueprint for a shared culture.

It would become one of a number of American "bibles": those dog-eared books for daily life that ostensibly taught readers one subject, all while subtly instructing them about their role in society and their responsibilities to family and to country. These were dictionaries, school primers, cookbooks, how-to guides, and self-help manuals—spanning the full range of our 245-year history—many of which sold tens of millions of copies, setting out specific archetypes for the ideal American, from the self-made entrepreneur to the devoted homemaker or the humble farmer. What makes these books so compelling—and why they are worth studying—is that underneath their surface are the blueprints for American values that endured long after publication. The foundation for American popular culture can be located more easily not in highbrow literary books—or even in the Constitution, a text that fewer than half of Americans read[5]— but in the ordinary, instructional books that average Americans have consulted every day.

All the books in this collection are either guidebooks or texts with an explicitly didactic bent. While a cookbook, a self-help book, and a dictionary might seem disparate, they are united in the way they functioned in people's lives. These how-to books taught people certain skills, all while delivering messages about American beliefs, encoding everything from individualism and self-reliance to meritocracy and personal freedom. People also tended to treat these books in a similar fashion, not reading them once and putting them away but rereading them, using them every day, and even passing them on to their children. Novels might be the books we love hardest and remember most fondly, but these are the books that raise us. What better way to understand a people than to look at the books they consumed most—not the ones they were told to read by teachers or parents, or read once and put on a shelf, but the ones they returned to again and again, with questions about everything from spelling to sex?

I've chosen books from the full scope of American history to the end of the twentieth century, based on their outsize influence and their status as bestsellers, usually in the tens-of-millions range (using data from *The New York Times*, *Publishers Weekly*, and a select few authoritative lists).[6] To avoid personal bias, I relied heavily on the data, focusing on those nonfiction how-to books that have consistently sold the most and influenced the greatest number of people throughout history. But sales in themselves were not enough of a reason for me to include a book here. I combed through newspaper and magazine archives to see which books struck a chord in the national conversation, which authors went on to spread their message through syndicated columns, radio shows, and sequels. I looked also to the books that spurred some change in an established custom or mode of thinking, or those that inspired other authors to write a bestselling book promoting a similar ideology. Academics across disciplines of American cultural study— literature, history of science, and history of publishing—have deeply informed this list, helping to discern not just what sold well but what reflected or reshaped the ideals of our national consciousness throughout history.

These bestsellers showed Americans what they could aspire to: namely, an ever-evolving archetype that addressed the challenges, conflicts, and insecurities of its time. They reveal the extent to which the things we take for granted about being American—freedom, justice, and liberty for all—are part of a constructed narrative in the goal of survival, economic prosperity, and social stability. Like most myths, they are lodged somewhere between an aspirational ideal and a pernicious delusion. But the gap between reality and the mythology that these books represent can offer a glimpse into our shifting understanding of what being American means. They allow us to see how we've arrived in a time where fact is up for debate and American identity seems more divided than ever. These books grapple with questions such as: What does it take to be a good American? And who gets to decide?

The relevance of how-to books is a product of American culture itself. If one of the highest compliments we pay one another is the moniker of "self-made," then asking for help becomes at least a little shameful. These books have helped generations of Americans avoid that awkward need that everyone has for assistance. If we can ask a book for help—the logic goes—then at least we do not have to ask another person, much less a stranger, a priest, or a government program.

Beyond their practical purposes, these books served as a refuge from ambiguity, offering both reassurances of who "we" were and the promise of control in times of turmoil. The appearance of many of these books was clustered around war, economic depression, or societal upheaval: their publication tended to follow the American Revolution, the Civil War, the Great Depression, and World War II, to name a few. Our society is more uncontrollable, disparate, and diverse than these authors would want us to believe, but their books served as a salve for national tumult, and their vision of the "good American" gives us fresh insight into our own identity.

Noah Webster and Dale Carnegie wrote our national story just as Benjamin Franklin and Thomas Jefferson did. Their beliefs and quirks became the values and habits of millions of Americans, woven into our cultural DNA over generations of reading and rereading. And yet their motivations—ranging from a desire to be useful or an attempt to cope with personal trauma, all the way up to commercial gain and nationalist fervor—often remain unexamined. These authors at once recorded elements of American customs or behavior and shaped the culture by codifying it. They alone did not invent the ideas of the self-made man or the domestic housewife, but they amplified existing strains of thought to the point of becoming mass culture, all while mixing in their own agendas, incorporating their fingerprint into the daily lives of millions of people. Reference books or guidebooks are meant to convey facts without ulterior motive. But these books were forged in the crucible of their authors' personal tragedies, secret hopes, and burning desires for their country. At the same time, what I see in the lives of these authors was not simply a desire for control (though that

is certainly there) but also a real resilience. The books they created are the result of personal and national trauma, and the stories they wrote come out of survivorship. Their stories—which
have become "our" stories—are a reflection of the idiosyncratic,
sometimes visionary, and always flawed people who wrote them.

Many of these authors' understanding of what "American"
meant was as much about defining who it was as who it was not.
You will note in this collection a striking absence of nonwhite
authors and LGBTQ authors. Up until very recently, our bestselling "authoritative" texts in this genre were written primarily
by white men, with a large number from fervently religious
communities. *Americanon* is as much about what is left out and
repressed by these books as what is in them. Each of these authors had a very specific vision for what the ideal American
looked like, and that ideal was often predicated on uniformity,
limiting who could be an American from the earliest conceptions of the word. We have a white, mostly male canon of bestsellers because privilege serves as an echo chamber in which
only certain voices emerge. Furthermore, many of our most
closely held American beliefs—from meritocracy to the power
of the individual—are self-perpetuating, functioning as a justification for who is at the top.

Part of the value in studying shared culture, or canon, is not
only to look critically at what gets included but also to think
about the ways in which two (or 2 million) people reading the
same text can land at such different conclusions about its meaning. It is why these books have such a biblical quality. Much like
the Constitution itself, a book such as *How to Win Friends and
Influence People* or Emily Post's *Etiquette in Society, in Business,*

in Politics and at Home can inspire opposite conclusions about what the book is trying to tell its audience. I challenge readers to revisit these texts in this new way, to think about people's beliefs as a path from author to text to culture, rather than a natural evolution of "right" and "wrong" ideas. Why this lens of reading history is important, too, is that these books were designed to appeal to some aspect of popular culture. They were made not for the few but for the many, and in that way, they offer an especially poignant vision into what people feared, loved, hoped for, and worried about at their times of publication.

Like many Americans, I grew up with *Merriam-Webster's Dictionary* and *The Old Farmer's Almanac*, as well as cookbooks, advice books, and all other types of self-help and how-to books. I also credit my maternal grandfather in particular for my interest in these books. He was a quick-witted person with a love of learning, always reading biographies and travel books, and he had a special fondness for the kind of self-improvement books that fill the chapters of *Americanon*. At the top of the family split-level home in Stoughton, Massachusetts, he hung framed copies of the Constitution and the Declaration of Independence alongside *Poor Richard's Almanac*. Later, as a journalist, I became fascinated by these types of books as cultural objects after I learned of Webster's fanatical motivations—by way of an offhand comment in a lecture. I had never imagined that the dictionary that sat on my shelf, guiding me through primary school and then college and even the early phases of being a journalist, had been written by a born-again Christian nationalist who hoped American English would become as different from British English as Swedish or Dutch was from German.

I have struggled to limit myself to ten chapters, and there are many, many books that remained on a shortlist for several years (everything from *Narrative of the Life of Frederick Douglass* to *Who Moved My Cheese?* and *The Secret*). There were also the books that felt like canon to me—that everyone *I* knew read and owned—but did not have the numbers behind them. (For my Massachusetts third-wave upbringing, this book was *Our Bodies, Ourselves*.) Writing about American culture in and of itself poses its own set of problems. The idea of talking about a singular culture presents a challenge in a country as vast and diverse as this one—who is to say that what feels part of the dominant culture in Seattle or Macon, Georgia, is the same as what "American" means to Bostonians or New Yorkers or residents of Cheyenne, Wyoming? Indeed, what many of these authors accomplished was to create an idealized vision of a unified America that in turn exerted a pull over the reality of a regionally, politically, and ethnically diverse nation. When I tell friends and dinner-party acquaintances that I am writing a history of bestsellers, they usually rattle off a list of books—some you will find here, some that did not make the cut, and some I have never heard of. *Americanon* is not intended to be a complete history of all the bestselling books that served this role but rather a starting point. I hope it will spark conversation about the books that shaped your community and your generation.

In revisiting these books and their messages about Americanness, we have the opportunity to look at the "truths" that we take for granted about our country. What are the ideals that we still unfailingly believe at the core of ourselves? What are the stories we have told ourselves so often and so convincingly about what being an American means that they seem beyond question? Perhaps the one that resurfaces the most is that the United States represents a place where anyone can go to try something new, to be "self-made." What I saw in my Irish ancestors who had toiled in Massachusetts mills—or in my Italian great-grandmother, who was forced to drop out of high school to work in a shirt factory but went on to become a respected leader in local politics—was what so many of us like to believe about the United States: that we all have a chance. That this is the place where hard work and the right attitude can be leveraged for a better life. And sometimes that is true, and the many stories like those in my own family (and in so many other American families) serve as a testament to that belief. It is hardly true for everyone who has come here, however, and it is at present truer for residents in countries such as France, Denmark, and Canada. These stories, the mythical ones that have come to feel like objective truth, are the ones I hope to look at most closely here. This book is more a reevaluation than a revisionist takedown; just because we have often failed to live up to our own ideals does not mean that they cease to exist.

Reexamining popular culture is an exercise in disillusionment, even humility. Living as an American in France, I am frequently lectured in all the ways the United States is uniquely bad (usually some combination of geopolitical hawkishness and the Coca-Cola corporation). It has made me curious about the ways in which we are unique, even if not uniquely good. In writing this book, I found myself at times disappointed by and at times nostalgic for the United States as I had understood it as a child, or for the United States of Frank Capra movies—all while understanding that this vision of America was necessarily unreal, a combination of partial truths, mythos, and imagination. The word "nostalgia" comes from the Greek *nostos* for "coming home" and *algos* for "pain."[7] I hope this book can serve as a homecoming for those who reckon with our complex history and yet still hope, despite everything, to return to the place they are from.

❀

CHAPTER ONE

The Old Farmer's Almanac (1792–)

Reaching *The Old Farmer's Almanac* office in Dublin, New Hampshire (population 1,543),[1] requires a nearly two-hour drive from any major city in the Northeast. The headquarters sit sandwiched between a barn, the town hall, the fire department, and a typical New England colonial church. For all its rural charm, semitrucks now whiz by along Route 101, on the east west highway that cuts across the state. Standing in front of the red Cape-style building, you can see the tip of a white-slatted steeple peeking out from the church behind. An American flag waves over the swinging door, and potted plants dot each of its window boxes. Inside, the lobby of the *Almanac* building might be mistaken for the living room of a favorite grandmother. Back issues of *The Almanac*, calendars, and all kinds of bric-a-brac—a painted wooden rooster, the errant fern, and a watering-can-turned-planter with a mini American flag—surround a pair of wooden rocking chairs in front of the reception desk.

Upstairs in his cubicle, Tim Clark, *The Almanac*'s then chief fact-checker and one of its editors, worked here in some capacity for forty-two years. Since our interview he has retired, but *The Almanac* is such an integral part of his life that he plans to continue writing the "weather doggerel" on the calendar pages in his spare time. Clark took classes in folklore while at Harvard, but he can also tell you which time of year is best for planting okra or how to whip up a homemade apple-and-parsnip soup with calvados cream. He cracks very dry jokes about empty rocking chairs, and he once wrote an article entitled "100 Ways to Avoid Dying."[2] *The Almanac*, he said, exists as a "teeter-totter" between the practical and the poetic[3]—but it's a description that could just as easily apply to Clark himself. On a recent fall day, as the leaves were starting to change in southern New Hampshire, Clark leaned back in his chair, his eyes bright behind thick glasses. He said, "So, here we are. We're in September now, right. So, September 2019. And today's the sixteenth. Today, physicist educator Ursula Franklin was born in 1921, and the high tides in Boston are 5.7 feet and 5.5 feet. The sun rose at 6:42 in Boston, eight minutes later here, and will set at 7:12. So, we're very close to the equinox, which means it's a twelve-hour-and-thirty-minute day."[4]

This is the kind of information that Tim Clark—and, by extension, *The Old Farmer's Almanac*—has at his fingertips. At a time when few people know the high tides in Boston on a given day (much less the birthday of physicist educator Ursula Franklin), *The Almanac* remains a source of both practical information and whimsical tidbits. Like most farmer's almanacs, the annually published book provides tide tables, sunrises, and sunsets as well as fun tips, jokes, and recipes. Surprisingly to many—including some of the *Almanac* editors themselves—this information has remained valuable to Americans since *The Almanac*'s first publication in 1792. Even now, *The Almanac* sells a staggering 3 million copies per year on average[5] (for reference, *The New York Times* in 2020 had a print circulation of 831,000).

"The secret of *The Old Farmer's Almanac* is: 'pay attention,'" said Clark. "Pay attention to the sky, and the winds, and the tides, and the number of acorns on the ground in the fall, and what the animals are doing, and which way the birds are flying. Pay attention. And that's what a farmer in 1792—or 1292—had to do to survive."[6] *The Almanac* invites its readers to look more closely at the sediment of everyday life. It's a call to observe the natural world, both the grand and the humble: eclipses and harvest moons but also changing leaves and hatching insects. In the present day, many readers might not *need* to know how to pickle vegetables or build a chicken coop in order to survive the winter, but they seem to need *The Almanac* for something else, something more symbolic and intangible. Watching things grow connects readers to a tradition that exists outside a highly technologized, often isolated modern world. Almanacs instead exist within a broader tapestry of folklore, according to Clark, which can be defined as "'the inextinguishable hope that all that is wrong in the world can somehow be put right.' So, there's a cure for everything."[8]

Reading *The Old Farmer's Almanac* now can still make a reader feel as if everything can be put right. More than two centuries after its first publication, it still has the same folksy suggestions for everything from natural pain relievers to animal mating schedules, the same format for its farming calendar, even the same style of illustrations. There is a comfort not just in its continuity with the past but also in this idea that we can still reconnect to that past just by planting tomatoes on our windowsills or baking our own bread. At a time when American identity seems ever more fractured, there's something uniquely reassuring, possibly escapist, about reading *The Almanac*. Paging through it gives even the least talented gardener the feeling that she, too, could return to the land with just a little help. It reminds us of this imagined easier time of self-reliance, small communities, and friendly neighbors. And yet, the idea that eighteenth-century America was a less complicated time, or that the life of the small farmer was simple, is its own kind of American story—a seed of truth about the United States' agrarian roots, mixed with generations of mythology that have grown so intertwined in the intervening years as to be indistinguishable from one another.

From the start, *The Almanac* served these dual purposes of the practical and the poetic: the book gave readers concrete information about farming, all while starting to build this mythic narrative around the American farmer as the model citizen. In *The Old Farmer's Almanac*, we find a vision of the farmer as self-sufficient, smart but not overly educated, patriotic, and civically engaged—all elements that would become foundations of the ideal early American. This annual text—one of the oldest continually published periodicals in the United States—served as a guide not just for farming but for citizenship as well (whether its founding author intended it that way or not). This almanac told farmers when the sun rose but also where to vote, how to pay their taxes, and even how much money the president made. In much subtler ways, it taught them that the work they did was important, vital not just for their own survival but for that of their community and also their nation. It provided a workable structure that cemented values of patriotism and religious freedom, serving as an early template for some of the most treasured American principles.

Out of more than one hundred early American almanacs,[9] *The Old Farmer's Almanac* is one of only a few to have survived throughout our history (along with its rival, the Maine-based *Farmers' Almanac*). For at least the first fifty years in U.S. history, a regional almanac was one of the only books that many Americans would have possessed (some 40 percent of rural New England households did not own a single book during this period, not even a Bible).[10] As such, it took on an outsize importance in a culture where books were rare commodities. Almanacs were some of the first sources to distribute foundational texts such as the Declaration of Independence, and at this crucial moment in American history, their pages brought together the United States' earliest values, from individualism and personal freedom to self-reliance and religious tolerance. As it went on, this particular almanac would shape those beliefs retroactively, too, imbuing an intense nostalgia for the past that was part real and part imagined.

❀

The first edition of *The Old Farmer's Almanac* appeared in 1792, barely three years after the U.S. Constitution came into force.

George Washington was serving his first term as president (it cannot be said that he was "in the White House," as the White House did not yet exist). Just as quickly as the Continental Army had been formed, its regiments summoned up through the ringing of bells in dozens of town squares, it was mostly disbanded. Newly christened Americans were left to cope with both the practical work of nation building and the psychological task of national unity. They had survived not just battles but also hunger and cold, the soldiers' bloody footprints in the snow at Valley Forge seared into the memory of thousands of young Americans. And yet, the lore of the American Revolution celebrated a kind of David-versus-Goliath victory in which a group of ragtag American farmers had trounced the British Empire, the small farmer's moral superiority proving itself on an international stage. While many elementary school students still learn about the American Revolution as an international war of the United States versus Britain (and Britain versus France), it was also a civil conflict, one that pitted neighbor against neighbor and father against son. Now the nascent country was faced with the prospect of establishing some kind of national identity across a disparate landmass that included Americans of French, British, and German origin—not to mention the thousands of enslaved people, indentured servants, Indigenous tribes, and free Black people who would be excluded from this origin story.

In the midst of this chaos, *The Old Farmer's Almanac*'s author, Robert B. Thomas, grew up in the years leading up to the Revolution.[11] He spent most of his life on his father's Massachusetts farm, and yet technically, he became the resident of four towns and two parishes[12]—so quickly was the landscape of his homeland changing, transforming from colony to state. By the time he published his first almanac in 1792, it was released for a new country. Little is known about Thomas's life, and that which does survive comes mostly from the autobiographical accounts he wrote for publication in *The Almanac* itself in 1833–39. He lived in what is now West Boylston, Massachusetts, a town that even today has fewer than ten thousand residents.[13] Back then it was little more than a village, with farms dotting the rolling hills near the Quinapoxet and Stillwater Rivers. Throughout his childhood, Massachusetts remained steeped in superstition. As enlightenment crept across New England, there was no more mass hysteria about witches (although the nineteenth century would see a tuberculosis-fueled vampire panic),[14] but folklore and superstition continued to mark daily life. Massachusetts residents took pains to ward off bad luck, and small details such as an empty rocking chair or a cat sitting with its tail toward the fire[15] were considered bad omens. Farming, too, was full of signs about good and evil forces at work—eclipses, late snow or early frost, diseased crops, pests—and many of these were considered marks not just of nature but of virtue as well.

Where most were content with a life that revolved around the farms, the several churches, and the one tavern, Thomas spent much of his time in his father's unusually large library,[16] searching for answers to the questions about daily life that eluded him. He was not satisfied when the weather was good and the harvest plentiful—he needed to understand why it happened and how to predict what might occur in the future. Separated by an ocean and nearly two centuries, Thomas grew passionate about the work of Italian astronomer Galileo Galilei.[17] He pored over

Galileo's writings about sunspots, fascinated by this idea that the eleven-year cycles of spots on the sun affected the weather on Earth. From his remote rural perch, Thomas began to consider not just the workings of the seasons in Massachusetts but the machinations in the cosmos that put them in place. *The Old Farmer's Almanac* still keeps Thomas's secret formula for determining the weather forecasts housed in a black box in the office in New Hampshire,[18] but it is thought to be derived at least in part from Galileo's seventeenth-century theory. This fascination with astronomy would lead him to a broader interest in the creation of almanacs—and some of the only official schooling he would enjoy in his life.

After the spring planting had been finished and his father's farmhouse prepared for summer, Thomas left home to study mathematics with Professor Osgood Carleton in Boston in 1792,[19] with the goal of writing his own almanac. It was there that he had his first taste of cosmopolitan life—brief though it turned out to be. Thomas was forced to flee Boston in August 1792 after only a few months, as a smallpox outbreak racked the city.[20] Smallpox remained one of the deadliest threats in eighteenth-century New England life, and Boston was determined to root it out. The city had started inoculating its residents several decades prior[21]—usually by scraping a bit of the disease off an active sufferer and inserting it under the skin of a healthy person. By the late eighteenth century, an entire smallpox epidemic protocol was in place, in which the city inoculated as many people as possible while shipping the infected to an island quarantine off the coast of Boston. If the person was too sick to move, he would be confined to his home, surrounded by a makeshift fence with a waving red flag designed to warn visitors away.[22] Convinced by a doctor that his young age and good health would make his inoculation a simple one, Thomas traveled back to central Massachusetts to undergo the process in a small country hospital.[23] The twenty-six-year-old farmer was soon covered with a blistering red rash, the telltale sign of active smallpox creeping across his entire body. He would spend the next month in the hospital with a soaring fever, likely enduring all the diarrhea, vomiting, and open sores that go with the infection. Thomas walked out of the hospital five weeks later a dead man. "It was, I afterwards learned, currently reported in the neighboring towns that I was dead,"[24] he wrote in his memoirs.

Very much alive, Thomas put the finishing touches on his almanac following his stint in the hospital. The first issue came out in 1792 (for the 1793 calendar year). *The Farmer's Almanac* (the "old" qualifier would be added later) debuted amid dozens of other competing almanacs. At the time, there were more than one hundred almanacs in print in the United States, with nineteen available for sale in nearby Boston alone.[25] Almanacs existed across the states, tailored to different climates and regional backgrounds, a choose-your-own adventure of early American print culture. They flourished particularly in the North, however, where small farming was more prevalent and where comparatively higher literacy rates led to an explosion in the printing of almanacs. A local almanac was one of the most likely books to be in a typical American household at this time. As such, competition among almanac writers was fierce, with the editors and the publishers developing intense, celebrity-feud-style rivalries, publicly accusing one another of plagiarism and stealing trade secrets. After Thomas's first edition sold a staggering three thousand copies that first year, he had to deal with such infighting and accusations (some of it merited, according to contemporary almanac editors).[26] And yet, circulation tripled the following year to nine thousand copies, and by 1826—fifty years after the Declaration of Independence—it had succeeded as the premier American almanac, printing a cumulative 1.8 million copies.[27]

Those first volumes read like an everything-you-need-to-know guide to being a model American citizen. Thomas was not the only almanac author taking this approach, but his book is exceptionally well-rounded, containing nearly everything that a farmer in 1792 needed to know. That included the dates of vacations at Harvard and Dartmouth, tricks for getting rid of caterpillars, and reminders to chop wood, check bees, prune trees, and "attend to your doves."[28] One page of the 1794 edition lists recipes for how to make cheese and refine sugar, and the next page contains a complete list of all U.S. senators.[29] Later editions would include the names of all members of the executive branch and even the salaries of many government representatives. There are court dates by state and religious service schedules. The 1794 edition also includes a book recommendation for farmers with extra time on their hands in December: Thomas suggested cozying up to the fire with a copy of Benjamin Franklin's *Autobiography*.[30] From work to religion to government to leisure, *The Almanac* asserted a guiding hand in every single aspect of daily life.

It's hard to pinpoint exactly what made Thomas's almanac such a runaway success. Editors of *The Almanac* like to say that it was more accurate, but *The Almanac* still only correctly predicts the forecast about 52 percent of the time,[31] even with the advanced meteorological equipment of today (*The Almanac* continues to claim that its accuracy is 80 percent).[32] It may have been Thomas's writing style and longevity that resonated with readers. Unlike many competing almanacs, *The Old Farmer's Almanac* had the same editor for more than half a century. Perhaps more important, it seemed to capture something of the American spirit at the time. Five years after the Constitution had been written—and only three after it had gone into effect—it was a new almanac for a new world, a handbook to American life. While printing information about statehouses or Quaker meetings might not initially seem significant, it started to weave a tradition of democracy into daily life for average Americans, physically tying together their farming cycles and the cycles of their government. This juxtaposition—alongside *The Almanac's* status as one of just two or three books that many early Americans owned[33]—served as one of the earliest frameworks for that most cherished American archetype: the small farmer. In *The Almanac*, we see the yeoman farmer as a patriot and model citizen, the foundation of the story the United States would tell about its origins. Like most fables, it came from a partial truth—rooted in the actual prevalence of farming in the early United States—but the idealized story of American agricultural life would loom ever larger as time went on.

The small farmer was rarely without his almanac, either in a pocket or hanging on a string within reach, there to guide him from planting to harvest (and anywhere else he might need to go, as it included a list of all the roads between local towns). *The Almanac* still has a hole drilled into the top left corner of each copy, as it is made to hang on a kitchen hook or from a string in the woodshed, there whenever you need to consult it. "The hole is critical, because it says you don't read it and throw it away or put it on a bookshelf; you hang it up where you can find it,"[34] explained Clark. The answers were with readers all the time. And unlike the Bible, *The Almanac* was not sacred and not heavy—so a farmer could carry it with him everywhere. Many earlier British almanacs had a distinctly superstitious quality to them, and while a whisper of that remains in *The Old Farmer's Almanac*, it is more folkloric than downright superstitious. Part of what Thomas was trying to do was to clear away the superstition of other almanacs and to move toward scientific and Enlightenment-era understandings of celestial activity, according to Clark. In the world of *The Almanac*, the universe is complex, and its inner workings may elude our understanding, but with the right tools, the world around us is both rational and knowable. Clark explained it this way: "We may not understand it, but if you observe, pay attention, you will notice things, and it's handy to have this little handheld publication with you to make sure that things are happening the way they're supposed to happen. And that's a very American, very optimistic, and again, a very Enlightenment kind of notion: that it is possible to know everything."[35] Within this almanac, then, was both a new way of observing nature and a new tool with which to filter those observations.

The Almanac was a grab bag of practical tips, political information, and entertainment—a Swiss Army knife of early print culture in America. It can even be understood as a kind of whimsical precursor to the Internet.[36] Tim Clark called it a "handheld computer that anyone could use,"[37] and Adrienne LaFrance of *The Atlantic* described *The Old Farmer's Almanac* as a forerunner to the iPhone age, calling it both a "radical, high-tech object" and "downright *Internetty*."[38] *The Almanac* served as a kind of bridge between the Enlightenment-era notion that it was possible to understand the observable universe and the modern age, where knowledge is increasingly available at a person's fingertips. Especially in the twenty-first century, when Internet culture and social media have transformed attention into both a rare and a crucial commodity, *The Almanac*'s call to "pay attention" bears particular poignancy.

The Almanac is filled with all kinds of unusual miscellany, much of which can only be described as flourishes of religious freedom. That first edition contains both the dates of Quaker meetings and what *The Almanac*'s former editor believed to have been the first printed history of the Jewish people in the United States, titled "A Brief Account of the Persecution of the JEWS" and written in 1792.[39] I've spent a lot of time puzzling over the inclusion of that article and have asked several *Almanac* editors about its existence, but they are all just as puzzled as I. At that point in the United States, there were estimated to be no more than a few thousand Jewish people at the absolute most, the majority of whom did not live in New England, so it was hardly pertinent local history. What's more, religious freedom in America has never, in practice, been fully extended to all faiths, and it has frequently excluded Jews in particular, going back to their earliest arrival on the continent. As early as the 1600s, Jews in New Amsterdam—what is now New York—were denied basic civil liberties. The governor at the time, Peter Stuyvesant, called them a "very repugnant, deceitful race, hateful enemies and blasphemers of the name of Christ." Perhaps the inclusion of this passage can be seen within an idealized version of American values and especially American Enlightenment thinking, somewhat divorced from the daily reality of living in America: a vision of the ideal American as a Renaissance man, someone who both knew when to mate his cows and had a passing familiarity with the history of Jewish persecution. This ideal, enduring today in some form, sees the good American as a freethinker who can see, know, or notice things that others do not.

There's something especially American about *The Almanac*'s insistence that the small American farmer can understand all kinds of information—and in fact, he might be better suited than most to learn about the world around him. That comes up again and again in *The Almanac*: that the farmer, by virtue of his hard work and intelligent nature, has everything he needs to survive. He may be even more qualified than the educated leisure classes, who can understand but do not live in tune with the earth's cycles, its passage of time. An anecdote from the 1800 edition of *The Almanac* recounts an "honest country farmer"[40] who comes across the parish's parson in a narrow lane. The farmer apparently does not yield the road quickly enough to the parson, who snaps at him haughtily, "[You] were better fed than taught."[41]

"Very true indeed, Sir . . . For you teach me, and I feed myself,"[42] the farmer replies.

A farmer was not a serf beholden to a tsar or a peasant to

a king—he was not even shackled to the whims of local clergymen.

❀

The Almanac was of course not the only entity (consciously or unconsciously) writing the agrarian origin story for the United States. Many early American politicians and thinkers saw small farming as the ultimate embodiment of the continent's promise. J. Hector St. John (born Michel-Guillaume-Jean de Crèvecoeur), a French nobleman turned American small farmer, became a great preacher of this idea, effectively pitching America as a new, free, and equal utopia. Ten years before the publication of Thomas's almanac, he wrote:

> Some few towns excepted, we are all tillers of the earth, from Nova Scotia to West Florida. We are a people of cultivators, scattered over an immense territory, communicating with each other by means of good roads and navigable rivers, united by the silken bands of mild government, all respecting the laws, without, dreading their power, because they are equitable. We are all animated with the spirit of an industry which is unfettered and unrestrained, because, each person works for himself. If he travels through our rural districts he views not the hostile castle, and, the haughty mansion, contrasted with the clay-built hut and miserable cabbin [*sic*], where, cattle and men help to keep each other warm, and, dwell in meanness, smoke, and indigence.[43]

Here are all the elements of the republican virtue of the small farmer distilled to their core: independence, productivity, limited government interference, and—perhaps above all—equality. Part of Americans' love of the small farmer has always been the way that he came to stand in for the very notion of equality itself. This symbol was so powerful because it tied the people together with both their founding values and the land. The idealized, simplified image was one that ignored all the bloody conflicts over land ownership, slavery, and genocide in favor of a more palatable vision of farming.

In the years following the American Revolution, politicians such as Thomas Jefferson held up the yeoman farmer as the perfect citizen, the building block for a pure, virtuous, and free society[44]—all ideas that show up on a much smaller scale in *The Almanac*. Farming, then, would become the essence of the ideal American: self-sufficient, self-starting, someone who could rely on the land for everything he needed. "Those who labor in the earth are the chosen people of God,"[45] Jefferson wrote in his *Notes on the State of Virginia*. The chosen people, then, would no longer be based on birth or nationality but on the work they did—a very American idea. The United States, by contrast to the British Empire, was pure in the minds of agrarian politicians, its landscape unmarred by the dark shadow of factories.

Ironically, even by the early nineteenth century, this status was already changing as the Industrial Revolution trickled across the Atlantic Ocean. In the years following the publication of those first issues of *The Almanac*, including in the tiny town where Robert B. Thomas spent his life, mills had already started to crop up along the rivers where farms once stood.[46] By the time his almanac took hold, it was almost preemptively nostalgic, published on the cusp of the first wave of industrial growth. This idealization of the small farmer from the start was also far messier and more complex than Crèvecoeur or Jefferson would have allowed. At its heart was a fundamental paradox: a nation that vaunted the small farmer was built on slave labor. Many of the founding fathers may not have seen those two truths as incompatible, but that contradiction has haunted this country ever since.

It's not a coincidence that the mythology of the small farmer would take hold so strongly in a place like the early United States—a country whose connection to the land has always been fraught, to say the very least. By the eighteenth century, though Americans may not have been consciously thinking about the actions of colonists a century prior, the land they stood on had often been acquired through surreptitious means, sour deals, or downright land grabs from local tribes—the latter being systematically excluded from the equality and freedom that the small farmer came to symbolize. Enslaved people, too, tilling so many thousands of farms not just in the South but across the country, stood in stark contrast to the basic understanding of the American agricultural story. They, too, would be excluded from this narrative. As Roxanne Dunbar-Ortiz wrote in her book *An Indigenous Peoples' History of the United States*: "Everything in U.S. history is about the land—who oversaw and cultivated it, fished its waters, maintained its wildlife; who invaded and stole it; how it became a commodity."[47] White landowning Americans seemed to need an ideological claim to the soil because their actual claim to it was so tenuous. Without a strong connection to the land, and often without long familial roots there, this emotional tie was created through other means, namely, through storytelling. *The Almanac* is of course not responsible for this foundational myth; the book is only one part of a much broader tradition of farmer folklore. The founding story is instead a way of imposing meaning by reordering the beginning, reimagining certain people—much like Adam and Eve—as the first arrivals, rather than the most recent and the most lethal.

This mythological, often conflicting, and even false lore around small farming was not Jefferson's alone. We have projected it backward in time onto the continent's early colonists. Some of the earliest printed material in the world was almanacs, and historians have suggested (although never definitively proved) that Christopher Columbus may have taken a 1475 almanac with him to navigate to the New World.[48] As an *Almanac* editor might quip today, that could explain a lot about how he got lost.

Many early Americans were farmers and would continue to farm for generations, but the extent to which they were self-sufficient—that ideal citizen mix of independent and loyal to the land—remains up for debate. The Pilgrims, for instance, whom many Americans learn about as the nation's earliest ancestors (this, too, being a myth), were untalented farmers, and their crops failed frequently in the rocky soil of Massachusetts. In their desperation, they pillaged the winter stores of the tribes nearby.[49] Their early survival would be thanks to the willing help of local tribes, too, including the Wampanoag chief Massasoit and the local Wampanoag villager Tisquantum, who taught the Pilgrims techniques for planting staples such as corn. The establishment of that so-called first farming community was also made far easier by the fact that the Wampanoag tribe had already cleared fields and constructed towns. And yet, the "virgin land" story of the Pilgrims' arrival in an empty wilderness— though fictional—was one that became foundational not only to American colonists but also to later pioneers, frontiersmen, and farmers: the bedrock of how the United States would tell its own story. The very idea that Americans were mostly ambitious upstarts sailing to the colonies to make a new, prosperous future from the land's bountiful resources is partially a myth. As historian Jill Lepore pointed out in her book *These Truths*, as many as three out of four of the earliest English people who sailed to the New World were indentured servants, debtors, or convicts.[50] Other, later arrivals were prostitutes. "They weren't slaves, but neither were they free,"[51] she wrote.

The first colonists and the first almanacs are inseparable from the history of the United States itself. Less than two decades after the arrival of the Pilgrims at Plymouth Rock, the first printshop would be established in Massachusetts. The second book printed was an almanac (after the pamphlet *Oath of a Freeman*).[52] With printed material limited, American almanacs quickly started to take on much more additional work than those in Europe: they served as almanacs but also as political pamphlets, newspapers, and recipe books. American almanacs mixed politics, journalism, farming, science, and entertainment. As the mindset of the colonists shifted from strict survival to issues of governance and society, American almanacs started to develop a political consciousness.

In the years leading up to the Revolutionary War, some almanacs—particularly in northern colonies—bordered on propaganda, fueling the rebellion cause. As early as the 1760s, almanacs printed patriotic songs, poems, and essays.[53] By 1770, almanacs were carrying Paul Revere's engraving of British troops landing in Boston. Early images of the Boston Massacre, in which British soldiers shot and killed several Bostonians during a riot, appeared in an almanac.[54] The project of certain early American almanacs was similar to that of the founding fathers: to drum up patriotic fervor, bringing together a disparate populace into one people. The respective almanacs of Nathaniel Ames and Nathaniel (sometimes spelled Nathanael) Low, both Revolutionary firebrands in their own right, exploded during this period, with Ames selling sixty thousand copies[55] a year (for reference, Massachusetts had fewer than 250,000 residents at the time). An excerpt from Ames's opening poem in his 1775 almanac reads:

> *While art and science fix their standard here,*
> *All hell combin'd no longer need we fear.*
> *Let savage virtue give a loose the reigns,*
> *Our sloughter'd traitors poison all the plains.*[56]

That poem, more of a rallying cry to war, seems like it could have been shouted before a battle, or written in a pamphlet by

Thomas Paine. It hardly seems like the introduction to a farming guide—but that, too, speaks to how multipurpose the almanacs were. On one page, the author might give the tide times, and on the next there were essays encouraging people to protest by boycotting tea and other British products. Ames went so far as to compare Americans wearing British finery and drinking British tea to "bulls and heifers of old adorn'd with ribbons and gilded horns before their destruction."[57]

Thomas's almanac employed a far subtler touch when it came to patriotism. Throughout the first century of its existence, its pages included writings by George Washington,[58] poems about the Constitution, and other kinds of flag-waving.[59] Throughout his tenure, for instance, Thomas commemorated the anniversary of the American Revolution in the subtitle itself, as in, "Being the Second after Leap Year, and Eighteenth of the Independence of America,"[60] tying his almanac to the birth of the nation. Much like a newspaper, *The Almanac* also delivered updates on current events, such as printing a timeline of the Civil War, and noting President Abraham Lincoln's assassination in the calendar pages. But *The Old Farmer's Almanac* was not partisan or even nationalist in the way that Low's or Ames's almanacs were. *The Old Farmer's Almanac* was political in the sense that it implicitly engaged in the construction of American identity, but the way it did so was never through a fiery editorial. One of the aspects that made this almanac endure was precisely its refusal to wade into politics or to take a strong stand on the issues of the day. That ethos has carried through to the present day—and arguably contributed to its popularity in our contemporary political climate, fraught as it is in its own way. "We don't do politics; we don't get involved in religious topics in the publication," Janice Stillman, the thirteenth and current editor of *The Almanac*, told me. "As I like to say sometimes, it's all good news. There's no bad news in the *Farmer's Almanac*," she said.

Instead, the pages of *The Almanac*, down to the farming calendar, were more civic than downright political. The heart of *The Old Farmer's Almanac* (and every almanac) has always been its calendar. Thomas's almanac divided the page into columns, with bits of wisdom and advice for each month alongside that month's forecast. As time went on, the farmer's calendar graduated from being purely practical to being more ethical and philosophical. By the mid-nineteenth century, readers had all the values of good American living alongside the cycles of the moon and the farm, in addition to bits of wisdom encouraging them to read the news and have no debts. The 1847 almanac includes this quote in the farmer's calendar: "The farmer, all-confident in the promise of seed time and harvest, cheerfully goes forth into his fields to his labor, lays his plans for the season, turns the rich loam, and makes preparations for earth's reception of the various seeds. It is in obedience to his Creator that he engages in business, fully assured that his labor shall not be in vain."[61]

The farmer, described as "all-confident," cheerful," and "assured" as he works for his Creator, celebrates farming as a calling rather than simply a way to survive. Much like the Puritans and their notion of God's will for their settlements, there is a thrust of the divine in early almanacs that anchors Americans to cultivation of the land. After all, what could possibly be more rewarding than working God's earth for oneself and one's family? Farming life was difficult, especially in New England, where long weeks of difficult labor often began before sunrise and ended after sunset in the damp, bone-deep chill that sets in early in the autumn and leaves around June. A successful harvest could be unpredictable in a climate such as New England, where Robert B. Thomas—by a wild stroke of luck (or perhaps by error)—correctly predicted snow in July.[62] Farming in Massachusetts revolved around a looping schedule of buying manure, going to market, and chopping wood[63]—the monotony broken up by little more than Sunday sermons. There was an inherent recognition in almanacs that it was easier to bear those hardships with humor and the practical help contained in its pages. And as this passage suggests, that sacrifice was made even sweeter if the reward was not only for one's personal gain but for the good of all the country—and possibly for God.

Thomas, for his part, continued to farm throughout his life, working on *The Almanac* during the winter and tending his crops the rest of the time. He was the perfect example of the yeoman: well educated but not pretentious, a good farmer, and an active American citizen. Thomas even went on to serve in local government: as a town clerk, several times as the chairman of the board of selectmen, and as a representative at a convention to revise the state constitution.[64] As he wrote, "It is by our works and not our words that we would be judged."[65] He seemed to practice exactly what he preached, which in many ways makes him the exception to the rule among the authors included in these chapters. *Americanon* is filled with writers whose vision of the ideal American all too often collided with who they themselves were. That includes career women with Ph.D.s who believed all women should be housewives, childless authors who spoke of child-rearing as a national imperative, and business experts with a trail of failed business ventures. Perhaps because he did not yet have this inherited national baggage to reckon with, Thomas lived by his principles until the very end, dying at the age of eighty while correcting proofs[66] for his almanac.

❀

The Almanac did not cease to exist after Thomas's death, and it has been published continuously every year since that first issue in 1792. No issues were missed during the Civil War, nor the First or Second World War. *The Almanac* continued to accompany, shape, and intersect with American history, often in strange ways. A young Illinois lawyer named Abraham Lincoln may have used this almanac during a trial in defense of a murder suspect.[67] Using the moon tables from the almanac, Lincoln was able to point out that a key witness would not have been able to identify his client under the light of the moon, as there had been no moon on the night in question.[68] One of the few times when *The Almanac* almost stopped publication was not because of death or illness of an editor but thanks to a German spy. One night in 1942, a German agent landed on Long Island by way of a U-boat.[69] The FBI would apprehend the spy on a train in New York City's Penn Station the next day.[70] Among his few possessions, he was carrying a copy of that year's *Old Farmer's Almanac* in his coat pocket.[71] The U.S. government suspected that the Nazis might have been using *The Almanac*'s weather predictions to plan an attack on U.S. soil, as the forecasts were available a full year in advance. *The Almanac*'s then editor, Robb Sagendorph, convinced federal authorities not to halt publication by promising to change its wartime weather reports from specific predictions to general indications.[72] Sagendorph had himself been working full-time at the censorship bureau in New York City and relocated the offices of *The Almanac* to a Manhattan apartment for the duration of the war.[73] Sagendorph had always been convinced that the Germans were more interested in the tide tables than the forecasts anyway.[74] In his typical dry humor, he later quipped, "Then again, maybe it was the forecasts. After all, the Germans went on to lose the war."[75]

Sagendorph did more than save *The Almanac* from wartime censors—he likely rescued it from total obscurity. Few people— far fewer than 3 million—might read this particular almanac today were it not for Sagendorph. By the time German spies were using *The Almanac*, Sagendorph had been at the helm for only a couple of years. He had purchased it from Little, Brown in 1939, when *The Almanac* had reached historically low sales, in the low eighty thousands per year (for reference, in 1863 it sold approximately 225,000 copies).[76] Sagendorph would later joke that he purchased *The Almanac* for the cost of a three-martini lunch.[77] By the time he died in 1970, the publication's annual sales had exceeded 1.6 million.[78]

If Robert B. Thomas was the spitting image of the yeoman farmer—a man who lived and died in the rural farmland of the Massachusetts countryside—Robb Sagendorph began life as his opposite. Born into a wealthy Boston family in 1900,[79] the son of a steel manufacturer, he grew up in part in the affluent neighborhood of Beacon Hill. Today, Beacon Hill remains one of the most desirable neighborhoods in Boston—its historic cobblestone streets perfectly preserved, the redbrick town houses tastefully covered with ivy, the lamps powered by gas. As a child, Robb could have played in the sprawling public park of Boston Common under the golden-domed shadow of the Massachusetts State House. He dutifully checked all the expected prestige boxes for his upper-crust Boston milieu: prep school at Noble and Greenough, a degree from Harvard, and a wife from Vassar.[80] When it came time to find a career, however, he faltered, being hired and fired three times by his father and working on and off in magazine writing. In the meantime, he started spending more and more time with his wife's family at their summer home, located in a New Hampshire village with rustic New England charm and acres of rolling hills. That town—then population five hundred[81]— was Dublin. So, he did what whimsical rich men do: he bought a farmhouse and started a magazine called *Yankee*, adding *The Almanac* to his media roster within a few years.

When Sagendorph moved to Dublin, he had never grown a crop in his life. A more than six-foot-tall "mountain of a man,"[82] according to his colleagues, he continued to wear a jacket and bow tie at the rural office. Both in "figure and look"[83] he resembled a forty-year-old Abraham Lincoln, according to a 1947 *New York Times Magazine* profile. Sagendorph replied that he and Lincoln were of course distantly related.[84] His transformation from Boston gentleman to country editor seemed to have begun the moment he moved into his wife's family's farmhouse. From his kitchen window, he could see out across the garden and straight to Mount Monadnock.[85] Soon he would plant crops on that land, and he even raised hogs, poultry, and cattle.[86]

"When he got to Dublin, I think he felt he wanted to be a countryman,"[87] Judson Hale, Sagendorph's nephew and the twelfth editor of *The Almanac*, told me. "He was always like two people: he was a sophisticated kind of guy—Harvard and all that—but he also wanted to be an old farmer."[88] Once Sagendorph decided to become the Yankee farmer, he did it with great success, known for his skill in the garden and his passion for the town itself. Like Robert B. Thomas, he even became a town selectman.[89]

What excited Sagendorph about *The Almanac* seemed to be what has always excited its readers, too: the wit, the wisdom, and perhaps most of all, a nostalgia for old farming culture and all the folklore about fallen acorns and apple trees that goes with it. Like so many readers of *The Almanac* who do not farm, for most of his life Sagendorph was on the outside looking in at the pastoral dream. But he was able to so effectively pinpoint those elements of "Yankee culture" that he quickly restored *The Almanac* to its former glory. In the first issue of *Yankee* magazine, published in 1935, Sagendorph described his reader in a way that could have just as easily fit the millions who would purchase his almanac, too: "He sees himself . . . hungry, on the edge of a civilization which demands mass production, mass distribution, mass advertising. . . . He sees individuality, initiative, natural ingenuity—the things he and his fathers and their fathers fought for—about to be sold, to be 'swallered inter' a sea of chain stores. . . ."[90] This mentality situated itself as a wedge, safeguarding countryside individualism from a perceived encroaching conformity. Despite the folksy, nonthreatening voice in the pages of *The Almanac* and *Yankee*, by the mid-twentieth century there was a rebellious tinge, too, an attempt to hold the line against the rise of commercial culture.

When he bought *The Almanac*, Sagendorph went back to Thomas's old way of doing things while taking advantage of some new technology. He reinstated the calendar pages and contracted some of New England's rising literary stars to contribute to its pages. By the 1940s, Sagendorph was already receiving letters from readers as far away as California, alongside his usual inquiries from New York homemakers looking for the best Saturday to give a garden party and a Boston rabbi searching for the exact moment of a sunset.[91] By 1947, the circulation had leapt from the measly eighty thousand and change when he had bought it to approximately four hundred thousand copies[92] a year. By the 1960s, he even convinced a NASA scientist to help him take the weather forecast national.[93]

Returning to tradition and putting a renewed emphasis on Robert B. Thomas's motto of "useful with a degree of humor" quickly restored the publication. Editors throughout the course of its publication have found that consistency and tradition are what bring generations of readers to *The Old Farmer's Almanac*. Present-day editor Janice Stillman noted that even slight changes to the format—as she attempted one year early in her tenure— can bring a wave of letters and emails from disappointed readers. What differentiates this book from the others across this collection is that it's the work not of a single author but of dozens of editors and writers over the course of two centuries. And yet, remarkably, a certain cohesion remains intact. Its tone may change slightly from decade to decade—and, at this point, from century to century—but its ethos shines through. "[*The Almanac*] is timely but timeless at the same time," Stillman told me. "It sort of touches every man. It's got a real personal approach, but it makes everybody feel like they're getting something from reading it."[94]

What made people in Sagendorph's time want to buy an almanac for farmers when statistically fewer people farmed with each passing year? It might be the same reason that people buy it now: the comfort of nostalgia. The mid-twentieth century, in a way unique from the post-Revolutionary period, was also a time of upheaval and uncertainty. Americans had survived the Great Depression and the Second World War, and in the postwar years they were bombarded by new technology and mass advertising. In that time of instability, they found a renewed connection to this nostalgic vision of the American farm. During World War II, Americans had planted victory gardens all across the country to grow produce to replace commercial output that was redirected to the war effort. In 1943, some 20 million Americans produced 8 million tons of food (Eleanor Roosevelt even planted a victory garden on the White House lawn). Americans had reconnected to the nation's farming roots during the war, and some kept their gardens after the war's end. Those who did not continue to farm—or were not able to as they moved to suburban developments or city apartments—rued something they felt they had lost. The nostalgia for land, home-grown food, and self-reliance has an obvious appeal, especially in the face of frighteningly rapid change. The more American life urbanized, the more Americans longed for an imagined rural simplicity. And that longing seems to have only grown stronger over time as country life disappeared for many people.

This rural nostalgia is often male-centric and almost exclusively white, Dr. Leni Sorensen, a culinary historian, noted. "Who's gotten left out of the equation in American agriculture? Black farmers. They have gotten systematically excised from the story, but it wasn't like there weren't any,"[95] she told me. Sorensen pointed to W. E. B. Du Bois's estimate that nonwhite farmers went from owning 3 million acres of land in 1875 to owning 12 million acres in 1900. Census data backs that up: by 1910—the peak year for Black farm ownership—nonwhite people fully or partially owned 12.8 million acres of land. It seems unsurprising that both top almanacs to survive throughout American history would come from northern states. The rival of *The Old Farmer's Almanac*, titled the *Farmers' Almanac*, is also based in New England and sells about 1 million copies every year. By situating farming in an independent region, readers could avoid their own discomfort in confronting the role that enslaved people and their descendants would play in American agriculture. Any painful feelings about our shared past and the integral role that slavery would play in constructing national wealth could be relegated to some faraway evil of southern plantations and their owners, nowhere near any quaint New England country home tilled by single families. That scapegoating also skirted New England's dependence on indentured servitude and later, redlining in cities like Boston.[96] The vision of the small farmer throughout American history has steered clear of a host of complex, often shameful aspects of agricultural life in America—from stolen land to stolen labor.

As varied as the actual yeoman farmer may have been throughout history—Black or white, male or female, slaveholder or independent, northern or southern—the image that we have inherited remains necessarily simplistic. It is the comforting answer to all types of different identity crises that span generations faced by wildly disparate obstacles: international conflict, regime change, shifting gender roles, and more. Almanacs provide a return not just to the past but also to an idealized vision of that past, which effectively unites us within its imaginary confines. In a world of digital media and magazines teaching us how to become our best future selves, almanacs root us firmly in the safety of the past. The United States has always been an uneasy place that needed buttressing with new national myths, reassurances of who "we" are, and rationales for the many people who have been displaced by that nation building. As mid-twentieth-century historian Richard Hofstadter once wrote, "This sentimental attachment to the rural way of life is a kind of homage that Americans have paid to the fancied innocence of their origins. To call it a 'myth' is not to imply that the idea is simply false. Rather the 'myth' so effectively embodies men's values that it profoundly influences their way of perceiving reality."[97]

Over time that myth would grow and evolve, morphing to respond to varying insecurities from one generation to the next. But it never ceased shaping our perception of reality. There is something alluring about the promise endemic to yeoman farming—and, by extension, about *The Almanac*—even now. What office worker has not thought of what it would be like to be his own boss, to leave everything and work the land? It unites the Right and the Left in its utopic vision of self-sufficiency, abundance, and independence. But of course, the reality was always different—and is different now. Fewer than 2 percent[98] of Americans are farmers today—and the number of independent farmers is likely even lower than those estimates.

Back in the office in New Hampshire, Tim Clark is grappling with that dwindling number of farmers. The editorial team over the years has started using the word "gardener" instead of "farmer" in many of its articles. But "The Old Gardener's Almanac" hardly has the same ring to it. Despite the shrinking number of farmers, *The Almanac* has not seen its readership wane. Perhaps like their ancestors, readers today rely on *The Almanac* for its reminders to count acorns, to avoid killing spiders, and to look to the small things. In that Enlightenment way, it reminds us that in nature—whether in the shifting seasons or in a bean sprouting—something deeper is at work, even if we cannot always hold it in our hands or measure it. *The Almanac* is a little mystical that way. It continues to function on its dual registers, both practical and poetic, living up to Robert B. Thomas's tagline, "Useful with a pleasant degree of humor." Clark put it this way: "Even if it's a house of cards, even if it's an illusion, it's been around for 228 years."[99]

CHAPTER TWO

Webster's Speller and Dictionary (1783/1828)

It started off, as many things seemed to do that year, with a tweet.

"A fact is a piece of information presented as having objective reality," *Merriam-Webster's Dictionary* tweeted in January 2017 alongside a photo of Kellyanne Conway, following her use of the term "alternative facts." Two days later, the dictionary followed up reports that Donald Trump had packed the first three rows of seats at a CIA event with staff and supporters to applaud him during a visit with a tweet that read, "If you're part of a group that's paid to applaud, you're a 'claqueur.'" A few days after that, the dictionary clarified that the term "snowflake" had in fact first appeared to reference those who opposed abolition in the nineteenth century.

What began as pithy one-liners became something of a movement, with an array of news outlets writing about the dictionary's newfound conscience and Internet users cheering the dictionary's sass. From explaining the meaning of "deplorable" to differentiating between "bigly" and "big league," the dictionary served as a biting challenge to an emerging culture of misinformation, winning praise for its sharp critiques. Editors from the dictionary said they wanted to engage in cultural dialogue, all while insisting that the dictionary was not partisan (they took on Hillary Clinton's use of language, too, albeit less frequently). "We're reporting the truth about words," editor at large Peter Sokolowski said during a TV interview at the time.

Reporting the truth about words, however, is hardly a straightforward task. Particularly during an era in American politics marked by ruses, conspiracies, and bald-faced lies, truth varied greatly based on belief. The dictionary still attempted to fact-check political figures at a time when even the word "fact" was up for debate, aiming to regulate at least one form of disagreement. Amid an election shadowed by nepotism and incivility, language served as a sanctuary from a frightening onslaught of moral ambiguity. The very foundations of our republic may be crumbling, but at least there's certainty in what the word "fact" means. And yet, language—and spoken language in particular—has never functioned as the objective authority that we might hope for it to be. Other than countries such as France, where an academy of experts decides questions of usage on a regular basis, language evolves based more on how it is used than on how it perhaps *should be* used. Nonetheless, in the course of the rancorous screaming matches of the 2016 political landscape, *Merriam-Webster's Dictionary* emerged as an unlikely and tempering voice.

Merriam-Webster's resistance to an administration steeped in nativism is complicated by the dictionary's original goal: to create and preserve a monolithic American culture. Noah Webster Jr., the dictionary's founding author, was one of the first American nationalists, and he wrote his reference books with the express purpose of creating a single definition of American English—one that often existed at the expense of regional and cultural variation of any kind. Uniformity was Webster's goal, and in his mind that goal was inextricable from the survival of the United States. What Webster would create, through his dictionary and school primer, was a veritable monolith, teaching millions of Americans how to read and write and instilling language standards that still exist today. His vision of the United States would form elements of the American psyche that solidified over the following two centuries, reemerging stronger than ever today in a nation that continues to see itself as a shining example for the rest of the world.

Webster would succeed not only in creating an independent linguistic tradition; he also codified some of the most elemental aspects of American culture—patriotism, exceptionalism, Protestant morality—through the very foundations of language. This idea that America was a fundamentally new place, a new experiment capable of achieving a type of power and freedom that the world had never seen, was not Webster's notion alone. Many other early Americans believed in this grand hope for the country's future, but it was this schoolteacher who wove those beliefs into the way people communicated: how they learned, read, spoke about, and conceived of their new country.

❀

It was not until he had tried and failed at a handful of professions that Noah Webster found his calling during his days as a
schoolteacher. He began to write what would become known as
the *Blue Back Speller* in the spring of 1782[1] while working as a
teacher in a one-room schoolhouse in New York State. In the
mud of that spring, General George Washington was encamped
at the southern edge of the Catskills waiting for a peace treaty,
as the British still maintained control of New York City. Meanwhile, Benjamin Franklin was in France attempting to negoti-
ate an end to a war that had been raging for nearly six years. The
fate of the United States seemed murky at best, and enmity
toward England was at an all-time high. The few schools that
existed in the United States at the time used British grammar
and spelling books to teach children how to read, but Webster—
a staunch patriot—bristled at the idea of teaching his students
how to read and write with a book written by an enemy author.
With 75 cents to his name,[2] Webster was also short on funds
and saw an opportunity to satisfy both his monetary and his
political needs. He decided to write a new text, complete with
the blueprint for a new language that would establish the United
States' cultural independence from Britain just as the war was
attempting to establish its governmental independence.

For Webster, it was impossible to have an independent
American culture without an independent language. "I have too
much pride not to wish to see America assume a national character. I have too much pride to stand indebted to Great Britain

for books to learn [*sic*] our children the letters of the alphabet,"[3] he wrote. In essays, speeches, and letters, he spoke of the need to establish a unity of language among all Americans as a moral imperative. "The spelling book does more to form the language of a nation than all other books,"[4] he would later write. This grand vision in mind, Webster turned his intense concentration to writing the speller. By his own account, Webster was a highly nervous, obsessive man, but compiling books quieted his mind. In that way, the books he wrote would be an antidote both to a larger national anxiety and also to an intensely personal one. With the speller, Webster began to move toward a linguistic independence, teaching children to read without books that included lessons on the British Crown or pages of British geography. One scholar of American literature went so far as to call Webster's spelling book a second Declaration of Independence[5]— one that played a crucial role in shaping the destiny of the United States.

What would set Webster's speller apart from others that had come before it was not only its American ethos but also its accessible approach. Almost like a proto–Dr. Seuss, Webster aimed to "delight and allure"[6] children with engaging stories, rather than bore them with the usual rote memorization of schoolbooks of the time. By speaking to children directly and by dividing up the syllables of words according to pronunciation rather than by their Latin roots (as had been the tradition), Webster was able to create something far more kid-friendly than what had come before it. *The New England Primer*, for instance, which had been a mainstay of colonial education, was a stodgy mix of moral lessons and fire-and-brimstone Calvinism.

In Webster's book, moralizing undertones still pervade, but there's something earthly and visceral about the way he writes. The words leap off the page, whether he's writing about a fox stuck in the weeds of a river[7] or describing the sun as a "fountain of light."[8] After several months of writing the speller, often adopting segments of an existing reader by Englishman Thomas Dilworth (the irony of this may have been lost on Webster), his speller was ready for publication.

Webster yearned to give the American public a language of their own, and the speller was the first step toward that goal. In his goal of making a book for Americans and of use to Americans, he also got rid of the pages devoted to British geography and instead replaced them with the names of the major towns, counties, and states in the United States.[9] Webster included a guide to proper (American) pronunciation and started to shift, albeit inconsistently, spellings such as "honour"[10] away from the British version and toward American spellings, designed to mimic the words as Americans pronounced them.[11] In doing so, he created a text that was radically new and essentially American, establishing an intellectual independence from the very first lines of the book. He wrote in the preface to the speller: "To diffuse an uniformity and purity of language in America— to destroy the provincial prejudices that originate in the trifling differences of dialect, and produce reciprocal ridicule—to promote the interest, literature and the harmony of the United States—is the most ardent wish of the author; and it is his highest ambition to deserve the approbation and encouragement of his countrymen."[12] The goal was a lofty one, and from the start Webster was not shy about his ambitions.

His book was indeed met with "the approbation and encouragement of his countrymen." In the century following the Revolutionary War, Webster's speller became so ubiquitous in the newly formed United States—selling nearly 100 million copies—that only the Bible outpaced it in sales. Webster's speller and later dictionary were instrumental in creating a single definition of American English, one he saw as synonymous with freedom, republicanism, Christianity, and a whole host of other values that would come to define how many Americans understood their homeland. In other early essays, Webster compared the United States to the great empires of Rome and Greece,[13] and with nothing more than a children's speller he hoped to lay the foundation for a uniform American speech that not only would be worthy of an empire but would supersede European linguistic traditions as well.

Dictionaries and other linguistic reference books have always struck a balance between describing language as it is and creating language by codifying correct and incorrect modes of speech. Where other instructional texts might describe existing ways of speaking, Webster's book sought to elevate a new kind of speech. That aim is part of what makes Webster so paradoxical: especially in retrospect, he can seem bound by his own contradictions. To some readers today, Webster feels hopelessly outdated and prescriptive, a sort of linguistic dictator telling people how—and especially how not—to talk. At the same time, he wanted to capture the way that Americans spoke (or at least, how a swath of well-educated Americans spoke) in the goal of standardizing their language. After all, he reasoned, it would be easier to spread American English across an ever-expanding landmass if that

English were all the same. The spellings that Webster would promote have now become hallmarks of American English, including dropping the letter *u* in words like "color," removing the *k* from "mimic," and changing words like "centre" to "center." His later definitions of words, from "plantation" to "senate," created the basis for concepts that would prove foundational to American society.

When Webster's speller was first published, some Americans were even debating the elimination of English altogether. Some advocated adopting German or Hebrew, while others wanted to invent an entirely new language to be called "Columbian"[14] (after Christopher Columbus), anxious as they were to throw off the yoke of England. These ideas were largely impractical, and Webster instead offered a compromise: envisioning a new, sanctified version of English to go with their new, independent identity. He railed against the emphasis on learning ancient languages such as Greek and Latin[15] and instead urged the government to create an educational system that would focus on American history and literature. Every American child should be more familiar with the short history of his own country than with that of the Roman Empire,[16] and he should learn it with a language of his own. Education was the basis of national sentiment, and national sentiment was required for American survival, according to Webster.

With nothing but a child's speller, he started to shape the future he wanted for the United States, one that laid the linguistic foundation for the American exceptionalism that we still have today. Webster's speller and later dictionary were nationalist in the truest sense of the word: "exalting one nation above all others and placing primary emphasis on promotion of its culture."[17] An integral aspect of establishing the United States as a world power, then, meant creating a national standard of language, the foundation for books and poetry but also political pamphlets and written law. At a time when education largely meant reading the Bible and learning from a grammar book or two, Webster's bestselling speller earned him a place as one of the founders of American education. In an essay on the importance of solidifying national identity through education, he wrote, "Our national character is not yet formed; and it is an object of vast magnitude that systems of Education should be adopted and pursued which may . . . implant, in the minds of the American youth, the principles of virtue and of liberty."[18]

It is easy now to underestimate how precarious the future of the United States was during Webster's heyday. A persistent American narrative has since developed, putting forward the idea that the United States was somehow destined to survive, that—much like the later myth of manifest destiny—the expansion and endurance of the United States was inevitable. Our survival, however, has never been self-evident. People like Webster recognized an urgency in building a framework that could encourage loyalty and patriotic sentiment after years of war that had pitted neighbor against neighbor. According to Webster, a standard American English language could rally people around shared principles for their new nation, sidestepping what he saw as the corruption of empires such as Britain and France.

Literature was a litmus test for American identity, in the eyes of Webster.[19] To have a tradition of American literature meant that the United States would have moved beyond simple survival and had graduated to having its own culture. A successful society needed the capabilities not only to feed and to defend itself but also to create art. Countries such as France, Italy, and England had a tradition of poetry and letters that stretched back nearly a thousand years, long before the first settlers had even arrived in the North American colonies. Webster's book was instrumental in establishing "American" as more than an identity distinct from "British"; it was also as an identity that people could aspire to, one that left room for idealization. It's easy to imagine him dreaming of American literary anthologies filled with great American poets, being used to shape the minds of American children. When writing his speller and later his dictionary, he was projecting his vision of the United States centuries down the line, longing to create a language that would be worthy of the millions of people he imagined would inhabit its vast land.

Despite its enduring influence on language and American culture, the speller was not an instant triumph. In fact, part of its success came from the sheer force of will on Webster's part to ensure the book's sales. When the speller first appeared in the early 1780s, Webster embarked on what linguist Rosemarie Ostler called the first multicity book tour of any American author.[20] He would spend more than eighteen months on the road, traveling from town to town either on a horse with two saddlebags strapped on either side or packed into a jostling ten-seat stagecoach.[21] On one stretch of the trip, his horse fell, crushing Webster's leg and causing him to limp for days.[22] And the stagecoach wasn't much better: it usually meant bouncing along among luggage, mail, and other passengers for miles on end.

The bookselling business was tough, and Webster decided to supplement his income on the road by giving speeches on the importance of a national language. His first speech, based on the first section of his *Dissertations on the English Language*, drew a modest audience of thirty listeners, who had paid a quarter apiece to hear his talk at the First Presbyterian Church in Baltimore.[23] He spoke passionately about the need for Americans to have an independent language alongside their newly independent government. He likely told listeners that night: "We have therefore the fairest opportunity of establishing a national language, and of giving it uniformity and perspicuity, in North America, that ever presented itself to mankind. Now is the time to begin the plan."[24]

Fresh from the victory of the Revolutionary War, more and more Americans flocked to hear Webster speak. Soon, he drew huge crowds in New York City and at Boston's Faneuil Hall.[25] With his ideas receiving wide applause from crowds all over the major cities of the country, the book started to take off. By 1815—thirty years after that first speech—the speller was averaging sales of 286,000 copies a year;[26] in 1828 the sales were estimated to be 350,000 copies. And in 1847, four years after Webster died, a reported 24 million copies of the speller were in existence.[27]

The speller not only made American English independent— it also made it standard. In the regionally diverse United States, Webster was already thinking about having standard English long before the start of mass immigration in the 1800s. "Webster's *American Spelling Book* probably had the greatest standardizing influence of anything in the nineteenth century on American English,"²⁸ Dr. William Kretzschmar, coeditor for the *Oxford Dictionary of Pronunciation for Current English*, told me. The standard Webster created was an ideal rather than a reality, as it regulated the way that American English was taught rather than the way it was natively spoken. Still, the speller started to establish the idea that American was something anyone could become—as long as they adhered to the rules. This was a major achievement: the speller began to cement the notion of American as an identity that could be both taught and learned. The idea of national belonging being open to everyone is lovely, but from the start, becoming American was a fraught task. Kretzschmar warned that the problem with standardization is that it means a minority of people will somewhat arbitrarily choose one way that will be the correct way for the majority—deeming all other ways wrong.²⁹ Webster's later dictionary, which would become the American standard, was not the pure, objective text that we might like it to be, existing instead in the pursuit of a specific agenda that extended far beyond the scope of lexicography. Webster's particular political agenda was an authoritarian one, and one that often veered into a total intolerance of difference. If a dictionary can be biased and partisan, what, then, of other reference books?

❀

Webster had a passion for reading from a young age, and as a child he would often carry a book around between performing chores on his parents' Connecticut farm.³⁰ He was mostly educated by his mother, until managing to get accepted to Yale. His family was not wealthy, and his father mortgaged the family farm[31] to pay for the tuition. By the time the Revolutionary War broke out, Webster was an eighteen-year-old student in New Haven and a proud patriot. He enlisted during his summer vacation, though he accidentally arrived late to the Battle of Saratoga,[32] missing the action. His lack of battle experience did not hamper his passion for the newly formed United States, and he spoke out at every available opportunity on topics that he believed to be vital to the nation's survival. Webster was so outspoken—and unfiltered—that both his contemporaries and his biographer called him a zealot. He even earned the nickname "the Monarch"[33] for his attitude of superiority. "He was basically one of the most politically incorrect men alive,"[34] said Joshua Kendall, author of the Webster biography *The Forgotten Founding Father.* "Today Webster would be like a standard policy wonk on *Sean Hannity,* this right-wing, angry white man," he told me. Not everyone agrees that he was right-wing; his politics were complex and sometimes paradoxical, and they don't fall easily into contemporary understandings of Left and Right. Even current *Merriam-Webster's* editor Peter Sokolowski, however, agreed with the categorization of "wonk."

In the America of Webster's youth, many people would have felt a stronger sense of loyalty to the states they lived in than to the newly formed federal government. In 1776, approximately 2.5 million residents were spread across thousands upon thousands of square miles from Georgia to Maine. "We ought not to consider ourselves as inhabitants of a particular state only; but as *Americans,* as the common subjects of a great empire,"[35] he wrote in 1785, when state-dependent identities were strong. One need only look at the Civil War, or even present-day discussions of "states' rights," to see the extent to which regional alliances would endure for centuries. The identity of "American" was brand-new in Webster's time, and yet he insisted on the radical idea that the United States—which had only just won its independence from the British Empire—would someday become its own empire. By 1785, the speller had brought Webster such notoriety that former president George Washington invited him to dine at Mount Vernon. The twenty-six-year-old schoolteacher boldly told the former president that the union between the states was so tenuous as to be a "cobweb."[36] In his view, regional dialects, along with the popularity of languages such as French and German, further divided an already fragmented empire. He feared that the influence of dialects in particular would "corrupt the national language,"[37] as he once wrote. He even warned Washington against hiring a Scottish tutor for his step-grandchildren, insisting that the president's family be taught by Americans only. This idea of corruption of a "national language" rings of the extreme, especially for a country that was barely past its sixth birthday by the time Webster's speller was published. Fear of division—and its frequent antidote, fervent nationalism—have wrestled with each other from the very start.

Despite the country's young age, dialects had already started to diverge strongly, particularly between North and South. The staunch lexicographer could likely not have predicted just how much spoken language would come to vary in the century that followed the publication of the speller, with the differences spidering out like some kind of Borgesian garden of forking paths. In the more than 175 years since Webster's death, different waves of immigration to varying regions across the United States contributed to divergence in regional language. Regions with high numbers of Polish and Slavic immigrants, for instance, started to elongate words and turn the *th* sound in words such as "cathedral" into a *t* sound,[38] one researcher found. The New Orleans accent in Louisiana bears inflections from the region's French, Spanish, and African origins.[39] In the related Cajun accent, the tendency to put the inflection on the second syllable of a word, for instance, is a direct inheritance from the French language.[40] What's more, likely to Webster's horror, these types of changes would not come from the top down, or even from trained speakers such as actors or orators. "Extreme speakers" (so called because they have the greatest influence on local dialects) such as local politicians—and even bank tellers— are more likely to cause shifts in dialect than anyone else, the modern sociolinguist William Labov[41] would later find. "Most of the important changes in American speech are not happening at the level of grammar or language—which used to be the case—but at the level of sound itself,"[42] he told *The New Yorker* in 2005.

While dialects would diverge more strongly than Webster could have ever imagined, his initial insistence on standard language and national identity may have helped some early Americans get ahead. Good grammar was more than the basis of good language in eighteenth-century America; it was a stepping-stone for social mobility. At a time before public schools, most people in the United States were educated through a shared family speller. Even relatively wealthy families used spellers to teach their children to read and write. Benjamin Franklin taught his granddaughter how to read using Webster's speller.[43] In that way, the prevalence of spellers served as something of an equalizer, promising education for only a few pence. The United States might be a land of opportunity, but hard work and perseverance have never been enough to land a spot among the successful. People also needed to speak the way that educated people did in order to function in their circles, even in a country without an established aristocracy. Just sounding educated was a shortcut to getting some of what a traditional education usually offered.[44] Grammar might be an unusual form of social currency, but shared language helped form a sense of national identity in a way that lingers today—as a tool for exclusion or inclusion.

The notion of the dictionary as a tool of social mobility was not just an idealistic hope; some of the most famous people in the United States actually used Webster's books to learn the basic skills that helped them succeed. Frederick Douglass, who would go on to become one of the most famous and effective abolitionists of the nineteenth century, had been born into slavery in Maryland in 1817 or 1818. Enslaved people were forced to remain illiterate, but he had learned to read from the wife of his enslaver and from local children[45] (he would exchange bread for lessons). In his memoirs, Douglass describes teaching himself how to write using nothing except Webster's 1825 *Spelling Book* and some copy paper left over by his enslaver's son.[46] Each Monday afternoon when the mistress of the house went to town, Douglass would take this book—more precious to him than anything else—and teach himself how to write over the course of several painstaking years. He would go on to pen one of the most important autobiographies of the century, *Narrative of the Life of Frederick Douglass*. Without Webster's ubiquitous text being available in just about every corner of the United States, it's unclear how Douglass would have learned to write at all.

There is something particularly American about the democratic values the speller, and later dictionary, strived to embody. What other book would teach both the son of an enslaved person and the descendant of a diplomat the same skill? And for the same price? The dictionary and speller would become important symbols of the flawed but deeply entrenched American belief that anyone—even someone born into the horrors of chattel slavery—could change his situation through sheer hard work and determination. And yet, simply because both Douglass and Benjamin Franklin's grandchild used the same book does not mean they therefore lived in an equal society. It's a vast psychological leap to hold up Douglass as an example of meritocracy, social mobility, and the possibility of the self-made man in America. The fact that he was able to escape and become successful, in part through the use of Webster's book, did not mean that he lived in a system in which everyone was given an equal chance, or (as was the case for generations of enslaved people) any chance at all.

Much of early American society looked to erase apparent markers of privilege, with no European titles of nobility, nor the accompanying castles that dot so much of the French and British countryside. In a place where no noble titles existed to distinguish high from low class, markers of social status—such as etiquette, accent, and slang—took on increasing importance. In his 1806 compendious dictionary, Webster's would reportedly become the first English dictionary to define the word "slang,"[47] which he described only as "vulgar language, cant phrases [*low*]."[48] Slang, then—that bogeyman of English teachers and grammarians—was seen as an enemy of social mobility from the start of the American project, especially by linguistic purists like Webster. His inclusion of the word "slang" in the dictionary—alongside several instances of profanity—is typical of his strange, conflicting balance between high and low culture, haughtiness and populism. He wanted language to be standard, dictated by an authority, but at the same time he added words based on usage, memorializing terms such as "chowder" or "Americanize" that had never found their way into a dictionary before but were frequently used by the people. For that reason, some critics of his dictionary would later decry it as "coarse." The lexicographer was a radical in many ways, but he did not want to tear down all the rules. Slang is where he drew the line.

National spelling reform, then—and the standardizing influence that went along with it—would lay the foundation for national identity and pride across all strata of Americans, according to Webster. Rather than taking the best forms of British English, he advocated for teaching a form of English that would take its cues from how most Americans spoke. But by "most Americans," he meant the people he counted as peers: Yale-educated white men. "There's all of these examples where he wants a certain pronunciation to nationalize or formalize American pronunciation,"[49] said his biographer Joshua Kendall, "and it's nearly always the way they speak in Connecticut."[50] Following a voyage in the American South, he was horrified by the dialect of his countrymen, citing their pronunciation of common words as repugnant ("reesins" for "raisins," for instance)[51] and criticizing their schoolrooms as disgraceful or nonexistent. During a lecture tour, the state of education in George Washington's native Virginia appalled Webster. As he wrote in his travel log, "Considerable business is done here: but little attention is paid to religion, education, or morals."[52] He went on to note how the vast majority of planters in Alexandria, Virginia, could not even write their own names. "O New England! How Superior are thy inhabitants in morals literature, civility & industry,"[53] he wrote in his diary. Webster would claim to be merely putting into print the way that Americans spoke, changing spellings to match their speech, but his vision of American English—one that remains in some form today—holds up the speech of well-educated, supposedly accent-free people as the baseline.

Dialects weren't Webster's only source of anxiety, and he was suspicious of the influence of foreign languages on the American tongue. Webster hated the French with a passion and even started a daily newspaper in 1793 in part to combat French influence over the United States. His newspaper, *The American Minerva*, promoted a pro-Federalist and pro-American agenda while also documenting the atrocities carried out by the Jacobins. It would become New York City's first daily newspaper[54]— and Webster's move to New York for that paper was made possible by a $1,500[55] loan from Alexander Hamilton, who would be a frequent contributor to its editorial pages. Hamilton and Webster, both staunch Federalists, maintained an on-again, off-again friendship until the turn of the nineteenth century, when their tensions boiled over into a highly public, downright theatrical falling-out. Webster was a staunch moralizer, and he could not forgive Hamilton his widely publicized extramarital affair with Maria Reynolds. The final blow to end their tumultuous friendship came when Hamilton wrote a seething screed against the Federalist candidate John Adams during his reelection campaign of 1800. That tirade toppled into an all-out war of words between Hamilton and Webster in pamphlets, editorials, and essays.[56] Webster, believing that Hamilton cost Adams the election to Thomas Jefferson, cut off Hamilton from contributing to *The American Minerva*.[57] As a result, Hamilton started his own daily newspaper, which would later become the *New York Post*. Webster's *American Minerva* would eventually be bought out and merged with *The New York Sun*—two founding fathers each founding some of the earliest New York dailies.

The American Minerva gave Webster yet another platform from which to disseminate his ideas, including his early belief in abolition. For all his disdain of difference, Webster wrote lengthy pamphlets arguing against slavery as early as 1793, and he even used a section of the front page of the newspaper to print an advertisement for an antislavery book.[58] His conviction was grounded in both a practical and a moral argument. On abolition, he wrote, "The industry the commerce and the moral character of the United States will be immensely benefitted by the change—Justice and humanity require it—Christianity *commands* it."[59] But to paint him as a hero abolitionist would be to ignore the entire latter half of his life, when Webster grew more conservative, advocating for caution in freeing the enslaved people. More than any devotion to the freedom of Black people, Webster used the slavery debate to reassert what he saw as the superiority of the North over the South. Part of his definition in the 1828 dictionary for the term "slavery" would read: "Slavery no longer exists . . . in the northern states of America."[60] As the abolition movement found fresh momentum in Webster's later years, he wrote to his daughter that the new wave of abolitionists was "absolutely deranged. . . . [S]lavery is a great sin and a great calamity, but it is not our sin."[61] Unity and uniformity were Webster's top priorities, and in abolition he saw a threat to both—and a promise of chaos. For all his Revolution-era ideals, Webster seemed prepared to sacrifice freedom in the name of national harmony.

⚘

Following his venture in newspaper editing, Webster moved to New Haven and started to conceive of the idea of making an American dictionary. But by the time he began working on his dictionary in the early 1800s, public interest in his vast linguistic project had waned, in part because of the events unfolding in France.[62] The French Revolution had given way to the so-called Reign of Terror, when revolutionaries attempted to purge the country through a gory fear campaign of rape and public executions. American pundits observing the fallout in France, including Webster's fellow Federalists, were spooked by the bloody consequences that took place in 1793 and 1794.

Too much revolution, they began to think, was not such a good thing. Webster had once envisioned American English as a language that would be as different from British English as it was from every other European language. In the decades following the publication of the speller in 1783, some of his proposals for American English to be written as it sounded had grown ever more extreme, suggesting such unusual spellings as "tung" for "tongue," "wimmen" for "women," and "fether" and "lether" instead of "feather" and "leather."[63] His critics may have always found these ideas radical, but now they saw them as potentially dangerous. Articles published in the newspapers at the time mocked Webster, and he had difficulty finding any publisher who would finance the project. One Philadelphia newspaper editor wrote that it was "perfectly absurd to talk of the *American* language,"[64] and other critics wrote passionate letters fearing that Webster would debase English by adding in words from spoken language. Reverend John Ewing, president of what would become the University of Pennsylvania, went so far as to call Webster a "fomenter of rebellion."[65]

Despite his detractors, Webster found fresh energy from a new source: God. While working on the dictionary in his study in 1808, Webster said he spoke with God, falling to his knees and confessing his sins.[66] From that day forward, he was a devout Calvinist and a born-again Christian, and his understanding of the dictionary shifted to incorporate his newfound evangelism. What might seem a bizarre claim to a modern reader was almost mundane in early nineteenth-century America. His revelatory moment had come during the Second Great Awakening, when a wave of religious zeal swept across the United States in the early 1800s, reinspiring millions of Americans in the Protestant faith. So many people were born again during this period that having a conversion experience became fashionable, with some of the most prominent writers, thinkers, and politicians of the day swept up in the spirit.

Webster's meeting with God in turn caused profound changes to his work on the dictionary—and further delayed its publication for another two decades. He became convinced of the literal truth of the book of Genesis and the Tower of Babel,[67] believing that all humans had spoken the same language at the beginning of time. With this conviction, he embarked on a series of wildly unscientific etymological investigations, trying to find common roots for words in languages originating in Asia, Africa, and Europe. He also looked to the grammar of Anglo-Saxon and Middle English, hoping to find a basis for an American English that would be even purer than what the Brits were speaking.[68] The lexicographer would spend years in this almost manic state, searching for the first, original language that he believed to have existed. When he made an exciting discovery, he would check his pulse and find it jumped from sixty beats per minute to eighty. He says he learned at least twenty languages[69] at this point in his life—a myth spread by his family and even historical societies today[70]—but beyond a handful of languages he understood well, there is little evidence to show he had more than a passing familiarity with the rest of those tongues.

Webster's first complete dictionary, at last published in 1828, is a work of gargantuan proportions, containing some seventy thousand words, including nouns that did not exist in England or had never been put into a dictionary. Many of those new entries had first appeared in Webster's compendious dictionary in 1806, and now they were being included in the final work:

words such as "skunk," "squash," "psychology," "chowder," "Americanize," and "penmanship." Webster erased some of his more radical spellings from earlier projects, too, such as "wimmen" for "women" and "soop" for "soup," but the removal of *u* in words such as "honor" remained, as did the shift from "defence" to "defense" and "centre" to "center,"[71] among many other major changes that have since come to define American English. (He also kept in several new spellings that would never catch on, such as "ake" for "ache" and "cloke" for "cloak.") As with the speller, Webster borrowed heavily from existing lexicographers—Samuel Johnson in particular—for his 1828 dictionary as well as for the 1806 version. An important facet of what made the dictionary lasting was its precision. For all its unscientific motivations, the result was impressive: his book had tens of thousands more entries and greater specificity than anything that had been previously available in English, including Johnson's dictionary.

The first edition of Webster's dictionary stands apart not only for its new spellings and scope but also for its ideology, which reflects its author's convictions, his vision of the country as a fundamentally new place that would serve as a paragon for the rest of the world. Webster cited George Washington, Benjamin Franklin, and Washington Irving in usage examples, elevating them in the ranks of literature. There's something sanctifying about being included in a dictionary's usage examples, especially in the nineteenth century, when dictionaries were more concerned with proper language than with all language. Just as the inclusion of a word in a dictionary seems to confer authority upon it, so does the inclusion of an author do the same. The preface reiterates Webster's devotion to a patriotic cause, calling the task of writing an American dictionary not just important but "necessary" for "preserv[ing] an identity of ideas."[72] He even required the inclusion of U.S.-specific definitions for words such as "senate" ("the higher branch or house of legislature")[73] and "plantation" (a farm "where the labor is performed by slaves")[74] as part of this identity.

The preface to the dictionary could have just as easily served as the introduction to the Constitution, the Declaration of Independence, or any number of patriotic texts. He wrote,

> The United States commenced their existence under circumstances wholly novel and unexampled in the history of nations. They commenced with civilization, with learning, with science, with constitutions of free government, and with that best gift of God to man, the Christian religion. Their population is now equal to that of England; in arts and sciences, our citizens are very little behind the most enlightened people on earth; in some respects, they have no superiors; and our language, within two centuries, will be spoken by more people in this country, than any other language on earth."[75]

A strong statement for a country that was little more than fifty years old. Webster was one of several early American thinkers who essentially rewrote U.S. history, shaping the national psyche through a glorious narrative that was much more palatable to people than their humble origins. There are many things in our early history that Americans can cheer, including one of the earliest and longest-lasting democratic republics (Webster would have been heartened to learn that France is technically in its fifth republic), but to claim that early Americans started with civilization, learning, and science is to fabricate the history of an initially agrarian society begun by venture capitalists, religious puritans, indentured servants, and enslaved people. And yet, this narrative of an "enlightened" country with "no superiors" was so effective in galvanizing early Americans that it has become ingrained in our national DNA. One need only turn on the television to hear politicians refer to the United States as an example for the rest of the world, even during periods of national shame.

The idea of having "no superiors" can be understood twofold: not only did Webster and others like him believe that the United States had no match; they conceived of the United States as a place that was not beholden to existing traditions. It was in essence the reference book for a nation that saw itself as having no reference point. The country could form its own rules, in politics as well as in culture and language, according to this narrative. Some of those rules—at least when it comes to language—happened to be created by a born-again Christian nationalist who saw dialects and foreign languages as corrupting influences. With influxes of immigration from all over the world, spoken American English in the following centuries would increasingly become a patchwork of dialects, inflected with words from Italian, Yiddish, Gaelic, Spanish, and myriad other tongues. And yet the standard language has not always reflected those changes, regardless of the dictionary's current attempts to be more inclusive. As to Webster's claim that English would be the most spoken language in the world,[76] he was

partially right. English (though not American English specifically) as a first or second language is now the most spoken tongue
in the world, with 1.27 billion people speaking it worldwide.[77]

Webster defined or redefined many words with his 1828 dictionary, from noting that racoon flesh is "palatable food"[78] to
including the word "Americanize" ("To render American; to
naturalize in America").[79] Among its most influential entries,
Webster's dictionary invented a new definition for the word
"immigration," one that some scholars say established a fear of
immigration in the American psyche. Webster's 1806 pocket
dictionary appears to be the first place where the verb "to immigrate"[80] surfaces in an English dictionary—"emigrant" had
long existed across languages, but the notion of the verb "to immigrate" as "to remove into a country"[81] was new. He was writing before the major waves of immigration to the United States
in the nineteenth century, but his staunch nationalism still
shines through. His definition continued to evolve in the writing process, with the 1828 dictionary further changing his original 1806 version to define "immigrate" as "to remove into a
country for the purpose of permanent residence."[82] Up until that
point, migrations were often considered seasonal, impermanent,
or from city to city rather than from country to country. Historian Neil Larry Shumsky argued that Webster's new definition of
the word "immigration" had the kind of impact on the American
collective consciousness reserved for precious few dictionary entries. Shumsky wrote, "By telling Americans that immigration
involves coming from another country, Webster set up an us-
versus-them opposition, foreigner against native-born. By telling
Americans that immigration is permanent and involves the intent

of residence, Webster encouraged them to fear that in time they might be displaced, their cities overrun and their jobs jeopardized."[83] This definition has echoed through generations to a time now when an oppositional mentality—sometimes veering into xenophobia—finds its way into American discourse.

Webster's version of nationalism was of course different from what we think of as American nationalism now, with its white supremacist slurs and protectionist agenda. But the idea of "America first" and of an American identity based on purity are very much Websterian ideals. His original sense of American nationalism was based on opposition to the British, but that notion would evolve over the years—picked up by those who came after him—coming to encompass opposition to a whole host of different national and ethnic groups. In Webster's work, it was impossible to have an "us" without also having a "them." He might not have bequeathed an entire ideology to modern-day nationalists, but he certainly lent them both the cornerstone of their values and the language to express those ideals.

The nationalist sentiment was only one aspect of the dictionary that helped it endure throughout history. The religious revival of the Second Great Awakening was in vogue when the dictionary first came out, and evangelicals cheered Webster's book as a godsend. Webster called Christianity "that best gift of God to man"[84] in the preface, but he did not stop there. Religious overtones pepper almost every definition of the dictionary. In the entry for "love," the word "God" appears five separate times, including "we love God above all things."[85] He defines "nature" as "a word that comprehends all the works of God"[86] and the word "devotion" as "a yielding of the heart and affections to God."[87] Religious ardor helped sell the dictionary, and some conservative Christians today still herald it as a Christian text, using Webster's speller and dictionary to homeschool their children.[88] A Bible society digitized the entire 1828 dictionary and put it online. That first dictionary is now out of print, but Christian homeschoolers frequently ask Merriam-Webster if they will reprint it, Peter Sokolowski of the dictionary told me.[89]

The dictionary solidified the relationship between Christianity and American language, weaving biblical examples and ways of speaking into the very foundation of speech. This way of speaking has persisted in the United States, whereas it has faded in most European countries. In modern French political discourse, for instance, it would be unheard of to mention God in a public address, whereas in the United States a speech is rarely over until the orator says, "God bless America." Webster is not the only one responsible for forming an inextricable relationship between God, country, and language, but he standardized it in a way to make it more universally used. Even today, elected officials consistently employ biblical language, and it's hard to imagine another Western country in which government officials regularly cite "God's providence" or invoke public calls to prayer.

❧

Webster's may never have become the dictionary it is today if not for the shrewd (and oftentimes cutthroat) business tactics of the Massachusetts Merriam brothers. After a modest initial release that landed its author in debt, it took several decades for

Webster's *American Dictionary of the English Language* to become
the preeminent U.S. dictionary, eventually outpacing Johnson's
A Dictionary of the English Language, which had been the standard in the United States from when it was published in mid-
eighteenth-century England. George and Charles Merriam
purchased the rights to Webster's dictionary in 1843, after
Webster's death, igniting a fierce battle between themselves and
dictionary writer Joseph Emerson Worcester, in what historians
would later refer to as "the Dictionary Wars." While "war"
might seem a strong word for a fight over lexicography, the
struggle for domination between the two competing dictionaries would span several decades and both the North American
and European continents, entangling the careers of some of the
most prominent lexicographers of the century. Worcester had
worked for Webster, and throughout the decade before his death,
Webster had accused his former protégé of plagiarism, a claim
that has never been verified. When the Merriams bought the
rights to Webster's dictionary, they decided that there was only
room for one American dictionary. They would launch an aggres-
sive publicity campaign, smearing Worcester in the United States
and abroad in London pamphlets,[90] spending the better part of
two decades trying to erase Worcester from the world of words.
After years of publicity campaigns and revised Webster editions
that happened to come out at just the same time as Worcester's
revised editions, by the 1860s, Merriam-Webster was the definitive victor.[91]

"What they did for Webster had never been done before.
Nobody did this with Johnson. Johnson's dictionary died on the
vine,"[92] Sokolowski of Merriam-Webster told me. "They weren't

scholars, but they were salesmen. They knew how to get this book into the hands of governors, and professors, and judges, and teachers, and schools, and to really promote the name of Webster and to kind of create a myth, a national myth. And Webster was sitting there waiting to be mythologized,"[93] he said. The business of selling a dictionary and ensuring its authority was just as important as—if not more important than—the work itself. Webster's first dictionary had been sold at the hefty price of $20 (well over $500 in today's currency), which was standard for the era. After Worcester published a new dictionary in the 1840s, the Merriams pushed out a single-volume dictionary in 1847 to compete with their rival, undercutting his price by selling the dictionary for $6.[94] While $6 was still a hefty sum in 1840s America, it was a downright bargain compared to what was available at the time. Sales took off, bringing the Webster family more than $250,000 in royalties (approximately $7.9 million today).[95]

The Merriams did more than just develop a strong business plan to sell Webster's dictionary; they also decided to revise the content itself to be more marketable. Many of the stranger spellings were axed ("tung" for "tongue,"[96] for instance, had made it into the 1828 version). Other changes, such as the use of *er* instead of *re* and the suppression of *k* in words such as "music" had already taken off in American culture and were left in. In a move that would clinch their success as the leading dictionary, the Merriams hired Yale professor Noah Porter[97] and his research team, who would revise or remove many of the Christian references, strange spellings, and far-fetched etymologies. After their work appeared in the 1864 edition, the dictionary would become a critical success alongside a commercial one, thanks in great part to Porter. The dictionary that the Merriam brothers produced was so different from the original by the second half of the nineteenth century that Webster's son requested that his father's name be removed from the cover.[98] That request was denied. The Webster name had become more a brand than a dogma—and a valuable one at that—and by the end of the nineteenth century, Webster's dictionary had become so popular that the publisher had to fight to keep other lexicographers from using Webster's name and his work. By the time the dust of the Dictionary Wars had cleared, *Merriam-Webster's* had secured a spot for generations to come on bookshelves, in classrooms, and in newsrooms across the United States. Webster's first dictionary may not have been an instant bestseller, but over the years it became a timeless classic: in the past 120 years, Merriam-Webster has sold 57 million copies[99] of its collegiate dictionary alone.

Webster's influence reached far beyond the pages of the dictionary or the speller. Even those Americans who have never read his work or heard his name are still bearers of his legacy. He shaped the underpinnings not only of American education and language standardization but also of the nation as a whole. The idea that America was a new experiment capable of surpassing Europe, the notion of a nationalism based on uniformity, the belief that the United States was a sort of country on a hill— Webster cemented and spread these ideas through the building blocks of language itself. The lexicographer was of course not the only one to maintain and express these principles. But more than even the writings of Thomas Jefferson or George Washington, Noah Webster's ideas were made accessible to the public at large, put in the hands of nearly every young American in the nineteenth century to be read and reread until they were committed to memory.

Over the years that followed, *Merriam-Webster's Dictionary* continued to serve as a text that both invented and reinforced American cultural beliefs and norms. Where Webster had drawn on his Christian and nationalist leanings to pass judgment on words surrounding God and government, the authors of the subsequent dictionaries continued to shape the American psyche with definitions that were less than objective. For example, the 1934 *Webster's Dictionary* defined the word "Apache" as "nomads, of warlike disposition and relatively low culture."[100] The dictionary did not just define things as they were; it defined them as how a ruling faction of Americans felt about them or understood them to be. The 1934 edition was more than eight times as big as Webster's first unabridged dictionary, clocking in at six hundred thousand entries and weighing seventeen pounds.[101] It referred to itself as a "supreme authority"[102] and as such took on the same kind of haughty tone. Throughout the nineteenth century and into the early twentieth century, dictionaries continued to serve as a prime tool for education, including encyclopedic information that extended far beyond word definitions. The dictionary functioned as a vehicle for literacy and cultivation—as well as the social mobility that those things could bring to the reader. To display the seventeen-pound tome in one's home was in and of itself a type of cultural cachet.

As time went on, the dictionary came to more closely capture language as it was spoken. Throughout the twentieth century, as authors such as John Steinbeck and Zora Neale Hurston
made dialect into the fodder for literature, the dictionary reflected the blurring of the lines between high and low culture.
The Merriam-Webster dictionary released in 1961, referred to
as *Webster's Third* (despite not being the third edition), caused a
veritable scandal for its attempts to represent vernacular English, even including the word "ain't." The authors of the dictionary were no longer capturing language as spoken by educated
Connecticut white men but as spoken by everyone, complete
with slang and dialects. *Webster's Third* incorporated thorough
definitions of baseball terms[103]—and the press release for the
new dictionary even included a photo of Betty Grable (the definition for "leggy" had been updated, and an entry for "pinup"
had been added).[104] Many disapproved of this edition, so much
so that a critic for *The New Yorker* said that Merriam-Webster
had "made a sop of the solid structure of English and encouraged the language to eat up himself."[105] But Philip Gove, the
editor in chief at the time, stood by his choice, believing that
dictionaries should be descriptive rather than prescriptive.

Gove wanted the dictionary to reflect the way English was
spoken and written in 1961, not just in college lectures or great
novels but on television shows and on the back of Campbell's
soup cans. In the twentieth century, dictionaries would increasingly embrace this mixture of high and low print culture, as
well as regional variations among English speakers. The 1960s
were also the time when researchers led by Frederic G. Cassidy

interviewed nearly three thousand people in 1,002 U.S. communities[106] to compile the *Dictionary of American Regional English*, whose first volume eventually came out in 1985. *DARE* defined regionally specific terms such as "honeyfuggle"[107] (a verb meaning to swindle) and "jugarum" (a type of bullfrog found in the Northeast).[108] Putting these words into dictionaries gives them a new kind of recognition—power, even. Linguistic projects, both within and outside the context of dictionaries, started to embrace the ways in which regional variation persists not just through accent but in words themselves. It's not as if people from different regions of the United States cannot communicate at all, even if it takes a moment longer for a Bostonian to describe what a rotary is, or for a midwesterner to clarify that they mean "pop" as in a beverage and not a grandfather. No matter how standard each person thinks his speech is, the geographically vast and culturally disparate United States has made it such that everyone's language bears markers of their background.

A baseline educated way of speaking remains, however, even if that baseline varies from state to state and from situation to situation. Unjust as it may be, Connecticut professors might still judge a southern drawl as ignorant, and someone whose English is exceptionally inflected with dialect or slang might succeed less well than a Websterian counterpart in a job interview at a New York company. This, too, might be part and parcel of Webster's legacy: we have always lived in this wonderfully diverse nation, and yet many Americans still see that fact as a point of weakness rather than a strength. Much like Webster, an undercurrent in American culture views diversity and national unity as somehow at odds. And yet, for all the talk of standardization, the United States is only one of a handful of countries around the world that has no official language.

⚘

Variances in speech and language will likely only further expand among American English speakers, especially between generations, as the Internet creates a borderless world of words. Rather than language simply influencing the Internet, the Internet is also influencing the way we use words, including offline. Memes and text abbreviations are used in spoken language, as linguist Gretchen McCulloch points out in her book *Because Internet*.[109] People sometimes say "LOL" instead of just laughing, and even septuagenarian politicians try to appeal to young voters by using Internet-speak on the campaign trail, often with extremely awkward results. Then presidential candidate Hillary Clinton was widely mocked for using "the Internet's favorite expression" when she sold campaign T-shirts emblazoned with the phrase "Yaaas, Hillary!" in 2016 (a riff on "yaaas, kween!"). This is where the fluid nature of the online world can get tricky: popular catchphrases seem to simply appear in the zeitgeist when in fact the Internet is often amputating expressions (many of which originate in Black or queer communities), transplanting them across contexts without any kind of authorship or credit.

The dictionary, too, is enjoying a renaissance online, with Merriam-Webster seeing 100 million page views per month and 2 billion word look-ups per year on its apps.[110] The democracy of the Internet has not only widened the breadth of accepted speech; it's also allowed for more of an exchange between the wardens of language at the dictionary and the users of the dictionary itself. Many of the emails that lexicographers receive consist of readers asking Merriam-Webster to add or remove a favorite or least favorite word, because even now "a sanction by Merriam-Webster is what makes a word 'real' or not,"[111] McCulloch noted. People like Peter Sokolowski, the editor at large, can also see what people are looking up in the dictionary and when, which in turn gives Merriam-Webster a sense of how readers are actually using the dictionary. Truth and understanding may vary based on how old you are, what apps you use, and what your political affiliations are, but there is a bridge to be found in online dictionaries in particular, a broadening of the exchange between readers and lexicographers.

The dictionary may be increasingly accessed online, but Merriam-Webster maintains a brick-and-mortar office in Springfield, Massachusetts, not far from where the Merriam brothers' first commercial building was located. Built in the 1930s, the current home to Merriam-Webster resembles a schoolhouse, but its purpose is prominently displayed: a dictionary carved into stone sits atop the front entrance with the words "Merriam-Webster Dictionaries" emblazoned underneath it. The twenty-five-person editorial staff maintains a "strong tradition of silence" in their libraryesque open-space office, Sokolowski tells me. There is no hum of fluorescent bulbs in Merriam-Webster: even the light fixtures were specifically chosen to be silent. Editors tend to speak in a whisper, and phone calls and meetings are reserved for the few closed-door offices. Adding to the library feel, the lexicographers at Merriam-Webster still make use of a card catalog of all the most recent definitions, located in rows of metal file cabinets in the center of the main room. It is on this one floor of the building in Springfield that most of the dictionary work gets done: adding new words, collecting novel definitions, and—perhaps most of all, according to Sokolowski—constant revision. The work of dictionary writing is a task of rewriting, updating definitions to reflect our shifting understanding of words and their meanings. Sometimes, old, seemingly immovable concepts need to be revised: following the racial reckoning in the United States in spring 2020, for instance, Merriam-Webster updated its definition of the term "racism." The word had been revised several times since it first entered into *Merriam-Webster's Dictionary* in the 1930s, and it was again updated in 2020 with recent examples from Black activists as well as a refreshed definition that reflects systemic racism.

The dictionary itself changes, and the way readers use it has evolved, too. The dictionary has served so many different purposes throughout history—reference guide, judge, schoolteacher, even moral arbiter—in the pursuit of everything from virtue to social mobility to comfort in times of hardship. It can even instruct its reader in etiquette. The first monolingual English dictionary appeared in 1604, and its author, a schoolmaster named Robert Cawdrey, dedicated it to "Ladies, Gentlewomen, or any other unskilfull persons."[112] From the start, dictionaries were there to educate people about more than just words. The decision to label words as "nonstandard" or "slang" teaches readers what language is considered appropriate, possibly even what type of language should make them feel ashamed. In that way, it can also operate as a self-help book for people looking to improve their station in life. Today, the editors at Merriam-Webster have been asked to serve as friend, guide, and philosopher for contemporary readers, functioning as a kind of "public utility," Sokolowski said.

Readers employ the dictionary in unlikely ways, in times of crisis in particular, Sokolowski noted. After the terror attacks that took place on 9/11, the top word that people were searching on Merriam-Webster's online dictionary was not "rubble," or "triage," or even "terrorism," but the word "surreal."[113] And the dictionary's data saw that happen again after the Boston Marathon attacks and after the mass shooting at Sandy Hook Elementary School—that same word, "surreal."[114] Merriam-Webster's definition for "surreal" is an adjective meaning "marked by the intense irrational reality of a dream." Perhaps, then, we find comfort in the authority of dictionaries, of definition—especially at moments when we feel as if we're living in "the intense irrational reality of a dream."

That same "intense irrational reality" arrived again when the COVID-19 pandemic first swept the United States in the spring of 2020. In mid-March, when many cities were preparing for stay-at-home orders, the fear and uncertainty of the moment were reflected in the dictionary's top looked-up words. There were the technical words, such as "pandemic," "quarantine," and "virus." But there were also the philosophical ones: look-ups swelled for the word "surreal," as well as terms such as "apocalypse," "Kafkaesque," "martial law," "calamity," "pestilence," "contagion,"

"well-being," "hysteria," "hoarding," "self-isolation," "vulnerable," "unprecedented," "triage," "essential," and "poignant." Sokolowski told me repeatedly that the dictionary is "neither an
accusation nor a diagnosis." I'd contend that it can be both, but
it can also serve a different purpose entirely: it can take the pulse
of the population, expressing some concern, anxiety, or national
trend through a surge of interconnected words and their web of
meanings.

The definitions of words may change over time, but a word
still exists to describe things we don't understand, and its definition can be found if we know where to look. "People were
turning to the dictionary not for facts but for what I would call
philosophy,"[115] Sokolowski said of these moments of crisis.
"You're trying to wrap your head around an idea or phenomenon, and you go to the dictionary to go back to basics. That's
also true for the word 'love.'"[116] Merriam-Webster receives
thousands of letters and emails every year, many of them inquiring about what he calls the "phenomenon" of a word, meaning our collective experience of it. Sokolowski recalled one letter
Merriam-Webster received in the 1990s, inquiring as to several
particulars of the word "love." Merriam-Webster responds to
every letter received, and one editor at the time wrote back with
this message: "We thank you for your letter, but your question
about how long love lasts is not something we can answer. We
lexicographers are good at defining words. Questions about the
nature and permanence of deeply felt human emotions, though,
are a little outside our field."[117]

Nearly two centuries after the release of Webster's first dictionary, at a time when truth is derided as fiction and the very

underpinnings of our society often feel destabilized, Americans have looked again to the dictionary for something more than the definition of words. Whether searching for comfort or just clarity, Americans seek out the dictionary in times of turmoil especially. "If the entire country is looking up a word like 'precedent,' 'unprecedented,' and 'unpresidented,' in our data, implicitly the country is asking us a question," Sokolowski said. "And what is the dictionary for but to answer questions about language?"[118]

✿

CHAPTER THREE

Benjamin Franklin's Autobiography (1793)

In 1722, sixteen-year-old Benjamin Franklin was bored. As an apprentice at his older brother James's printshop in their native Boston, his tasks were few and menial. Given his status as the fifteenth of his father's seventeen children,[1] the young Franklin had only two years of formal schooling—and no real prospects. So, he invented one. Franklin started writing letters to James's newspaper under the pseudonym "Silence Dogood," a widow with a penchant for giving advice. Over the next year, James would publish fifteen of Mrs. Dogood's letters, and the fictional widow became something of a hit with Bostonians—she even received a few marriage proposals. When James found out that the widow was none other than his younger brother, the discovery put increasing tension on an often fraught relationship. Within a year, Benjamin Franklin ran away from his apprenticeship to his brother, fleeing the city of Boston. But their falling-out sent the young Franklin on the path to Philadelphia, where he would transform from "the first juvenile delinquent in American literature"[2] to one of the nation's founders.

Franklin was many things throughout his life: a statesman, an inventor, and a successful entrepreneur. He was also many people; while writing under pseudonyms was a common practice at the time, Franklin created nearly enough alter egos to field an entire football team, chief among them Silence Dogood, Richard Saunders, Anthony Afterwit, Polly Baker, Alice Addertongue, Caelia Shortface, Busy Body, Martha Careful, and Benevolus. Franklin drew upon his various personas like a well-stocked wardrobe closet—somewhere between a coat of arms and a spy's disguise. He consistently chose the most profitable costume for the given situation, whether it was a widow doling out romantic advice or a washed-up astrologer hawking almanacs.

Franklin was a master of transformation, and Silence Dogood was just one instance of many where he created and stepped into the most profitable identity for the occasion. The founding father was self-made not only in the sense that he came from no inheritance and built a fortune but also in that he invented and reinvented himself by sheer force of will. And his autobiography, which has maintained its iconic status over the course of more than two centuries, serves as America's first potent guide to becoming the type of self-made man that Franklin embodied. Posthumously titled *The Autobiography of Benjamin Franklin*, the book is hardly a straightforward account of his life. Franklin both paints a glorified version of his early pursuits and lays out a road map for others to follow in his path to success.

His origin story—which drew on a mix of hard work and a fake-it-till-you-make-it attitude—would serve as the first American rags-to-riches narrative, the cornerstone of one of the most irrepressible myths of American life. It was the first text that put into print exactly what the American dream was—the perfect marriage of capitalism, civic values, and a bit of showmanship—and how to get it.

Because nearly every school-age child learns some version of Franklin's history, his vision continues to shape our notions of the self-made man, even for those who have never read his book. *The Autobiography* is at once a guide to the values that would come to define U.S. identity and a how-to book for making it in America. The idea that anyone can pull himself up by his bootstraps has become so entrenched in the American psyche that it's taken as objective fact—a concept reinforced along the way by generations of farmers, immigrants, and venture capitalists who made a new life in the New World. But like all stories, it has an author. Though rags to riches was not Franklin's idea alone, his version of that tale would shape the American understanding of wealth (and guile) like no other.

When *The Autobiography of Benjamin Franklin* first appeared in English in 1793 (it strangely appeared in French two years earlier),[3] it quickly became a hit with thousands of Americans who wanted to make a better life for themselves. Franklin soon came to embody the folksy, salt-of-the-earth American that many Americans imagine in the best of us: self-taught, temperate, a patriot without being a zealot, and a scholar without being an intellectual. In the early nineteenth century, a time when Americans were still figuring out just what kind of a people they wanted to be, Franklin offered a kind of ready-made mold. As the nineteenth century wore on and Americans were faced with a new kind of identity crisis—this time coming in the form of influxes of new immigrants—people turned again to Franklin's success story. "All that has happened to you is also connected with the detail of the manners and situation of a rising people; and in this respect I do not think that the writings of Caesar and Tacitus can be more interesting to a true judge of human nature and society,"[4] Franklin's British editor Benjamin Vaughan wrote in a letter that would later be included in *The Autobiography*. An ever-expanding, rising people did indeed find something worth vaunting in Franklin's whimsical retellings of his own life. Between 1794 and 1822, some twenty-two editions of Franklin's *Autobiography* were published,[5] and to this day it remains a rare American bestseller written before the nineteenth century. It can be understood as both the first popular American self-help book and a complete guide to early American identity, reprinted nearly 120 times in some form by 1860.[6] What is remarkable about it is that it has endured beyond its original context, continuing to draw twenty-first-century readers—in the past few decades alone, it has appeared on the syllabi of college courses roughly two thousand times.[7] Tesla CEO Elon Musk[8] says he was inspired by the life of Benjamin Franklin, just as Thomas Mellon had been more than a century prior. In part because there were so many unauthorized versions put into circulation, it's impossible to know just how many copies have been sold since it was first published, but it has been called "the most popular autobiography ever written,"[9] serving as the blueprint for the lives of millions of Americans. The book was one of only a handful of bestsellers in the early United States—a place that did not yet have a national public school system, much less a centralized demand for literature.

Franklin's story began to serve as a great unifier. Both the powerful and those over whom they exercised their power read the book. Newly freed indentured servants and new arrivals to the country alike—as well as the ruling elite—read it, with many nineteenth-century migratory workers carrying it in their packs all the time.[10] When folk hero frontiersman Davy Crockett died fighting at the Alamo in 1836, the one book he had on him was Franklin's *Autobiography*.[11] For those at the turn of the century who were learning to read at the same time they encountered *The Autobiography*, its tale of self-made success became all the more impactful, as for many people it would have been the first book that they read outside of the Bible, an almanac, and a school primer. "His power is that he served both American nativists and recent immigrants alike as a sort of mystical civic figure with whom differing peoples could identify themselves and their common social interests,"[12] wrote English professor and Franklin expert Carla Mulford. "Franklin's figure was used to obscure difference beneath a myth of national unity."[13]

❀

Long before he would become a social rival to John Adams and the bespectacled founding father known to millions of American schoolchildren, the young Franklin grew up poor in Boston. To illustrate his lack of social standing (and complete dearth of inherited wealth), Franklin described himself in *The Autobiography* as "the youngest Son of the youngest Son for 5 Generations back."[14] His father was a candle and soap maker, a trade considered even lower on the social ladder than those of other artisans, and his childhood on Milk Street in Boston was sparse. At ten years old,[15] Franklin was pulled out of school to assist his father in his shop. While this was not entirely unusual for the time— George Washington had about the same amount of formal schooling as Franklin did—it would later put him in stark contrast to the many Harvard graduates who attended the Continental Congress. While other founding fathers spent their days at Latin schools, Franklin ran errands, cut wicks, and filled dipping molds day after day.[16]

In *The Autobiography*, however, Franklin focuses instead on the cheerier aspects of being generally left alone: he was able to read what he liked, explore the city, and get up to whatever mischief crossed his mind. Often, the young Benjamin and his friends spent their time fishing for minnows in a nearby salt marsh. A new house was being built nearby, and Franklin convinced his friends to steal the stones from the worksite to build a wharf for their fishing expeditions. One evening after night fell, he rounded up his friends to steal the stones. Only the guttural *ribbit*s of the frogs would have punctuated their grunting as they lugged the stones, sometimes needing three boys to carry the bigger pieces.[17] When the workmen arrived the next day to find their stones missing and a new wharf erected in the pond, the boys were "corrected" by their fathers, Franklin recounts in *The Autobiography*. "Though I pleaded the usefulness of the work, [my father] convinced me that nothing was useful which was not honest,"[18] he writes. And yet, it seems, that correction did not stick. As the American literature scholar John Griffith would later point out, "*The Autobiography* confesses that Franklin's standard was not so much *truth* as *usefulness*."[19]

Usefulness became Franklin's litmus test throughout his life of what was acceptable behavior, just as it would become a central tenet of American life. Coming as we have from colonists, pioneers, and frontiersman, for whom survival was the first and sometimes only goal, usefulness laid the foundation for middle-class life. Being both poor and ambitious imbued Franklin with a particularly American devotion to usefulness, and after he fled to Pennsylvania, Franklin's beliefs about success started to transform into a more complex paradigm that revolved around practicality and performance. "So convenient a thing is it to be a *reasonable Creature*, since it enables one to find or make a Reason for everything one has a mind to do,"[20] he would later write in *The Autobiography*. Franklin's ability "to find or make a Reason" would enable him to accomplish nearly everything he had a mind to do—and much more than most minds could imagine.

When he first arrived in Philadelphia as a teenager, the young Franklin stood tall at five feet nine or ten inches, with blond or light brown hair.[21] He was "strongly built, rounded like a swimmer or a wrestler, not angular like a runner . . . his eyes grey, full, and steady, his mouth wide and humorous with a pointed upper lip,"[22] according to his biographer Carl Van Doren. With no money and after getting his first rest in Philadelphia by sleeping in a Quaker meetinghouse, Franklin was forced to rely on his wiles to be able to eat. When he turned his ambitions to becoming a printer, he was quick to assume the importance of appearances. Franklin himself admits that he performed the role of a successful printer long before he really became one. He writes in *The Autobiography*: "I took care not only to be in Reality Industrious and frugal, but to avoid all Appearances of the Contrary. I dressed plainly; I was seen at no Places of idle Diversion; I never went out a-fishing or shooting; a Book, indeed, sometimes debauch'd me from my Work; but that was seldom, snug, and gave no Scandal: and to show that I was not above my Business, I sometimes brought home the Paper I purchas'd at the Stores, thro' the Streets on a Wheelbarrow."[23]

His book showcases one of the recurring themes of American values: they are often a double-sided coin, with a positive virtue like entrepreneurship on one side and a necessary duplicity on the other. There seems to be something perhaps not uniquely but strongly American in the idea that other people need to know what you're up to for it to count, that part of being a successful person is necessarily a public endeavor: something others have to witness to make it true. Through the ubiquity not just of Franklin's *Autobiography* but of his entire life story as well, he started to add a new layer to what the ideal American looked like. He introduced this type of role-playing, even a subtle deceit, into what is required for success. Franklin's alter ego Poor Richard once wrote, "What you would seem to be, be really,"[24] and it's a kind of tightrope act that has defined much of Franklin's legacy, in ways he both did and did not intend.

During his more than two decades as a printer, Franklin

drew on the power of performance and disguise on his path to becoming one of the most successful men in Philadelphia. Part of the original meaning of rags to riches in Franklin's case was a literal one: the rags used for printing newspapers would build his vast fortune. When a rival printer named Samuel Keimer stole Franklin's editorial ideas and opened his own newspaper, Franklin called again on pseudonyms as a weapon for defeating a rival. He wrote letters ridiculing Keimer's *Pennsylvania Gazette* in a competing newspaper under the pseudonym Busy Body.[25] Those letters were so damaging to Keimer's reputation that he was eventually forced to close the paper and sell it to Franklin "for a Trifle."[26] In anecdotes like this one that he recounts in *The Autobiography*, part of what makes Franklin come off as the hero (and not just the cause of someone else's bankruptcy) is his own honesty. Throughout his life, he effectively anticipated and fended off criticism through candor, even within the text of the book itself. His self-deprecation works in a similar way—even if it, too, is a type of performance. Franklin's book is especially convincing because he makes us feel as if he's telling us the whole story, but as in all memoirs, he's giving us his version: one in which he might chastise himself but in which he—and the nation as a whole by extension—is ultimately triumphant. Franklin lets himself off the hook by situating his own success as a necessary means to the end of national prosperity. The distinctly American heroism in his story lies also in his rise. Not only did he become wealthy and successful enough to retire in his early forties, but he did so without inheritance or education.

Franklin was not making money for money's sake but rather

in order to retire and devote himself to pursuits in science and politics that would serve both his own interests and the nation as a whole—something he did at the age of forty-two. With his fortune won, Franklin would later use his wealth to start social programs and endow cities, and his *Autobiography* begins to outline a new vision of money as a collective good and not just a personal one, connecting the success of the individual to that of the republic at large. The very ways in which we talk about money and success today cannot be unwoven from the ways that Franklin conceived of those things. "Waste nothing"[27] and "Lose no time; be always employ'd in something useful; cut off all unnecessary actions,"[28] he advises readers. So many of Franklin's ideas about wealth and success have been ingrained seamlessly into our everyday discussions about money—how to get it, how to keep it, and how to use it wisely. The many more expressions falsely attributed to Franklin speak to just how mythic he has become. In a way that has grown ever more problematic over time, Franklin shows capitalism as part of the virtuous American ideal—not in order to stockpile couture like the French nobles, but rather to effectively build and strengthen small communities. In *The Autobiography*, he points out several examples of his money going toward a communal good, from organizing a subscription library to forming one of the first fire brigades. A successful American, Franklin argued through example, was one who made enough money to give back to his community.

This notion has only grown thornier in the intervening two centuries, and it has lingered in ways Franklin could not have predicted. In the late eighteenth century, when Franklin was writing, even the largest American cities—at that time New York and Philadelphia—had approximately thirty thousand residents each.[29] A wealthy donor such as Franklin could indeed make a real difference by starting a social club, a library, or a fire brigade. The power of the individual to effect social change through private donations diminished rapidly as the population grew exponentially over the following generations. The idea that personal wealth is a communal good, however, has remained, even as it has become falser over time. One need only look at trickle-down economics or the oft-quoted expression "a rising tide lifts all boats" to see how this idea endures both in popular culture and in the American economic model—even when it no longer fits the contemporary reality. Especially today, at a time when wealth consolidation has reached extremes, the whims of the richest Americans may lead to the creation of charitable foundations or nonprofits, but their influence in cities populated by millions is but a drop in a needy ocean, not the establishment of a "way to wealth."

❀

Despite Franklin's successful life and his desire for *The Autobiography* to serve as a blueprint for those who sought a similar "State of Affluence and some Degree of Reputation in the World,"[30] he ironically began work on his memoirs at a moment of utter failure. He started what would become *The Autobiography* in 1771, more than twenty years into his retirement. Franklin had won recognition as a scientist and public intellectual, but he struggled to find a toehold in politics. Franklin was coming off a public snafu in which the American public perceived him to have equivocated concerning the unpopular Stamp Act—and in retribution, an angry mob nearly burned his house down in Philadelphia. A string of political missteps was capped by another disappointment when he was passed over for a royal appointment.[31] A growing number of American patriots started to see Franklin as the old guard, not quite revolutionary enough. As Franklin himself lamented in a 1768 letter, "I do not find that I have gained any point, in either country, except that of rendering myself suspected by my impartiality; in England of being too much an American, and in America of being too much an Englishman."[32]

A defeated Franklin retreated to the English countryside in the summer of 1771. While staying in the southern hamlet of Twyford with his friend Jonathan Shipley,[33] he wrote the first pages of what would become *The Autobiography*. Franklin may have been a successful businessman at that point, but the vision he crafts of himself in the first part of *The Autobiography* as a well-established success is at least partially untrue. Certainly, he was wealthy, and his scientific experiments were increasingly well-known in Europe, but 1771 would have been a low point in both his career and his personal life. The colonies were still five years away from declaring independence, and both his future and that of his home were growing murkier by the day. Even the way he framed that first section as a letter to a beloved son is something of an inconsistency. His "young" son was by that point a forty-something governor of New Jersey. Though Franklin describes him in the book as a "dear son," the two were constantly fighting,[34] and he had not seen him in seven years.

Seen this way, the book was Franklin's way of correcting the record of his own life before anyone could say otherwise. He would return to this project off and on over the course of the next two decades. Ever the adept public relations expert, Franklin was getting ahead of the story, even when the story was his own life. For someone who would come to be remembered as a great man and a Revolutionary, this attitude bears much more in common with a man like Noah Webster—a man who feared early on that his name would be forgotten over the course of history (and indeed was later confused with that of politician Daniel Webster by much of the public). Franklin was of course more well-known during his lifetime than Webster was in his, but Franklin's enduring legacy seems to have come in part from his own anxiety over how he would be remembered, as well as his own tireless efforts at self-promotion.

Franklin biographer Walter Isaacson called him "America's first great publicist,"[35] and in *The Autobiography*, the product Franklin is selling is at once himself and his vision of a future America. With hindsight, Franklin's brand seems to us so established as not to be worth marketing in this way, but it is precisely because of this dedication that his ideas, beliefs, and patterns of living remain staples of American cultural life. He willed them into being through a combination of hard work, achievement, and especially self-promotion. The innocuous, patriotic Franklin we remember is a far cry from the complex and utterly strange man he was. As he became more successful—and later downright famous—whatever genuine self he had became inextricably entwined with all the various masks he wore.

Franklin the printer, Franklin the failed diplomat, Franklin the inventor, and, later, Franklin the successful diplomat were quite different people with vastly different goals and worldviews. A necessary part of Franklin's legacy is a kind of subtle deception, a constant reframing of both his own life and that of the American people. His story—which would become the American story—was just that: a narrative, drawn both from how things were and from how he would like them to be.

Franklin saw the successful American as a talented social chameleon who could move between social registers along his rise to success: navigating the high- and the lowbrow, the British and the American, existing as both a renowned scientist and the son of a soap maker. Ideas similar to Franklin's would later be codified by the sociologist Erving Goffman, who wrote that all of life was a performance in which the actors wear a set of shifting masks.[36] A person might act one way in the office, where a boss is watching, and another way when he's alone with coworkers, at a moment when he feels offstage, or more relaxed. That same person might wear a slightly different mask with school friends, with family, or with a romantic interest. There is no true self, according to Goffman, and the performance of these different selves is neither positive nor negative—it simply is.[37] The words you use, how you dress, even the way you walk or hold yourself—none of these are permanent. They are all changeable, ready to be transformed based on the situation.

Franklin is sometimes accused of being false, but he may have merely been a more adept performer amid a sea of less talented actors. Performance takes place not only for the benefit of the performer but for that of society as a whole, according to Goffman, facilitating social ease. Franklin's various roles—shopkeeper, diplomat, American, Englishman, et cetera—are only contradictory if we look at them at the same time, said Dr. Michael Hattem, a historian of early America. "If we want to assume that those roles were real or were a fundamental part of him, then yes, we have what seems to be a number of paradoxes,"[38] he said. "But I think if you think about it more as he's inhabiting these roles whenever the moment calls for them, then he looks way more aware of what he's projecting than most people in the eighteenth century were."[39]

It's why so many Franklin scholars talk of the multifaceted Franklin, the man behind the masks[40] (or if they're being less generous, the two-faced Franklin). Franklin's vision of the ideal American as an aggressively industrious but benevolent striver, someone who "emerged from the poverty and obscurity in which [he] was born and bred,"[41] is an archetype that has endured in the American psyche for centuries. Franklin himself was self-made not simply in the sense of a man who came from nothing and became a success but in the way that he was self-fabricated, self-invented, just as any number of fictional heroes (Jay Gatsby comes to mind). Franklin's goal in writing the book, aside from rehashing his own glory, was to give the American people what he saw as the keys to their survival. In doing so, he constructed an identity for them to step into based greatly on his own flair for disguise. More than just codifying this archetype, the book served as a model for American history itself—the way we would patch together our collective identity from a series of facts, fictions, and partial truths.

⚘

More than older empires such as France, Britain, or Spain, with monarchies and established social hierarchies, America—at least in the eighteenth century—was up for grabs, in just about every way: politically, socially, and economically. The performance of success was so vital in achieving actual success, in part because performance was all there was. An eighteenth-century French pauper, for instance, may have been able to perform the role of a noble, from manners to language and dress. If he was not in fact of noble blood, however, it would not have mattered how successfully he looked the part. But there was an opportunity in early America, a small window that lasted perhaps not much longer than Franklin's life, where a successful performance, a conformity to what an American looked, acted, and sounded like, was enough leverage to gain a better life. With the social order still in flux, there was money and influence to be had for those who could successfully conform to shifting ideals of Americanness. This opportunity, of course, even at the beginning, was limited to white men. Role-playing only works if you already "pass" to a certain degree as what a successful person looks like, and at the time that was a Christian white man and only a Christian white man. The vast majority of women and people of color would be excluded from the possibility of becoming self-made for generations (and to a certain extent are excluded from many roles to this day). American identity, or a specific archetype embodied by Franklin, was long limited to those men who looked like him.

Franklin has become the standard for the self-made man, but that image ignores a more complex picture: his success story relied on at least two types of free labor. The first came in the form of the housekeeping carried out by his wife and daughter. Franklin may have spent his first years in Philadelphia skimping, saving, and managing his own time and money—even forgoing meat so that he could afford books—but by his early twenties, he had married his wife, Deborah, passing over all the household duties to her. "He's as close to self-made as a self-made man can be. But he did have a wife and a daughter doing everything for him once he married,"[42] said Dr. Micki McGee, a sociologist and author of *Self-Help, Inc.: Makeover Culture in American Life*. After all, it is far easier to have the luxury of time for the activities that Franklin encouraged in his autobiography, such as reading and personal development, when you do not have to cook, clean, or do other menial tasks.

For most of his life he also kept two men, George and King, enslaved. Franklin never mentions this fact in *The Autobiography*, perhaps because like many men of his generation, he did not see slave labor as related to his personal achievements. And Franklin's vast newspaper fortune—the one that would build libraries and finance scientific experiments—came in part from the frequent advertisements that his *Pennsylvania Gazette* ran for slave auctions[43] and runaway slave notices. While historians and average citizens alike today increasingly talk about the checkered legacies of Washington or Thomas Jefferson when it comes to the issue of slavery, Franklin has escaped largely unscathed, remembered as the first American self-made man despite his reliance on slave labor. He is memorialized as a quirky,

almost modern founding father—not a slave owner who bene-
fited in more ways than one from the horrors of chattel slavery.

"Self-made" and "slave owning" cannot comfortably coexist,
even if certain founding fathers did not initially see it that
way. This is not judging the eighteenth century with a twenty-
first-century morality; many eighteenth-century Americans recognized the incompatibility of slavery and the founding ideals.
Some ten years before the publication of *The Autobiography*, William Cushing, chief justice of the Massachusetts Supreme
Court, wrote, "The Idea of Slavery is inconsistent with our own
conduct & Constitution,"[44] adding, "There can be no such thing
as perpetual servitude of a rational Creature."[45] Even Noah
Webster would advocate for abolition on the grounds that it was
inconsistent with America's founding values, writing, "To labor
solely for the benefit of other men, is repugnant to every princi-
ple of the human heart."[46]

Franklin, too, would change course, partially because of his
own close ties with abolitionists. By 1785 he became president
of an abolition society in Philadelphia, and by 1790 he would
employ one final pseudonym[47] to write an impassioned denun-
ciation of slavery. Franklin wrote a satirical letter to *The Federal
Gazette* purporting to reprint a speech by a seventeenth-century
Muslim leader defending the practice of enslaving Christians.
"Let us then hear no more of this detestable proposition, the
manumission of Christian slaves, the adoption of which would,
by depreciating our lands and houses, and thereby depriving so
many good citizens of their properties, create universal discontent,"[48] the leader says. The letter concludes, "The doctrine that
plundering and enslaving the Christians is unjust, is at best

problematical; but that it is the interest of this state to continue the practice, is clear; therefore let the petition be rejected." In this role reversal, Franklin turned the institution of slavery on its head, showing its false logic. Franklin signed his letter with the name Historicus—the voice of history.

❀

If the first part of the autobiography was written in a time of doubt and struggle, the second part would come out of years of personal and national triumph—the capstone to nearly a decade of successful diplomacy on the international stage. Franklin had sailed to France after the outbreak of the American Revolution with the aim of convincing the French king to bankroll the war. Franklin's time in France would become arguably his best performance of all—and the one that proved most vital to the creation and survival of the United States. Without Franklin, there might not have been French support for the American Revolution, and without France, the newly formed United States hardly stood a chance against Britain.

Several years had passed since his diplomatic stumbling blocks in England, and his increasingly fervent patriotism convinced his fellow Revolutionaries that he shared their vision for a free country. In 1776, when Franklin left for France, he was a wily and wise seventy-year-old polymath—fully aware that an American, no matter how accomplished, would be unable to match the French on their haughty, aristocratic terms. So instead, he arrived in France dressed as the frontiersman the French expected Americans to be, complete with plain clothes, spectacles, and a marten fur cap he had brought from Canada for the occasion. In his American costume, Franklin charmed every dining room, café, and ornately decorated hall that he entered; legend has it that even Marie Antoinette had a crush on him. Franklin was arguably the most famous American abroad, owing to his scientific experiments, but his celebrity reached new heights in France. People lined the streets to see him arrive in Paris. The French were so taken with the portly American with the fur cap on his head that his likeness soon decorated everything from snuffboxes to wallpaper in Paris.[49] French ladies rushed out to spend their livres on wigs that mimicked his style, deemed *"coiffure à la Franklin."*[50] Soon, French artisans made clay medallions of his face, signet rings, and other keepsakes.[51] As he later wrote in a letter to his daughter, Sarah Bache, "The numbers sold are incredible. These, with the pictures, busts, and prints, (of which copies upon copies are spread every where) have made your father's face as well-known as that of the moon."[52] In little more than a year after his first arrival, Franklin would secure supplies, munitions, and an official treaty—and the support of a French armada. The idea that Franklin—a poor man's son, a self-made man, and an all-around maverick—could swindle the French out of more than 1 billion livres while wearing a dead animal on his head remains a satisfying tale to Americans. His success at Versailles was improbable for many reasons, not least of which that Louis XVI seemed not to fully comprehend the parallels with his own situation. He would be financing a revolution to overthrow a king—a sort of practice run for French dissidents who would soon have their eye on their own king's head.

What made Franklin so successful in France—especially in

comparison to prototypical puritanical Americans such as John Adams—was his adaptability. As had been the case throughout his life, Franklin did not have an immovable sense of self and morality in the way that someone like Adams did. He enjoyed instead a mix of Enlightenment reasoning and the love of a good party. By the time he arrived in Paris, he was a prolific inventor and scientist, but his scholarly success did not stop him from enjoying soirées, multiple-course dinners, and plenty of flirting. He may be beloved as an American, but there is a real Frenchness to Franklin's leisure ethic. The French were so wooed by Franklin that they decided to claim him as a fellow countryman. One newspaper in Amiens reported that "Franquelin"[53] was a common surname in the Picardy region, suggesting that Franklin's family could have in fact been French before they immigrated to England and then the United States.

Franklin's years in France were far more complicated than those of an adept manipulator ready to extract as many livres as he could from the French king. By all accounts, the love affair France had with Franklin was a mutual one, and he spent the better part of the next decade living there. He spoke of the food, the cleanliness, and the beauty of the country in a letter to his daughter as one might speak of a lover. Franklin's daughter, Sally, would even name one of her children "Louis" after the king.[54] "This is the civilest nation upon earth,"[55] Franklin wrote in a letter to a friend. Instead of the mask slipping, in letters and anecdotes like this one, we see the mask becoming fused to the man in ways he might not have realized. For all his homespun charm, Franklin lived far from a simple life in France. His home was part of a compound of villas in the Passy neighborhood (what is now the posh sixteenth arrondissement in Paris), complete with formal gardens and a pond overlooking the Seine. Soon he had amassed more than a thousand bottles of wine in his collection,[56] including Bordeaux and champagne. Franklin's years as the happy ambassador in the lap of French luxury revealed yet another yawning gap between reality and the reputation he would enjoy as a salt-of-the-earth hero.

By the time Franklin sat down to write the second part of his autobiography in 1784, he had been living in France for nearly eight years. It was then that he would write the "plan for attaining moral perfection"[57]—sometimes referred to as the thirteen virtues—in what would become both one of the most cited and one of the most despised sections of the entire book. Paris was the perfect place for him to write a section about calculated personal change, at this moment in his life when each move he made, down to what he wore on his head, had been selected for a specific purpose. In it, Franklin lays out the thirteen virtues that he says guided him to his success, such as temperance, silence, order, frugality, justice, moderation, and humility. He includes a calendar grid that he claims to have used in order to track his progress with each virtue every day,[58] and he encourages others to follow the same path. What is remarkable about this section is that—arguably for the first time in American history—it lays out both what he saw as the values of an ideal American and a concrete strategy for cultivating them. He even includes an example of his daily schedule, which starts with his four a.m. wake-up and ends with his nightly moral evaluation as he slides into bed at ten p.m.[59] As a prototype of American self-help, it has all of the hallmarks that would come to define the genre, all the way down to an absurdly early morning wake-up call and a numbered list of steps. Franklin's main piece of guidance, as would become the case for many self-help regimes, was constant self-evaluation for constant self-improvement.

The "plan for attaining moral perfection" was a kind of shrewd reverse engineering of personal character. This, too, is part of the legacy of his book: the American obsession with self-improvement. Franklin could hardly have imagined that there would be entire magazine columns devoted to the morning routines of everyone from Bill Gates to Kris Jenner, much less enormous sections of bookstores dedicated to self-help books that would use strikingly similar methods, from behavioral modifications to small change over time to a taking of one's personal inventory. The root of this type of advice is about imposing the performance from the top down, as opposed to advocating for the kind of personal development that starts with a fundamental change in belief. Much like any number of present-day self-help experts, Franklin saw daily habits as the building blocks of personal and moral change. He seems to attribute much of his physical and intellectual prowess to minor, achievable changes, such as drinking water instead of ale and eating vegetables. It created a strange and often implausible link between small behavior modifications, moral character, and professional success. In a way typical of the Protestant work ethic, Franklin's emphasis was always on practical, classifiable progress.

The quest for moral perfection inherent in self-help can be traced back even further than Franklin, all the way to the early colonists' Puritan roots. Franklin's parents were devout Protestants, and he wrote openly of how he was influenced by the "Do

Good" essays of the fiery, witch-hunting minister Cotton Mather.[60] What he created went beyond Mather's morality and toward a much more modern understanding of success based on personal power. As a nation, we are lovers of goal setting, of New Year's resolutions, of self-motivation. Perhaps it's because we tend to have an obsession with achievement, seeing ourselves as a people who earn what they get—and continue to earn more and more. We owe that ethos, at least in part, to Franklin and his *Autobiography*.

The thirteen virtues section still includes Franklin's signature self-deprecation: he reminds readers that he, too, struggles to fulfill them. He even added the thirteenth virtue, humility, after a friend informed him that everyone thought he was too proud.[61] Franklin is quick to acknowledge his own shortcomings in his goal of "moral perfection," but his self-deprecation often feels like a literary tool: a way of showing that he's just like us. He is offering up his story as an example to everyone, rather than an account of the extraordinary, eccentric, and all-around singular person that he was. This, too, is a double-sided coin: by holding up his individual example of hard work and self-reliance as something that anyone can achieve, he ignores the fact that the staggering amount he accomplished in his lifetime is simply not possible for all Americans. As a man who demonstrated the existence of electricity, accrued enough wealth to retire in his forties, and was instrumental in the founding of a nation, Franklin was not the rule of American life but the exception to it. Beyond his accomplishments, he was unique in just how strange he was: he used to take "air baths,"[62] sitting naked in front of an open window in the belief that it would keep him from getting sick. He wrote an essay on farting;[63] he developed his own alphabet; he chased tornadoes. And in what was something of an anomaly for his era, he was not religious in the traditional sense of the word.

Self-help books, however, tend not to take into account the possibility of failure, or even of mediocrity. With their big promises of better lives, they have been popular in the United States since they first started appearing—a trend that should be at least a little surprising. There has always been an anti-authority streak to American culture. This is a country that was founded through revolution, and its original social contract—the Constitution—functioned initially to limit government meddling in individuals' lives. Americans are a people who started a war in the name of freedom and escape from outside influence, and now we gleefully purchase books that tell us exactly what time to get up in the morning. At the same time, self-help is in some ways the most American genre of literature there is, as it connects personal achievement with the good of the group while locating both the problem and the solution within the individual himself. These books continually take the pressure off the system and put it back on the person. Self-help books—and this one in particular—fulfill many of our earliest values: autodidacticism, individualism, and meritocracy. Even the term "self-help" seems destined for a country that praises pulling oneself up by one's bootstraps.

Part of what critics would later rage against in *The Autobiography* is a trap endemic to this kind of literature in general: while it can help many people, it can hardly help everyone, nor can it transform every single reader into a Franklinesque genius. That reality has only compounded over history as inherited wealth and a staggering wealth gap have increasingly come to define the American economic landscape. Because if successful people like Franklin receive full credit for their success, are those who struggle in America blamed for their failures? Franklin does not explicitly fault others who do not succeed, but he does take the example of the character flaws of those around him—a rival printer, a drunken friend—who stumbled on the ladder to success. He points to their bad morals and flawed choices, just as he notes his own virtuous behaviors.

The Autobiography is not just self-help; the thirteen virtues section makes Franklin's book arguably another kind of literature entirely: reference. It encourages readers to come back to the book repeatedly, rereading the virtues to check on their progress and to find new kernels of wisdom, much like a traditional Bible. A reader can flip to this section to check on their progress without needing to read what came before or after, not unlike looking up the definition of a word in a dictionary. In it, Franklin makes no reference to dates or to history; the thirteen virtues project exists outside of time. In this way, too, it would lay the foundation for all kinds of reference and guidebooks that would use a similar framework, encouraging readers not to read once but to come back to the books' principles again and again.

This book remains hard to classify because it is at once a self-help book, a memoir, a get-rich-quick book, and a guide to citizenship. It also began to form the ideological grounding of the

American middle class. Franklin was of course not the only one to promote the kind of thrift, hard work, and self-reliance that would come to define what many Americans understand as middle-class values. He was, however, the only early American to lay them out in list form and provide a measuring stick for their achievement. Part of his legacy lies in the way that the moniker "middle-class" has become its own kind of status marker, too, with nearly everyone in the United States claiming to be middle-class (including the rich).[64] Franklin took pride in being part of "the middling People,"[65] the self-made men he believed were destined to replace England's rigid class structure with an American social order based on hard work. In a country that sometimes likes to claim class categories do not exist—and rarely discusses them—the term "middle-class" has come to function as a catchall that avoids any real distinctions between people. Perhaps that's why it seems to be one of the most used terms by American political candidates, regardless of the election year or their party affiliation. In some ways it's logical for so many to claim the term "middle-class." Given the current extremity of U.S. wealth disparity—with billionaires such as Jeff Bezos living in the same cities as thousands of homeless people—it's easy to feel as if the rest of us fall somewhere in the middle. As one researcher pointed out, "middle-class" has become more of a brand even as it has faded from being a reality for many in the United States.[66] That might be the reason why we still cling to Franklin's vision. If middle-class America no longer means a pension, vacations, or good healthcare, at least we can still choose to believe it means thrift, honesty, and hard work.

❀

In the late nineteenth and early twentieth centuries, public opinion soured on Franklin's legacy among an increasing number of British and American intellectuals, in great part because of the thirteen virtues section. In the Industrial Revolution context, Franklin came to represent, to some, the unrestrained capitalism and the cult of the individual that were emblems of turn-of-the-century America. The criticisms of Franklin were more than a question of literary differences; he became the scapegoat for all of America's problems of character, from materialism to self-interest. There was a deliberate confusion between Franklin and people like Andrew Carnegie, who took themselves to be Franklin's "ethical heirs,"[67] one scholar wrote. The list of writers who wrote diatribes against Franklin during this time is essentially a who's who of the literary world of the era. Everyone from Mark Twain and Herman Melville to John Keats and D. H. Lawrence had a critical word to spare for Franklin. In his novel *Israel Potter*, Melville depicted Franklin as a kind of drunk wizard.[68] Twain, creator of so many enduring and folksy American archetypes, might seem a natural ally for Franklin's view of self-made American life. But in a comedic, yet acerbic, essay on *The Autobiography* he wrote, "The subject of this memoir was of a vicious disposition, and early prostituted his talents to the invention of maxims and aphorisms calculated to inflict suffering upon the rising generation of all subsequent ages. His simplest acts, also, were contrived with a view to their being

held up for the emulation of boys forever—boys who might otherwise have been happy."[69] In other words, Benjamin Franklin
singlehandedly ruined Mark Twain's childhood.

These writers took umbrage in particular at the thirteen virtues section, mocking it for being overly prescriptive and con-
trolling, too simplistic an approach to any real personal or moral
development. D. H. Lawrence accused Franklin of trying to
turn men into "virtuous little automaton[s]."[70] He rewrote the
thirteen virtues, revising the section on temperance to read:
"Eat and carouse with Bacchus, or munch dry bread with Jesus,
but don't sit down without one of the gods."[71] What Lawrence
seemed to hate most was this idea of man as a perfectible machine. Ironically, Franklin would have been the first to admit
that he failed constantly at his own game. Some of the accusations lodged against Franklin were valid, and many Franklin
himself likely would have agreed with, as he joked throughout
his life (and even in *The Autobiography* itself) that he was far
from achieving moral perfection. These critics read *The Autobiography* as something so regulatory as to be oppressive, a demand for a specific kind of American conformity in a changing
world. There are many paradoxes within the criticism that Franklin represented some kind of ruthless capitalist (the most obvious
being that he worked to live, retiring at forty-two to take on
challenges he found more interesting). Regardless, the unifying
narrative that had once united disparate Americans was now
something that many chafed against.

That so many writers found *The Autobiography* worth rallying
against speaks to just how central it has always been within
American culture. And its influence today on business leaders

such as Elon Musk shows its enduring relevance, especially for a certain kind of American entrepreneur. *The Autobiography* was America's first rags-to-riches story, one of our most foundational myths. Then it became a self-help book, a guide to American values, even a kind of get-rich-quick manual. For some, it would represent the best of what we have to offer as Americans, and for others it meant just the opposite.

As historian of early America Michael Hattem said, "Franklin can be whatever he needs to be at a moment, but we also make Franklin what we need him to be."[72] How we understand Franklin now—for better or for worse—is no truer than how early twentieth-century industrialists viewed him, or how nineteenth-century indentured servants did. For a performer as skilled as Franklin, the masks he wore were not more or less real; they simply *were*—there not only for him to draw upon but for us, too. This perhaps is his legacy more than anything: an elasticity. We can see him (or not see him) in Dale Carnegie, or Anna Delvey, or any number of presidents, but what we choose to see says decidedly more about us than about him. And the Franklin narrative has become a model for the way that we cobble together the American story, based not on objective truth but rather on necessity. Benjamin Franklin was the chameleon Revolutionary, the ideal American not for what he was at any given time but for his ability to be so many different things to a disparate, diverse, disunified nation in need of a new Adam.

CHAPTER FOUR

The McGuffey Readers (1836–1837)

When Benjamin Franklin died in 1790, coughing and feverish from pleurisy, the United States consisted of thirteen states and fewer than 4 million people.[1] By the 1830s, the number of states had nearly doubled and the population had more than tripled, to well over 12 million.[2] Americans had evolved from farmers and fortune seekers to include a growing number of self-made businessmen and new immigrants, all of them sharing their stories with an evolving new language. But the mythology developed and delivered by people such as Franklin and Webster was often limited to the level of individual Americans. Without widespread schooling, people educated themselves at home with their school primer and a Bible. But telling tales around family hearths—or even in a growing number of books—was not an efficient way of mythologizing this new nation. What many Americans felt the country needed next was an organized way of disseminating these ideas of American identity, no matter how new and fluctuating they still were. They needed a vehicle for teaching shared morality and values to what Franklin's editor called "a rising people." Americans required a school system that would educate them not just in order to read but in order to vote and to shape the future of their young nation. The man to do that job, to educate more than 100 million Americans, was born into one of the log cabins that were increasingly dotting the western edge of the United States.

William Holmes McGuffey was a child of the frontier, swaddled in an empty maple syrup trough[3] and raised in a one-room log cabin constructed out of the surrounding trees. In the years leading up to his birth, his parents had worked to clear the forest for farming land on the edge of what is now Pennsylvania and Ohio.[4] McGuffey's father, Alexander McGuffey, made his living in the 1790s as a hunter and a soldier. A Scottish immigrant, Alexander joined a squad whose entire purpose was to skirmish with and spy on local tribes.[5] In the push to expand the United States westward, the government attempted to fully expel the Indigenous people living along the Ohio River—many of them refugees who had already been ousted from ancestral lands elsewhere in the country[6]—and McGuffey's father became well-known in the region as a soldier in that fight. Alexander cultivated a reputation as a man skilled in firearms and espionage, known for his single-mindedness, bordering on ruthlessness, when it came to what he saw as his mission against the Shawnee, the Lenape, and other tribes.[7]

With the daily grind of survival on the western frontier—the constant chopping of wood, hunting, and growing whatever food they could—education was not the first priority in the

McGuffey family. For the young William McGuffey, school would be a privilege and not a right, something he did when all the practical work had been completed and only when time and money allowed for it. Like many western families, his parents could not afford to spare their oldest son from the work of the farm, so he labored in the fields in the summer and spent only part of his winter in classes. His mother, however, had a passion for learning. She began William's education at home, as was traditional, with the memorization of biblical passages. She would even trace letters in the soot of their fireplace to teach William the alphabet.[8] By the time he was a young man, he could allegedly repeat entire books from the Bible and sermons he had heard a single time.[9] A devout woman, his mother maintained a fervent hope that her son might grow up to become a preacher.

William's childhood was steeped in an extremely conservative strain of Presbyterianism. His mother was a driving influence in his eventual decision to be ordained, but he would also be marked both by several Presbyterian minister teachers and by a small but highly devout community on the frontier. The McGuffeys were of Covenanter stock, a strict Calvinist group that frowned on everything from dancing and games to certain kinds of singing. When William's grandparents first settled in their community in Washington County, Pennsylvania, they had signed a "religious code," along with 114 other families. This document served as both a governing contract and a sacred covenant, warning against a whole host of bad behaviors. The following is only an abridged list, but the rules of the code forbade "Breach of His Sabbath, disobedience to parents, back-bitings, entertaining bad thoughts, and receiving groundless evil reports of others, lascivious songs, filthy discourse, promis-cuous dancing, drunkenness, defraud, deceit, over-reaching in bargains, gaming, horse racing, cock fighting, shooting for prizes, lying, covetousness, discontent."[10] From the start, Mc-Guffey's notions of God—and good behavior—would be noth-ing if not strict. This framework would mark McGuffey in his lifelong beliefs about God, his fellow man, and what he owed to both.

McGuffey's mother's fervent desire to give him a better edu-cation may have come out of that same religious devotion. Cal-vinists have always put a high value on literacy as a necessary skill for growing closer to God through Bible reading. After his mother reached the end of what she could teach him at home, she sent William to a small school run by a local reverend. The one-room schoolhouse where he first started taking lessons was situated at the end of a road that McGuffey's father had cleared himself.[11] As a boy, William would walk the six-mile stretch of road to attend his first sessions of formal schooling. One of the few books available to him—which would quickly become the most influential on the young McGuffey outside of the Bible—was Noah Webster's *Blue Back Speller*. The speller taught him to read, but it also provided a potent example of how to mix read-ing comprehension with moral lessons, a structure that would come to define the books he later wrote. As McGuffey's daugh-ter wrote, "Father had the usual education that boys of that country get, but of course it was not much. He was fond of studying and reading. He used to walk miles to borrow books from the schoolmaster or the minister and would read at night by the firelight, stretched out on the floor. He was eighteen years old before he ever saw a slate."[12] When the reverend who ran the school where William was studying died in 1814, his education screeched to a temporary halt.

As an adolescent, McGuffey got his first taste of the profession that would define his legacy. Following the reverend's death, McGuffey took his former teacher's place at just fourteen years old, opening his own subscription school, where he would soon teach forty-eight students in the back of a livery stable.[13] At the time, it was not uncommon for people with only a rudimentary education to serve as teachers. In the years before a public education system, schools were paid for on a subscription basis, organized and led by teachers wandering the countryside on horseback. Ohio did not even require a test or any kind of certification for a person to become a teacher. McGuffey would spend the better part of the next several years teaching, eking out a living with an irregular schedule of classes and a dribble of income.

McGuffey lore has it that his formal schooling started up again after his mother stood outside their log cabin and made a wailing prayer to the heavens, asking God to provide a way forward for her children. Supposedly hearing the cry, Reverend Thomas Hughes rode by on horseback and invited the young McGuffey to come study at his school, Old Stone Academy.[14] There he would do chores in exchange for schooling, subsisting on a diet of bread and milk,[15] desperate for any path that bent toward education. Over the years, his formal schooling continued on and off, with the off periods usually determined by a lack of funds. He would attend Washington College in Pennsylvania to finish his schooling, studying philosophy, history, and ancient languages (Latin, Greek, and Hebrew). McGuffey could barely afford the books for his college courses, and he continued to teach during a portion of the year in order to pay for his studies. It was there, teaching in a makeshift classroom inside a smokehouse, that McGuffey would be noticed by distant relatives of the Reverend Robert Hamilton Bishop, president of Miami University in Oxford, Ohio. Bishop traveled all the way to McGuffey's classroom just to watch him teach—and after observing him for only a short while, Bishop offered the twenty-six-year-old a job as a professor.[16]

❀

By the time McGuffey started working at Miami University he had been teaching on and off for more than a decade. The frontier boy had grown into a dogmatic Christian and a strict disciplinarian. As a newly christened professor of biblical languages, he arrived on campus—if you could call it that—in 1826. Oxford had only been incorporated territory since 1810, and even after McGuffey's arrival, teachers still had to help clear the forest to build the school.[17] The pioneer town, population five hundred,[18] was little more than a smattering of log cabins and frame houses encircled by the woods.[19] Within a few years, McGuffey was ordained as a minister—a passion that fueled him both in and outside the classroom.

Miami University had hired McGuffey to teach ancient

languages, but he saw his mandate as far broader than the scope of his classes. McGuffey feared for his students' immortal souls: they needed more discipline, better schools, and books that would effectively achieve both. On this humble stage, McGuffey was a star in the pulpit—and an awkward, often controversial bombast just about everywhere else. But when McGuffey preached the word of God, people listened. McGuffey's sermons attracted praise early on in his career, and later in life eager spectators would even cut a hole in the ceiling of a crowded lecture hall just to be able to listen from the roof.[20] McGuffey would later say that he preached three thousand sermons in his lifetime, all of them spontaneously.[21] (The fact that written sermons exist,[22] however, undercuts that claim to a certain extent.) His passion sprang from how he understood the task of education: as forming the moral and not just the intellectual character of students. As he looked out on his classroom each day, McGuffey saw the symptoms of a wider national ill: a country whose future generations desperately needed guidance. In McGuffey's eyes, the children of the western frontier were wild, reckless, and, above all, godless.

As he walked between the school chapel and the classroom, McGuffey's appearance was striking: With his wide-set eyes and mismatched features, one colleague later described him as "so ugly as not to be readily forgotten."[23] His usual dress was "the most old fashioned I ever saw outside a museum," that same colleague said, describing a high linen color surrounded by black silk, matched with silk stockings of the same color and shiny buckle shoes.[24] McGuffey's contentious personality quickly divided both his students and his colleagues. While he found allies among some of the stricter Presbyterian teachers, and several students remembered him fondly, McGuffey was quick to make enemies. He butted heads with the other professors, berating them for being too lax with their students. One of his colleagues called McGuffey a "fomenter of discord"[25] for how combative he was with the other teachers and even with the president of the school. McGuffey demanded harsh punishment for everything from drinking to profanity. Many of the young wards of the college feared McGuffey, a man whose scowl made even the cockiest of his students "tremble" with fear.[26] One year, eleven students were expelled from Miami University[27] (out of little more than one hundred total). Later in his career, at Ohio University, he expelled so many students that by the spring there was only one senior left to graduate.[28]

While still working at Miami University, he began compiling a school primer that he hoped would lay the moral foundation for the budding nation. As McGuffey found himself in conflict with the head of the school, President Robert Bishop,[29] in particular, he turned to writing the books. The school's president saw a new way forward for Presbyterians, arguing that they should take on moral issues of the day, such as abolition, while easing off of some of the fire and brimstone that had defined their past. McGuffey disagreed. Tensions between McGuffey and Bishop would later mount toward a breaking point, with McGuffey eventually being forced to resign.[30] If he couldn't convince the president of the school to take on his plan for morality, he would instead develop and lay out his own project for the future of a Protestant American education in the books he was writing.

The Cincinnati publisher Truman & Smith had already approached the schoolmaster with a proposal to write a series of school primers in the early 1830s.[31] It was a strategic move: New England authors had dominated the market for schoolbooks, but the expanding frontier provided a different audience for a different book, one written with their values and daily experiences in mind. "Western books for Western people"[32] was their rallying cry. Especially as some New England–based primers grew increasingly explicit on issues such as abolition,[33] a book that avoided all divisive politics could succeed both on the frontier and in response to slowly growing demand in southern states. McGuffey spent several years compiling the first four volumes of his Readers (his younger brother Alexander Hamilton McGuffey would assist him and write several later volumes). The publishing company was nearly broke, so McGuffey was offered a royalty scheme: the teacher would earn 10 percent of royalties on the books until he earned an advance of $1,000. After that, he would receive no further payment.[34] The publisher would go on to become a millionaire (as a concession, he would continue to give McGuffey an annuity beyond the initial contract).

McGuffey's Readers might never have been commissioned by Truman & Smith were it not for the Beecher and Stowe families. The dogmatic Lyman Beecher arrived in Cincinnati from Connecticut in 1832 with his family in tow. A passionate crusader in all kinds of reform movements, from temperance to education to abolition, Beecher came out west for a position as the president of the Lane Theological Seminary in Cincinnati. Part of what drew Lyman Beecher to the expanding frontier was both a desire to create schools and a fear of Catholics—two things that were closely entwined in his mind. As he watched an increasing number of German and Irish immigrants, many of them Catholic, buy up inexpensive land in Ohio, Beecher made the case that Americans needed to educate Catholic immigrants in common schools or forever lose control of the country to the whims of the pope. He called Catholic immigrants "an army of soldiers"[35] ready to encroach upon American freedoms, writing, "The Catholic system is adverse to Liberty."[36]

Beecher was highly involved in the movement for common schools, and his growing and powerful faction saw the ideal American not just as Christian but also as a certain kind of devout Protestant, viewing even other sects of Christianity as a threat to the American republic itself. McGuffey soon became entrenched with the Beechers and the common school movement more broadly. McGuffey himself may have been quieter on anti-Catholic rhetoric, but the Beechers—who were instrumental in McGuffey's securing his book contract—were outspoken about the dangers of Catholic immigrants. McGuffey's publisher had reportedly first approached Catharine Beecher,[37] sister of Harriet Beecher Stowe, with the proposition to write a series of schoolbooks; she recommended McGuffey instead. Excerpts from Lyman Beecher's sermons and speeches would later be printed in the McGuffey Readers, including Beecher's widely circulated anti-Catholic speech, "A Plea for the West."

After several years of drafting the books, all while teaching and growing ever more active in the common school movement, attending meetings of one of the earliest U.S. teachers' associations alongside the Beechers,[38] McGuffey finally finished the first four volumes of his Readers. The first was intended for young children learning how to read, and the books gradually increased in skill level, with the fourth made for children of high school age. Where the early volumes started with simple sentences and images about farm animals, the fourth volume was essentially a collection of reading samples from both English and American writers such as Nathaniel Hawthorne and William Shakespeare, as well as Bible passages. In 1836, the first two volumes came out, and the second two would follow the next year.

The books arrived at the exact right place at the right time. From the time McGuffey was born to when he published his Readers, Ohio—much like the rest of the West—had expanded at a breakneck pace as cheap land drew immigrants and caravans of Americans from eastern states. In 1800—the same year McGuffey was born in neighboring Pennsylvania—Ohio had 45,365 residents.[39] When he was three years old, Ohio became a state. By the time he published the first two volumes of his Readers in 1836, Ohio had well over 1 million residents, with nearly half of them born outside the United States.[40]

The first Readers were published little more than fifty years after the end of the Revolutionary War. The question of "What kind of people will we be?" was very much still up for debate. For McGuffey, the answer to that question was deceptively simple: a Protestant people. He refused to engage with questions of slavery or politics, and his intense focus squared solely on ensuring a set of shared values—a kind of civic religion—guided by Presbyterian theology. "To educate the 'mind and heart of the nation' meant, above all, to form a public, one people out of many,"[41] wrote Christian educator Robert W. Lynn. Catholics were just one face of what these activists saw as a much larger threat, in the form of a shifting populace. And public institutions would be the answer to the question of how to incorporate, or Americanize, an increasingly diverse group of citizens.

The books accomplished far more than literacy; both the McGuffey Readers and public schools in the United States existed to teach people how to be American, or rather, how to be a certain type of American that people like McGuffey had decided was best. New citizens would be able to learn their adopted heritage in the McGuffey Readers, and the books instructed children that their cultural forebears were not just the American Revolutionaries but the Puritans; the primers put John Winthrop[42] and John Adams all in one breath. The McGuffey Readers would sell 122 million copies by 1960, teaching more Americans how to read than any other volume in print—and successfully founding a tradition of God in the classroom that would endure for generations.

❀

It is difficult to overestimate how prevalent the McGuffey Readers were: not only have they sold approximately 130 million copies since their first publication, but nearly every copy was shared by multiple children in a family or school, meaning that 130 million is actually quite a low estimate of how many people read the McGuffey Readers. What made these books so powerful in forming American identity, too, was that they were not read once. The methodology of the nineteenth century was memorization, and several decades later (and well into the twentieth century) many adults educated with the Readers would later report being able to recite from memory the stories they had learned as children. McGuffey's writing was committed to memory by millions of people, made a permanent piece of their understanding of morality. The Readers at once reflected and would come to shape American culture over the next century— teaching a growing number of young Americans how to read, think, and reason with their place in the nation. They appeared just as public schooling in the United States was starting to take hold, offering what some saw as the perfect Protestant books for the next generation of American children. After a brief controversy and accusations of plagiarism from a competing primer written by Samuel Worcester,[43] McGuffey's publisher revised certain sections and went on to establish the book as the foremost textbook of antebellum America. Within little more than a decade, the books had already sold 6 million copies.

Dozens of schoolteachers, hailing from Brooklyn to Terre Haute, wrote testimonials attesting to the quality of the Mc-Guffey Readers. A group of teachers from public schools in 1840s-era Chicago called the books "the very best series we have ever seen"[44] and of "incalculable benefit to the teacher."[45] The leader of an academy in Pennsylvania described them as "of the purest morality."[46] Lyman Beecher said they were simply "perfect."[47] The books received mostly rave reviews from the press, too. *The National Press* described them as "*invaluable*,"[48] and *The Pittsburgh Morning Chronicle* wrote that they were "now superior to any series of school books published."[49]

The McGuffey Readers represented one man's vision of the country, but part of their success came from McGuffey's ability to put Americanness on the page in a way that resonated with millions of Americans. As guidebooks to American mythology, morals, and social mores, the Readers taught students to memorize the life of George Washington and the speeches of Patrick Henry rather than the writings of Plato or Cicero. Across the volumes of the books, we can see nearly every archetype of the good American, from Revolutionary-era patriots to the self-made man to the humble farmer. An emphasis on hard work as the key to success in America was one of the most crucial themes within this vision. The authors he chose, too, reflected this ethos. For instance, McGuffey made sure to note that one poem's author, John Greenleaf Whittier, started as a farm boy. Whittier then became a shoemaker before going on to become an editor and a writer who "ranks with the first poets of America."[50] McGuffey might not have talked about the self-made man in such terms, but he depicted good children as hardworking, self-reliant upstarts who are rewarded for their efforts. Those who did not fulfill those ideals, however, were punished in equal measure. One passage in *The Fourth Reader* is entitled "Consequences of Idleness."[51] In it, an unmotivated student goes through life lazy and never trying hard in school. He eventually goes to college only to be suspended and eventually forced to leave. "Despised by everyone," he becomes "a poor wanderer, without money and without friends."[52] As McGuffey warns his readers, "Such are the wages of idleness."[53] The reading comprehension term for this passage was "consequence."

The book updated Presbyterian ideas about damnation and

eternal reward into secular American ideas.[54] Where older Calvinist books such as *The New England Primer* spoke of eternal
damnation, McGuffey wrote of "consequence." Just as bad children's punishments were extreme, good children earned their
reward both in this world and in the next. McGuffey elevated
the stakes of hard work to life-or-death levels. In doing so, he
made the case that Protestant values were essentially American
values. Among these were obedience, discipline, temperance,
and responsibility to family and to community. The books lambasted vices such as gluttony, wealthy excess, and laziness. The
children who worked hard for their families, for their country,
and for God were rewarded, while those who disobeyed were
punished. The moral universe of McGuffey is a severe one: this
framework wove a tradition of old-school Protestantism not just
into the classroom but into a much broader vision of America as
well. In both understandings of the world, people earn what they
get—in success and salvation or failure and damnation.

For McGuffey and his allies, Protestant beliefs would sketch
the skeleton of national culture. McGuffey created a potent mix
of Protestantism and patriotism from the very first lessons in
the first volumes of the primers. Some of the reading passages
are taken directly from the Bible and in the first edition were
often overtly anti-Catholic or anti-Semitic. McGuffey used de-
rogatory terms for Catholics or Catholicism such as "papist"[55]
and included a passage from Shakespeare in which the Jewish
character Shylock demands his "pound of flesh."[56] In a lesson on
consonants in one of the volumes, an exercise asks students to
repeat the phrase "He cannot tolerate a papist."[57] Many of these
passages would later be revised or taken out entirely by the 1850s,[58]

but they figure prominently in the original Readers. Reading comprehension sections included questions such as "Was Christ a mere man?"[59] As McGuffey wrote in the preface to his fourth volume, he would make no apology for the Christian overtones of his text: "From no source has the author drawn more copiously, in his selections, than from sacred Scriptures. . . . In a Christian country, that man is pitied, who at this day, can honestly object to imbuing the minds of youth with the language and spirit of the Word of God."[60] For McGuffey—and for many Americans like him—the Bible was a nonsectarian, universal text. The way he used it shows something else entirely: McGuffey was essentially making the case for the Bible as a national text, tying patriotism and a certain kind of Christianity ever closer together.

❀

The McGuffey Readers are one of the most potent examples of how a certain type of American story—authored by a certain type of American author—was disseminated to millions of Americans, but McGuffey was far from being the only person thinking about how to create a specific type of national culture through schools. By the 1830s and 1840s, most states in the nation were grappling with what a publicly funded school system might look like, a system in which poor and rich had equal right to attend. Education reformers could not agree on much, but they almost unanimously envisioned the role of school as educating an expanding number of future citizens—not simply teaching kids how to read and count. If Americans remember one person from this movement, that person is probably Massachusetts reformer Horace Mann, posthumously dubbed the father of public education in the United States. While he was hugely influential in advocating for common schools, especially in the Northeast, his vision was neither secular nor universally shared by his countrymen. He assumed that Bible reading would be part of school, arguing—as McGuffey later would—that Bible passages presented without commentary or interpretation could offend no one (even in the mid-nineteenth century, this was not the case). Part of why we remember Mann, too, is that his message of an egalitarian, nonsectarian system is more in line with our contemporary understanding of our school system—and ourselves—as democratic.

The messier truth is that many of the people instrumental in building the U.S. education system saw it as missionary work. For them, it was a way of reforming the American spirit in their own religious image, founding the public school system not on values of democracy and inclusion but on exclusion and uniformity. "Almost everybody else who was playing a similar role to Mann within the United States was an evangelical Christian,"[61] Dr. James W. Fraser, a historian of U.S. education at New York University. Fraser stressed that the term "evangelical" did not have the same meaning in the nineteenth century as it does today, noting: "They cared equally about converting society, building a Christian culture and a Christian nation,"[62] Fraser said. Evangelicals in the common school movement overwhelmingly saw public school as a "parallel institution"[63] to Sunday school. The burgeoning public schools that existed in this era would be unrecognizable to an elementary school student today. Classes frequently drew on Bible reading, hymns, and, later, the Mc-Guffey Readers—which were also full of Bible readings, hymns, and explicitly Protestant overtones.

Disagreement over what this Christian nation would look like fueled many reformers during this era. The middle decades of the nineteenth century gave way to a fight so vicious over religious texts in schools that it is now referred to as "the Bible Wars." The question was not whether there would be Bible reading in school but rather which Bible would be used. Debates raged in Cincinnati, Boston, Philadelphia, and cities across the country through speeches, sermons, and op-eds concerning Bible reading in school and the supposed encroaching influence of Catholic immigrants. Fear fueled the Bible debate and the common school movement at large: fear of immigrants, fear of tribalism, and fear of what some reformers saw as cultural fragmentation. Much like Noah Webster, these reformers had as a central motive for their work a suspicion of the other. We have this identity built on opposition because so many early conceptions of the good American were about who he was not. The books by authors such as Webster and McGuffey were driven by an attempt to fend off some perceived threat to that identity.

The battle for the soul of American public schools was even something that people fought and died for. In 1844, in Philadelphia, actual riots broke out because anti-immigrant Protestants were furious over the request that Catholic students be allowed to read the Douay Bible (considered a Catholic translation) instead of the Protestant King James Bible in class. When the so-called nativists (named because they claimed to stand for Americans born on U.S. soil) staged a public protest, shots were fired from a neighboring window, and soon a full-blown riot began.[64] Over the following days, the ensuing violence devolved into hand-to-hand combat with knives and broken bottles, the exchange of cannon fire, more than thirty fatalities, and many more churches and homes burned to the ground.[65] Like something out of the Old Testament, people wrote "Native American" across their own doors in the hopes of being spared from the chaos. It would take five thousand militia members to eventually stop the rioting.[66] The violent conflicts in Philadelphia and elsewhere reveal a crack in two of the foundations of American belief: that there is freedom of religion and that there is a separation of church and state. Religious tolerance in America has always been a selective virtue. The chaos over Bible reading shows the extent to which the origins of the public education system sprang not from democratic agreement but from violent, partisan uproar.

McGuffey's books may have been Calvinism dressed up in civic language, but his Readers delivered that message in a much subtler way than the cannon fire of Philadelphia. The original 1830s books were explicitly Protestant, but they became slowly less sectarian over the following four decades. Especially in comparison to what came before it, McGuffey's books were far less extreme than *The New England Primer*, for instance, which had been a standard speller for many Americans in the seventeenth and early eighteenth centuries, selling several million copies since its publication in Boston around 1688. McGuffey may have been a hard-core Presbyterian who saw dancing as a sin and feared the collapse of Protestant culture, but the book he produced is toned down when compared with *The New England Primer*. For instance, in *The New England Primer*, when learning the alphabet, students were instructed that *A* was for "In *Adam's* Fall We sinned All."[67] In the pioneer world of the McGuffey Readers, *A* was simply for "axe." McGuffey and his tales of frontier children, farm animals, and American Revolutionaries seemed like a unifying balm, given the context. Especially after the revision of the more extreme anti-Catholic and anti-Semitic passages, McGuffey's books were even more appealing as a tool for unification. And the fact that he mixed Bible passages into his books made them increasingly attractive to Protestant crusaders, a kind of Trojan horse for smuggling the King James Bible into schools without needing to engage in violent debate over translations. McGuffey's books put the emphasis on unity, focusing on the codification of a shared set of stories.

Given the McGuffey Readers' dedication to American authors, American stories, and American history, they were a hit with the earliest author of a U.S. primer: Noah Webster himself. McGuffey made the choice to use Webster's spelling of words at a time when that was not yet universal. In turn, Webster wrote a letter (strangely addressed to Alexander McGuffey) thanking him for using his orthography. Ever the self-promoter, Webster also seized upon the opportunity to lobby McGuffey's publisher to print his pamphlets for a midwestern audience. "It's to be regretted that the schools in our country cannot be furnished with a uniform orthography,"[68] Webster wrote to McGuffey. "I wish only for the prevalence of truth & justice. I have devoted most of my life to the improvement of education, but competition & plagiarists deprive me of a large portion of the reward which I have earned by my labor."[69] The exchange between Webster and McGuffey shows the extent to which our common culture is determined both by extreme actors and by the fickleness of chance over time. McGuffey happened to pick up the fight for Webster, but if he had been educated with a different speller, he might have used a different orthography. Webster's endurance in that way has to be credited to McGuffey, too. What might have become of Webster's spellings and ideas if those 130 million copies of the McGuffey Readers had used British orthography instead? Our culture might feel grassroots or democratic—cobbled together by average citizens and not by kings—but it was often, especially through the end of the nineteenth century, determined by a small, interconnected group of similar men.

McGuffey's books show the extent to which national myths and stories get promoted based on this combination of power, happenstance, and utility. This book, read by more than 100 million Americans, is a product of the person who wrote it, not of universally accepted principles about what being American might mean. The advanced volumes of the books in particular, compiled by his brother, mix traditional American heroes—such as George Washington and Benjamin Franklin—with Protestant ones. The McGuffey Readers make frequent reference to the Pilgrims and the Puritans, calling them our "fathers."[70] While the Pilgrims have since become part of American lore, they were not always viewed in this way, especially outside the Northeast. Thanksgiving would not become a national holiday until the Civil War, a quarter century later. The McGuffey

Readers were instrumental in spreading the Pilgrim mythology to the South especially, where many southerners had long resisted Thanksgiving as an imposition of Yankee culture. Our mythology and our origin stories are a construction, based both on their usefulness to unite people and on the arbitrary will of the authors who wrote them into these bestselling books. Over the years, these stories about Pilgrims and Benjamin Franklin—constructed around a seed of truth—take on mythic proportions. Their meaning is no longer intrinsic but rather a projection of what certain Americans felt they needed to believe in order to survive. Much like a constellation in the night sky, these myths' meaning has only the outline of physical reality.

McGuffey saw common culture as a necessity for survival. That idea was so attractive because it did not necessarily rely on shared heritage: being American could be about believing in the same things and being familiar with the same stories. The narratives that have shaped us—about who founded this country, what it represents, and why—are stories that can be useful or harmful depending on how they are employed. Familiarity and identification with those myths become less about the stories themselves being inherently good or bad. Mythology is instead a kind of social currency, a way of demonstrating who is part of the "us" and who is part of the "them." Individuals can then use those myths to their own ends, whether promoting harmony or enforcing conformity. In that way, the survival of the early United States seems tied less to any exceptional qualities specific to Americans and more to their talent for storytelling, their ability to convince themselves and one another of some special Americanness.

Talking about national culture in the 1830s and 1840s presents a challenge: the United States was less than seventy years old. In a country so regionally diverse and divided across a fragmented and enormous landmass, national culture was more imaginary than a reality. And yet, the discord over issues such as immigration and religious expression—and the fear felt by so many Protestants like McGuffey and the Beechers—showed that many people felt they did indeed have a culture to lose. If people did not at least believe they had some sense of nationhood, they would not have felt so threatened by new arrivals with different beliefs, rituals, and customs. Common culture, much like the West at large, was up for grabs. McGuffey proved to be so influential not just as a writer and a schoolteacher but as a shaper of culture, because he put in print a workable framework of Americanness at this crucial point in history. McGuffey effectively reined in the changing face of America by attempting to organize people under a shared set of values and stories. The perseverance of those values and stories is evidence of his success.

The difference between common culture (something you acquire) and common heritage (something you're born into) seems to be a line that McGuffey blurs. It can be hard to escape the fact that becoming American in the nineteenth century (and for much of our history) was often indistinguishable from becoming white—something that would long prove impossible for Black people, indigenous peoples, and new immigrant groups of the late nineteenth century, such as the Chinese. Italian immigrants, for instance, were at first considered nonwhite upon their arrival to the United States in the nineteenth century. They were described as "swarthy" or "kinky haired" and greeted

with epithets such as "nigger wop" and "dago."[71] Over generations, they—like the Irish before them—slowly lost aspects
of their perceived foreignness. Many changed their clothes and
their eating habits—and some Italian Catholics even converted
to Protestantism. It was only then that they were accepted as
American. The identity that we now take as "American" for
many decades instead meant "white, Protestant, and U.S.-born,"
a group that would be slowly updated to mean "white, U.S.-born"
by the twentieth century and simply "white" by the mid-
twentieth century. The McGuffey Readers rarely make reference to these demographic changes happening, whether on the
level of race, ethnicity, or immigration. The books would guide
several generations of children through the Civil War, Reconstruction, and all the various waves of migration of that century,
but their narrative exists outside of time, in a kind of ahistorical,
Protestant utopia. It's arguably part of why they succeeded: as
politics grew more fractious in the run-up to the Civil War, the
McGuffey Readers would offer a ready escape.

Both slavery and the massacre and removal of Indigenous
people from much of the United States in the 1830s were also
the unspoken context and subtext of McGuffey's Readers. Many
of his biographers have puzzled over whether McGuffey himself supported slavery or whether he was simply following his
publishers' mandate to make the books palatable for a southern
audience. He was surrounded by prominent abolitionists, including the Beechers, though it seems notable that he is not
known to have made any statement in support of their cause.
McGuffey included an excerpt from William Shakespeare's *The
Merchant of Venice* in which Shylock speaks against slavery—but

McGuffey's editors deleted that section of the passage.[72] His editors also deleted an excerpt of a speech from leading British abolitionist William Wilberforce.[73] As for the systematic extinction of Indigenous peoples codified by the Indian Removal Act of 1830, both William Holmes McGuffey and his brother—especially given their father's history—seem surprisingly compassionate toward the plight of Indigenous tribes. *The Fifth Reader*, compiled by Alexander, includes stories such as "Prospects of the Cherokees"[74] and "The Lone Indian"[75]—passages that speak empathetically about the tribes' loss of land. The irony of course was that the Readers were destined for an audience on the western frontier, one whose very presence was actively displacing the people that Alexander McGuffey eulogized. In the late nineteenth century, the McGuffey Readers would even be translated into Keres,[76] the language of the Laguna Pueblo people in what is now New Mexico. Presbyterian missionaries used the books as part of their attempts to convert them to Christianity. McGuffey's so-called Americanizing influence would thereby be inflicted upon a people whose existence on the North American continent long preceded McGuffey and his ancestors.

Public school was in this sense a political tool: it galvanized some Americans around common stories, but those common stories often further marginalized many different peoples. The fight over what is taught in public schools—a battle that began in McGuffey's era and continues to this day—provokes so many strong feelings because at its core, it is a debate about values and culture. Schoolbooks in general—and McGuffey's in particular—speak to fundamental questions of American identity: Are we a people united in certain beliefs? Which ones? Do immigrants need to leave parts of their cultures behind? Does American identity necessitate a degree of uniformity? We talk of the melting pot, but despite our democratic ideals, there has always been some form of cultural hegemony. Who is included in the "us" has broadened slowly over time—from white land-owning Protestants, to white men, to white people, to an expanding group of ethnicities—but many Americans, even today, resist letting go of the category of "not us." Debates over public school in America have always been about what kind of people (or peoples) we want to be.

※

Over the next century, McGuffey's books would educate some of the most famous and powerful people in the country. The Readers' influence extends beyond the sum total of people who read them. Its impact is also reflected in the number of presidents, writers, and businessmen—from Laura Ingalls Wilder to Henry Ford—for whom the book's message formed their moral compass. The McGuffey Readers educated nearly every U.S. president in the years spanning from William Henry Harrison to Harry Truman. Ford was so obsessed with McGuffey that he reprinted thousands of Readers in the 1920s,[77] opened a McGuffey school, and even paid to reconstruct McGuffey's childhood cabin home, log by log, in Dearborn, Michigan.[78] McGuffey's principles had a "profound"[79] impact on Ford's character, according to one biographer, making him the industrious person that he became. Ford was also a raving anti-Semite who spent millions of dollars[80] defending what he saw as white American culture from Jewish people—an obsession that another Ford biographer attributed in part to the anti-Semitism of the McGuffey Readers.[81]

By the mid-twentieth century, the Readers had mostly disappeared from public schools, as states increasingly sought stricter enforcement of separation-of-church-and-state laws. They were briefly put back into Virginia public schools as recently as the 1980s, prompting what several publications deemed a "McGuffey Revival."[82] Within a year, the Department of Education received more than one hundred letters of inquiry looking to put the McGuffey Readers into public schools. It's hard to know what exactly fueled the resurgence other than a kind of conservative nostalgia, with one McGuffey publisher telling *The New York Times* that parents longed for "the good old days"[83] of America.

For that same reason, the McGuffey Readers have experienced something of a second coming among ultraconservative Christian homeschoolers today.[84] They are featured prominently on many mommy blogs authored by those mothers who have decided to educate their children at home for religious reasons. They appear frequently on lists of homeschool families' must-have reading lists. They even show up in the perfectly curated homes of Christian homeschooling YouTubers, who give tutorials on how to teach children to read with these books from the 1830s. The fan favorites of the homeschool movement on YouTube tend to have modest followings of three or four thousand subscribers, whom they teach about everything from cooking apple crisp for fifteen children to curating college prep courses.

A tutorial on how to use the McGuffey Readers appears on many of their channels. "McGuffey was a wonderful Christian man, and he wanted Christian morality to be written in these books,"[85] Sherry Hayes says lovingly in a YouTube tutorial about the Readers on her channel, Mom Delights. As Aaron Jagt, an advocate of the Readers, told me, "Most homeschool families have a set of McGuffey Readers somewhere in the house."[86]

Jagt, thirty-three, runs the site Dollar Homeschool, which sells reprints and online versions of the Eclectic Series, a set of nineteenth-century textbooks that includes the McGuffey Readers. The oldest of six children, Jagt grew up steeped in conservative homeschool life. He and his siblings were educated at home in Michigan by their parents, and he started reading the McGuffey Readers from the age of six. His father was a salesman in homeschool circles, hawking the conservative Christian Robinson curriculum. Arthur Robinson, who designed the curriculum, described public school as "a threat to the spiritual, moral, and mental health of each child."[87] For Jagt and others like him, contemporary public school was too dangerous to have ever been considered an option. "There's just too much of a divide in values between people that attend public schools and people that are homeschooling—what they're trying to accomplish and the values that they have are too different,"[88] he told me. When I pressed him as to what that difference in values specifically entailed, it seemed to come down to the most important distinction: God. Referencing Charles Darwin and what he called other "anti-God" messages, he said, "I don't think you could be really Christian and attend those schools or allow your children to attend those schools."[89]

The McGuffey resurgence represents a longing for a lost America, one that is part real, part imagined. "One thing the McGuffey Readers provide is a sense of belonging: This is who America is. This is who an American is,"[90] Jagt said. That person, according to Jagt, was someone self-reliant, industrious, and God-fearing. Some contemporary homeschool families are so nostalgic for an America gone by that they raise livestock or grow their own crops in an attempt to return to a time of self-reliance, Jagt told me. For them, McGuffey's frontier-era wisdom is just one aspect of a broader movement to return to what they imagine as a simpler, better time in our country's history. Jagt and his cohorts in the homeschooling movement—highly conservative, usually white Protestants—were once mainstream, and now they feel they've been relegated to the fringe. There is an obvious bitterness in that loss. "American society *used to be* Christian,"[91] he said. At the same time, they feel an imaginary loss, too. Jagt spoke of public school in McGuffey's era as if it were conflict-free, determined by small communities of dedicated parents who built schools in their own image. That reality existed to some extent in smaller towns, but as we've seen in the fiery debates of the mid-nineteenth century over common schools—not to mention the bloody riots of sectarian violence concerning Bible reading—peaceful agreement over public schooling has never existed in the United States.

If anything, the debates led by McGuffey and others only laid the groundwork for decades of passionate disagreement over the state of American public schools, from the birth of Reconstruction-era schools in the South, to the Scopes Trial in the 1920s, to a fresh debate over Bible reading in the 1960s, to the so-called culture wars of the 1980s and 1990s. We have rarely been a united people; we are instead a people who come together momentarily for certain shared goals. The very foundation of American thought—down to our two-party political system—has always been disagreement. Part of McGuffey's power seems to have been his ability to unite at least *some* Americans around shared principles, even if just for a few brief decades. The fervor with which people continue to debate who writes schoolbooks, on which topics, and how they are presented to school-age children speaks to just how important storytelling remains when it comes to identity. Parents, teachers, and students alike still debate everything from the banning of controversial books to the inclusion (or exclusion) of topics from climate change to sex education.

The fight to include diverse authors within school curricula, too, is one aspect of an ongoing negotiation over who is included not just in class syllabi but in the identity of "American." It is a remedy to what writer Chimamanda Ngozi Adichie called "the danger of a single story."[92] When we have only one definition of what American identity means, we all suffer—not just minority groups. American mythology is at its most robust when it comes to include voices such as Toni Morrison, Amy Tan, Julia Alvarez, Zora Neale Hurston, James Baldwin, and Sandra Cisneros. The umbrella category of "American" doesn't cease to exist when it expands, but it comes to incorporate a richer tapestry of the American experience. The history of American public schools is a history of grappling with those questions both about who we are as a nation at any given moment—and about who we would like to be.

McGuffey might not have answered those questions in the same way the majority of Americans would now, but he wrestled with them in a real and public way. There is an irony in the homeschool crusaders with the King James Bible in one hand and the McGuffey Readers in another. McGuffey was a product of his time, someone who spent his life tirelessly fighting for the necessity of public school, so that future generations would not be subjected to the lonely and incomplete education he received at home. For him, school seems to have been as much a social and a national project as it was a religious one. McGuffey saw public school as a civic enterprise, something intended for the good of the nation at large, even if his understanding of that was inevitably colored by his own interests. "Public schools exist to bring us together,"[93] said one historian of education, Dr. Johann Neem. "If we don't see ourselves as part of a common project and part of a common nation, we'll have tribalism—and perhaps violence. Somewhere in there is a balance."

CHAPTER FIVE

A Handbook to American Womanhood

In 1822, Catharine Beecher lay in bed in misery. Hardly able to move for three days, she was afflicted not by any earthly malady but by conversion pains.[1] The twenty-two-year-old had not yet undergone the religious conversion experience that was all but a prerequisite for women in her Calvinist milieu, and time was running out. Beecher was set to marry the young Yale professor Alexander Fisher, and her father—the dogmatic Reverend Lyman Beecher—urged her to have a religious awakening in order to be fully prepared for marriage. Before Catharine could walk down the aisle, however, she would suffer another kind of agony.

While en route to visit Europe, her fiancé's ship crashed along the rocky coast of Ireland. The twenty-four-year-old professor drowned, along with dozens of others. His body may have been lost forever at sea, but his grieving fiancée feared most for his immortal soul, dreading that he would be submitted to an eternity of excruciating torture, as he had not yet been saved.

"Oh, Edward, where is he now?"[2] Catharine wrote to her brother soon after Fisher's death. "Are the noble faculties of such a mind doomed to everlasting woe, or is he now with our dear mother in the mansions of the blessed?"[3]

Fisher's death altered the course of Beecher's life; she would turn away from marriage and children and toward something else entirely. Perhaps Beecher did not want to sully what she saw as her drowned lover's legacy. Maybe she was ambivalent both about Fisher and about marriage in general.[4] Whatever the reason, Beecher would remain single throughout her seventy-seven-year life, never marrying or having children of her own. Instead, she became something of a mother figure to women across America, aiming to reform the immortal soul not just of a single person or family—but of the entire country.

In a quest to shore up the ruins of her life, Beecher turned to the moral instruction of people everywhere. She became convinced that women, in their roles as wives, mothers, and teachers, were the true gatekeepers of the moral fate of the United States. She lobbied for the construction of girls' schools across the country to ensure that all women would be fit for such a gargantuan task. Beecher displayed so singular a focus on her goals that many people who met her—including potential investors and even her own family members—could barely stand to be around her. Nearly all her siblings described her as ambitious, manipulative, hawkish, and self-centered.[5] Her sister and famed author of *Uncle Tom's Cabin*, Harriet Beecher Stowe, once wrote of Catharine: "I considered her strange, nervous, visionary, and to a certain extent unstable."[6]

Given her lack of social finesse, Beecher arguably found the most success in her solitary work as a writer. Catharine found inspiration for her work not in the kitchen or in a nonexistent marriage but in the writings of French aristocrat and political scientist Alexis de Tocqueville. In reading de Tocqueville,[7] she came to see the United States as a place where democracy and unfettered social liberties could lead to chaos, or at the very least to an environment of continual upheaval—especially in an era that was increasingly defined by abolition, immigration, and class mobility. Despite coming from a prominent abolitionist family, Beecher wrote against the abolition movement in the 1830s and 1840s[8]—and, in particular, women's involvement in it—so terrified was she of the violence and chaos that any challenge to the status quo might bring. Aiming to reach beyond the influence of her women's schools and straight into their homes, Beecher wrote an extensive manual for educating women entitled *A Treatise on Domestic Economy* (1841). The book was published just five years after McGuffey's Readers, arriving at a time when rapid land and population expansion, coupled with a financial crisis in 1837, left many Americans frightened and anxious about the future. *A Treatise on Domestic Economy* quickly became a bestseller. She would later expand and revise it into *The American Woman's Home* (1869), the latter written with the help of her sister Harriet. The books covered everything women might need to know about running a home, from the proper type of chimney ventilation to how to best emulate the example of Jesus in their daily homemaking. *The American Woman's Home* would be published four years after the end of the Civil War, and in it Beecher would present her vision of the family unit as a kind of healing balm to unify the nation, addressing a host of insecurities about

American politics, consumer culture, and growing diversity. Many other Americans—both men and women—shared Beecher's anxieties. If *A Treatise on Domestic Economy* had arrived in an era of breakneck change, *The American Woman's Home* would be published at a moment of even greater existential upheaval following the Civil War. Many Americans were eager for an answer, for a concrete blueprint of how to safeguard a certain way of life.

More than just offering practical tips on homemaking, Beecher's books would put forward a new and complete philosophy that located women at the center of the United States' moral destiny. Through their roles as nurses, teachers, and shoppers of the household, women were ultimately responsible for the preservation of the physical, moral, and economic health of the entire country, Beecher argued. She was so convinced of women's need to stay home that she spoke against women's suffrage her entire life—even including an impassioned anti-suffrage letter in the first edition of *The American Woman's Home*.[9] By assigning women this grand role in the American project, Beecher was able to effectively propose a form of social control in a period of rapid change—all while reframing her own role within that national destiny. While Beecher's books were not mega-bestsellers on a par with the tens of millions of copies sold by William Holmes McGuffey or Noah Webster, they left an indelible mark on several generations of American women—especially homemakers, teachers, writers, and the many home economists who rose to prominence after her death. She was also part of a much broader trend of authors writing domestic advice books in this era. This chapter is different from the preceding ones, however, in that it looks at a type of literature—popular nineteenth-century domestic manuals—within which Beecher was arguably the most famous author.

The popularity of domestic advice literature exploded in the nineteenth century, filling the void created by growing literacy coupled with a lack of girls' schools. Domestic manuals differed from cookbooks in that they focused more on the organizational and even philosophical elements of creating and managing a family home (they included recipes alongside tips for decorating the house, ensuring the health of all family members, and teaching young children). Especially with novel machinery made available thanks to the Industrial Revolution, women's work in the home had changed as inventions both simplified and complicated household chores. It was grueling, often challenging work—preparing and washing laundry alone could take several days to complete. At the same time, this period in American history saw homemaking become an explicitly symbolic task, too: cultivating a good home was no longer a question of cooking, cleaning, and taking care of the children in the name of simple survival. Everything from the wallpaper selected to the layout of one's kitchen could be a symbol of Christian and patriotic virtue. Through Beecher's books, alongside the hundreds of domestic manuals, periodicals, and novels preaching a similar message, nineteenth-century writers wove the cult of domesticity into every aspect of women's daily life, elevating it to the point of becoming part of popular culture. In an era of American history when the nation remained divided along regional lines, each state might have its own domestic manual, but they frequently shared the same goals: giving women expertise in their work, elevating the value of that work, and creating national stability through gender roles, placing women at the center of the traditional family unit.

Beecher—though never a mother or wife herself—was introduced early to the challenges of raising children and managing a home. The oldest of nine children, she took over as matriarch of the family when her mother died when Catharine was just sixteen years old. She practically raised some of her siblings, including the youngest child, who was less than a year old at the time of their mother's death. Catharine learned how to cook and developed her sewing skills, though she had never been specifically trained in domestic duties. She found motivation instead in her devotion to her father. "He stimulated my generous ambition to supply my mother's place," she wrote of Lyman's encouragement.[10] After her father's remarriage, Beecher seems to have felt at least a little pushed to the side, and she soon left home. By 1821, she became a schoolteacher, and in 1823, two years short of her twenty-fifth birthday, she opened a girls' school in Hartford, Connecticut. By her mid-twenties, Catharine had devoted her life to advocating both for women's education and for their rightful role as educators. And yet, even this decision seems surprising: the woman who would devote her life to women's schools once called teaching "drudgery."[11] One Beecher scholar suggested a theory: Catharine was "simply devising an elaborate rationale for correcting the defects in her own education."[12] The schooling available to girls varied widely based on region, but the scope of subjects was often limited:

where some girls learned math and reading, others focused more on etiquette and some French. Catharine pushed for girls to be able to learn traditional subject matter such as Latin and algebra alongside what she called "domestic economy" (everything from caring for the sick to cooking healthy food to leading the family in calisthenics). In that way, she differed from many of the authors of other domestic manuals, who saw their books as instructions for the household, not the textbook for an expert profession.

Beecher would never have had the platform she did were it not for the fame of her family. Her father was the widely known Lyman Beecher, friend to William Holmes McGuffey and a dogmatic common school crusader. Lyman was arguably one of the most famous preachers of the nineteenth century, a man whose fiery sermons against slavery and drunkenness made him a household name. Her brother Henry Ward Beecher, too, rose to prominence as a speaker, preacher, and social reformer. Her youngest half sister, Isabella Beecher Hooker, was a prominent suffragist. And, of course, her sister with whom she cowrote *The American Woman's Home* was Harriet Beecher Stowe of *Uncle Tom's Cabin* fame. The Beechers were arguably the most famous family of the nineteenth century, and scholars have compared them to the Kennedys—or even the Kardashians.[13]

Catharine Beecher's early adulthood often stood in stark contrast to the life she would write about in her books. By the 1830s, she was arguing that women's rightful place was in the private sphere of the home, and yet she was a public figure throughout most of her life—she even went on lecture tours, traveling around the country to disseminate her message. She

lobbied loudly and often for what can be understood as a form
of empowerment, asking Americans to help develop and respect
women's expertise. Yet, many of her views did not line up with
the burgeoning women's movement of the nineteenth century,
and she was a tireless crusader against women's right to vote
throughout her long life. Women should not be involved in political debates, Beecher told the abolitionist Grimké sisters in a
famed public exchange.[14] But she herself had launched a nationwide campaign to prevent the 1830 Indian Removal Act. Along
with Lydia Sigourney, Beecher had created what many called
the first national women's petition campaign,[15] flooding Congress with pleas to reverse the decision to remove Indigenous
peoples from their land. She was essentially one of the earliest
female activists in the country, and she spent much of her life
telling other women that they should never be activists. From
the start, Beecher's worldview was a complex web of paradoxes.

⚙

By the time Beecher began work on what would become her
bestselling book, *A Treatise on Domestic Economy*, she had nearly
gone broke.[16] She had followed her father, Lyman, to Ohio in
an attempt to bring her message of women's education to what
she saw as the uncivilized West, hoping to ensure that the burgeoning frontier would evolve to look more like her vision of
civilized New England. As her father and McGuffey rallied
western folk around the common school movement, Catharine
advocated—often unsuccessfully—for the necessity of women's

schools and women as teachers. She had started a school for women in Cincinnati that would fail just a few years later.[17] The economic panic of 1837 had pushed the institute toward financial collapse, but Catharine's own personality certainly did not help in its survival. She failed to win support for her school from potential investors, such as Cincinnati gentleman Edward King, who found Beecher insufferably arrogant. As he explained in a letter to his wife: "Tell Catharine Beecher that she is a guest and not a director [in our home]."[18] Her New England snobbery eventually made her an outcast in Cincinnati society, and her attempts to socially divide easterners and westerners were met with anger from local inhabitants.[19] A letter she wrote to a local paper blaming the city's backwardness for her school's struggles only further ostracized her.[20] The school folded within a few short years, and Catharine managed to take the little money that remained for herself and saddle her sister Harriet with the bulk of the financial losses.[21] Struggling financially, increasingly isolated from her siblings, and unable to get a social toehold in Cincinnati, Beecher turned to writing. Unwilling to have her vast vision for domestic life fade to obscurity and live out her days as a spinster aunt, she began work on what would become *A Treatise on Domestic Economy* in the late 1830s.

She envisioned *A Treatise on Domestic Economy* as the text-book for a new kind of women's education: one in which women's work raising children, cooking, and organizing the home would be valued for the important labor that it was. The book is at once a manual and a show of appreciation for the fact that women's work was quite complex, requiring expertise in order to do it well: baking in ovens that had no real regulation of temperature; teaching children how to read, write, and think; tailoring and dyeing clothes. Especially in the early nineteenth century, working-class and middle-class women were performing work that is now carried out by a separate host of professionals, from tailors and nurses to schoolteachers. Beecher saw women's work as a challenging mix of moral, academic, physical, and domestic subjects, ones that they could not just naturally learn by watching their mothers. Women were unhappy in their destined profession because they were unprepared for it and not respected in it, she argued. Her solution, then, was to make domestic economy a profession—much like men's professions as doctors, lawyers, or businessmen. Women did not need to leave the home to work in men's jobs because they were uniquely suited for the work of the home, according to Beecher. But just as an aspiring lawyer needed law school, Beecher contended that women needed extensive training for their profession. She had good reason to think that professionalizing women's work was the best way forward. Beecher had observed how farming quickly transformed from menial labor to a science after schools were endowed for agricultural study.[22] Work in general becomes valued when it is "professionalized,"[23] and Beecher saw herself leading a generation of women to their destiny. Her success in advocating for women as professional teachers outside the home would be far-reaching, too: at the beginning of the century, the majority of primary school teachers were men; by the end of it the majority were women—a trend that has continued to this day and that many credit, at least in large part, to

Beecher (as well as to the fact that women teachers could be paid less than their male counterparts).

When *A Treatise on Domestic Economy* first came out in 1841, this message on women's crucial role in the future of America resonated with an expanding group of women, both in the Northeast and in the burgeoning West (what is now the Midwest). The book was so popular that it would go through fifteen editions. *A Treatise on Domestic Economy* is excruciatingly detailed and covers everything a nineteenth-century wife and mother would have needed to know about (and many things she probably did not need to know). *A Treatise on Domestic Economy*, for instance, barely mentions cooking except in the context of the health of the home and the necessity of creating balanced meals that would not produce sluggish, immoral Americans. Beecher's book covered the basics of infant care, healthy cooking, and treatment of common wounds. It also included farming tips such as how to plant fruit, architecture lessons for constructing a home, and a section on the importance of physical exercise (an idea that was newly applied to women). From the start, *A Treatise on Domestic Economy* did more than instruct women in their role; it advocated for their place as the moral arbiters of American stability. Beecher wrote,

> The mother forms the character of the future man; the sister bends the fibres that are hereafter to be the forest tree; the wife sways the heart, whose energies may turn for good or for evil the destinies of a nation. Let the women of a country be made virtuous and intelligent, and the men

will certainly be the same. The proper education of a man decides the welfare of an individual; but educate a woman, and the interests of a whole family are secured.[24]

In other words: Educate a woman and ensure the fate of a nation. Women, then—through the way they managed their households—would determine the success or failure of the American project. The way they cleaned their homes, did their laundry, and put food on the table would move the United States forward or back, Beecher argued. It's what Linda Kerber dubbed "Republican motherhood":[25] the idea that women could embody civic virtues, playing a crucial role in society by raising future citizens—especially the men who would vote, write laws, and lead the country. From some of the earliest conceptions of American womanhood, a woman's place was behind the scenes. The American woman was there to ensure that American men could lead the rest of the country, but she was more than a cog keeping the larger machine running—she was improving upon that machine by raising ever more patriotic and Christian young men. Beecher was arguably more radical than many of the voices disseminating the cult of domesticity. She seems to have taken women's backstage role a step further, envisioning that work like that of the man behind the curtain in *The Wizard of Oz*, unseen but in fact running the show.

Much like William Holmes McGuffey, Catharine Beecher recognized an opportunity to construct American stability and national identity. She was a product of her time, but she gave women credit in nation building in a way that had never quite been done before. And in the pages of her book, she encoded many of the same values that McGuffey and other bestselling authors had done, from patriotism and Protestant morality to autodidacticism and work ethic, slightly tweaked and adapted to women's situation. Beecher even updated that staple of American self-help literature—work ethic—calling on the American woman who "values the institutions of her Country"[26] to insist that labor was not "degrading."[27] She condemned Americans who continued to emulate Europeans, criticizing those who "ape the customs of aristocratic lands."[28] In a sense, Beecher looked to do for manners and home life what Webster did for spelling and language. In *A Treatise on Domestic Economy*, she wrote, "Shall we not rather take the place to which we are entitled, as the leaders, rather than the followers, in the customs of society, turn back the tide of aristocratic inroads, and carry through the whole, not only of civil and political, but of social and domestic, life, the true principles of democratic freedom and equality?"[29]

The home was a place to express those specific qualities that set Americans apart from the rest of the world, those customs that would transform society into something new and radically American, according to Beecher. It was a type of idealized American exceptionalism in which women were called to lead. At its best, the book is a kind of addendum to the Declaration of Independence—reclaiming an American identity for women that was free from the influence of their European counterparts. It embraced—in name at least—those values of meritocracy, freedom, and equality that had long been reserved for men.

In the Beecher universe, domestic life was a way to impose what she understood as New England values on a burgeoning group of Americans, especially Western frontier folk and new arrivals to the country. Beecher's ideas about how best to form the men who would lead the country was just as much about what they would look like as what they would not look like. Fear of immigrants and especially of Catholic immigrants dominated her thinking at the time. Much like her father, she spoke often in the 1830s of the "thousands of degraded foreigners and their ignorant families pouring into this nation."[30] As the United States rapidly expanded, stretching farther west and incorporating an increasing number of German and Irish immigrants in particular, Beecher and others like her worried that such demographic changes would spell the death of a Protestant American soul. Soon, people like Beecher feared, the pope would decide who became president in the United States of America. What's more, the number of voting Americans was increasing from within the country, too. Starting in the 1820s, many states began to ease property requirements for voting. The result was that voter turnout for the 1828 presidential election was nearly four times what it had been in 1824. She was terrified that soon the majority of voters would no longer be middle-class, well-educated Protestants such as herself but a horde of the illiterate, the ignorant, and the papists. The same fears that fueled the common school movement infused energy into Beecher's activism around domestic education. Pointing to the number of illiterate adults and children without schools, she would write just a few years after *A Treatise on Domestic Economy*, "If these children come on to the stage with their present neglect, we shall have *three millions* of adults managing our state and national affairs, who cannot even read the Constitution they swear to support, nor a word in the Bible, or in any newspaper or book" (Beecher's italics).[31] Much like Noah Webster, Beecher advocated for a "best American" way of doing things, but that best way always happened to be the old-school New England way.

Without education, men could not lead the country. And without women, there could be no proper education, according to Beecher. *"It is in the power of American women to save their country,"*[32] she would write just four years after the publication of *A Treatise on Domestic Economy* (Beecher's italics). Part of her domestic project, then, was an Americanizing project. Those seemingly innocuous books about laundry and houseplants were there to teach women how to be American—or, more specifically, to teach them to be the kind of American that people like Beecher preferred. Much like McGuffey, Beecher longed to assimilate an expanding group of people into Protestant American culture—and her domestic manuals were a facet of that vast goal. Her books, however, were not a direct line destined to convert Irish Catholics. The idea was that women of Beecher's class would learn from experts like her in order to educate their own children and to act almost as missionaries for their Catholic maids.[33] As McGuffey did with his books, Beecher's texts formed a kind of civic religion designed to bring out the unique character not just of women but of a specific ideal of American women created in her own image.

Beecher may have been more extreme than some of her contemporaries, but she was just one of many women (and some men) penning the domestic manuals that would form the nineteenth century's understanding of women's place in the home and in the country. Domestic advice books were ubiquitous during the second quarter of the century, filled with many of the same themes and notions of what American women owed to their country, such as Christian virtue and patriotic republicanism. One of the earliest and most successful in this genre was Lydia Maria Child's *The American Frugal Housewife*, published in 1829, considered one of the first American domestic manuals—and Beecher's chief competitor for several years. Child updated American ideals usually associated with men and their work, such as thrift and self-reliance, applying them to women's vital work in the home. One of the first sentences of her book—the quotation "Time is money"[34]—feels strikingly contemporary, like it could be the start to a self-help book, a get-rich-quick book, or any number of management books marketed toward men. By emphasizing the financial worth of women's work, Child recognized the way that housework was—and to a certain extent still is—undervalued by those who don't do it. In a Franklinesque way, she urged scrimping and saving, insisting that everything and everyone—including children—can be "made useful."[35] Child even quotes Benjamin Franklin in the first chapter of the book. When warning about spending too much money on household wares, she quotes him as saying, "Nothing is cheap that we do not want"[36] (though it is unclear if Franklin ever said this). Books such as these started to create a female archetype that—for all its flaws and limitations—finally applied core values of the republic to women's lives.

In the goal of making women ideal citizens, many of these books covertly smuggled their authors into the public sphere of activism. Child, for instance, wrote *The American Frugal House-wife* to earn money for her family. Later, the proceeds of this book (reprinted thirty-five times) supported her as she founded her own abolition society. In that way, these innocuous domestic guides could also be radical political objects, there to advocate for causes from women's suffrage to Indigenous people's rights. Many of the authors of these books were primarily homemakers, wives, or mothers, but their books were often grounded both in the autonomy of earning their own money and in a fierce political engagement.

The field of domestic advice literature soon grew sprawling within a few short decades, and women in Richmond, Virginia, and in Hartford, Connecticut, may not have been reading the exact same domestic manuals. The books that they read, however, tended to share a similar ideological scaffolding: namely, that women, through their work in the home, could create a more moral and just America. Many of the authors may not have been actively thinking about white Protestant America the way that Beecher was, but their books tended to appeal to a similar readership of white, middle-class women (and those who wanted to become them). Where men of the early nineteenth century might hope to model their lives after *The Autobiography of Benjamin Franklin* and his eighty years of adventure, experimentation, and social change, domestic manuals sometimes seemed to be telling women that their highest calling was to birth and raise men like Franklin. At the same time, the philosophical grounding of domestic manuals is more complicated than this binary. Part of what these books accomplished was to center women in the American project, to make their work and jobs valued, to convert them into citizens and not just vehicles for citizens. These authors did not invent this vision of mother-hood, just as Noah Webster didn't invent American national-ism. But they codified it into a digestible form, put it—in some regional version or ideological stripe—into the homes of literate women across the country, to be read every day, or even con-sulted multiple times a day. Though Beecher might have added her ideological fingerprint, and she was influential because of her family, the threads of all these different authors wove the fabric of domestic ideology, each magnifying shared values or adding in their own strain of thought. Together, they laid the groundwork for a notion of the unique role of mothers that per-sists in some form today.

⚛

There is a gap between this image of millions of American women enthusiastically scrubbing their dishes and the more complex vision of womanhood that had started to emerge by the mid-nineteenth century. While the cult of domesticity was ar-guably part of the prevailing culture in antebellum America, the separate-spheres dogma seen in domestic manuals was not universal. It was an idealized vision of home life that was part imagined, and these books prescribed how they wanted the coun-try to look rather than describing the actual reality. Even by the mid-nineteenth century, many women—especially immigrants, people of color, and working-class women—were already earn-ing money outside the home. In fact, the Industrial Revolution that provided those jobs and moved production from farm to factory was one factor that led to the doctrine of separate spheres in the first place. And a competing vision of American woman-hood had already begun to take shape by the time these manuals were being written: Elizabeth Cady Stanton, born a decade and a half after Catharine Beecher, maintained near opposite views when it came to women's role. She advocated for suffrage alongside a slew of other rights that would later be identified with first-wave feminism, such as women's right to control their wages and even own property. While the two activists seem to have come from different generations, they led almost parallel lives. In 1848, just seven years after *A Treatise on Domestic Economy* came out, Stanton and Lucretia Mott held the first women's rights convention at Seneca Falls, New York. In the 1870s, soon after the publication of *The American Woman's Home,* Stanton argued in her "Home Life" lecture that women "waste their lives in domestic service."[37] Women such as Stanton, Mott, and Susan B. Anthony may have represented a minority of women, but it's not as if alternatives to the separate-spheres argument did not exist. As the nineteenth century wore on, voices such as theirs would only grow louder. The division between these two camps would lay the groundwork for a century of debate over the best path forward for American women.

At the same time, some of Beecher's ideas were radical and empowering in their own right, too, even if they do not fall within what we might consider feminism today. She may seem hopelessly antiquated in her thinking about women's roles being confined to the home, but she was forward-thinking, too, envisioning jobs and colleges for women at a time when they barely had access to good primary schools. The home became a kind of parallel institution to the budding common school movement: a place for both moral and intellectual education. It is why she was such a passionate advocate for both common schools and specialized women's schools. She was almost prescient in recognizing the need for women's higher education: by 1850, girls and boys were enrolling in primary school at the same rate—and even more girls than boys attended high school, as many boys were forced to leave school to work.[38]

A Treatise on Domestic Economy was hugely popular, and it was able to reach a broader audience than Beecher's New England milieu, thanks to her own tireless promotion of her ideas. While she was writing the book, Beecher had remained active in education reform movements, arranging for teachers educated on the East Coast to be sent to western frontier towns. Many of the teachers that were sent west took Beecher's ideas—and even her books—with them.[39] Nor were her ideas confined to her social class. As historian Nancy F. Cott pointed out, middle-class New England women of this era were often the ones who "created constraints or opportunities"[40] for all women. And thanks to Beecher's frequent speaking engagements during the 1830s and 1840s, books were only one channel for disseminating her message on the cult of domesticity. *A Treatise on Domestic Economy* was so successful that it even became the first textbook in its subject matter that was recognized by a state board of education. "In the next three decades Catharine Beecher could enter virtually any community in the United States and expect to be received as the heroine who had simplified and made understandable the mysterious arts of household maintenance,"[41] wrote her biographer, Kathryn Kish Sklar. In a way that has lingered, Beecher set up the home as a tool for patriotism and homemaking as a measuring stick for American virtue, themes that would resurface again and again in American history, in times of turmoil and especially in times of war. In her view, women's identity as American could even become more important than their identities as western, northern, or southern, Union or Confederate.

❀

In the run-up to the Civil War, domestic ideology was reaching women through every possible form of the written word. In the span of just a few decades, domestic literature expanded from manuals to dozens of handbooks, multiple women's magazines, and several bestselling novels about domestic life. By the 1850s, when the cult of domesticity was arguably at its peak, there was a "veritable flood" of domestic novels, according to one historian.[42] By 1860, literacy rates of boys and girls were almost equal.[43] Even women far from bookstores could access an increasing number of periodicals, such as *Frank Leslie's Lady's Magazine and Gazette of Fashion*, *Graham's Ladies' Paper*, *Godey's Lady's Book*, and *The Lady's Friend*, among many others. A contemporary of Beecher's, Sarah Josepha Hale, embodied this same dedication both to republican motherhood and to domesticity. Widowed with five children by the age of thirty-four, Hale turned to writing to support herself. By 1828, she became the first American woman editor of a magazine, serving as the editor in chief of Boston's *Ladies' Magazine*, which later merged with *Godey's Lady's Book*. Periodicals were hugely popular, and hers was reaching a circulation of upwards of 150,000 readers, covering everything from fashion and music to gardening and literature. She was an outspoken advocate for women's colleges, and her messages about domesticity and women's special role in American society were reaching massive numbers in the run-up to and during the Civil War. Hale is even credited with convincing President Abraham Lincoln to make Thanksgiving a national holiday. *Time* magazine would later call *Godey's Lady's Book* the "most phenomenally successful of any magazine issued before the Civil War."[44]

Despite growing debate over abolition, domestic literature tended to address that reality only implicitly. The sheer amount of domestic labor performed by enslaved people—not to mention the many kitchens run by enslaved women in the South—does not figure into the middle-class, white vision put forward by many domestic manuals. Earlier manuals, such as *The Virginia Housewife* (1824), implicitly addressed the reality of slavery, written as they were for newly married white women who did not know how to cook because they had grown up in the slave-run kitchens of their parents' homes.[45] Those books often included recipes developed in part by enslaved cooks, for which they were never given credit.[46] Some Black authors were able to capitalize on this insatiable demand for domestic advice literature. Tunis G. Campbell, a free black man, activist, and later Georgia state senator, even wrote a guidebook for people working in domestic service, entitled *Hotel Keepers, Head Waiters, and Housekeepers' Guide* (1848). "People of color were seen as living outside the mainstream of American life, their highest expectation being to professionally manage other servants,"[47] wrote culinary historian Barbara Haber. In that way, both the sharp regional divisions between states and the entire country's reliance on slave labor were an unspoken subtext of domestic manuals.

When the Confederacy formed, the Beecher family was quick to decry Southern secession and to rally around the Union cause. Two of Catharine's half brothers—James and Thomas— would enlist, with the latter traveling throughout upstate New York, drumming up soldiers to defend the Union. Catharine's younger brother the famed preacher Henry Ward Beecher delivered some of his most rousing sermons to call for aid in supporting the Union. In April 1861, just two months after the birth of the Confederacy, parishioners packed into a Brooklyn church to hear Beecher speak, and his sermon "caused the very blood of the listener to leap with patriotic fervor,"[48] according to a local news report. The crowd was rapt as Beecher said, "Seven States of this Union, in a manner resolutionary [sic], not only of Government, but in isolation of the rights and customs of their own people, have disowned their country, and made WAR, upon it! What shall we do? Go forward? Now is the hour for patriatism [sic]."[49] His impassioned speech ended with the entire church spontaneously singing "My Country 'Tis of Thee." He would go on to deliver many similar speeches, inspiring Northerners to enlist in droves.

For Catharine Beecher, the arrival of the Civil War seems only to have imbued her domestic project with fresh energy. A plea for a return to old-fashioned domestic life, or some simpler imagined time gone by, had long been Beecher's solution to a host of social and political problems, and she continued to see family structure and gender roles as the only building block that American society—North and South—had in common. And yet, the fallout of the war was inveterate, not easily fixed by some kind of domestic ideology. To this day, the Civil War remains the deadliest conflict in American history, taking the lives of at least six hundred thousand soldiers alone. The average number of deaths would eventually reach a record-breaking 504 per day as Americans picked up arms against one another for four blood-soaked years. The fatalities were often so staggering that many soldiers were simply buried where they fell on the battlefield, in unmarked graves. The Civil War represented not only a violent challenge to the sovereignty of the United States; it also stood as a potent contradiction to the idea that women were unfit for work outside the home. With men away at war, women managed farms, served as nurses, and raised money for the war effort—defying the notion that they were destined only for housework. This pattern would hold for many subsequent wars—World War I and World War II in particular—in which women took on added responsibilities during wartime, realized their own capabilities, and lobbied for more autonomy after the war's end. By the 1860s, many of Beecher's ideas were already starting to become obsolete.

And yet, rather than slowing her projects down, Beecher refused to abandon the ideology that had guided her for decades, and she instead looked to bend her ideas to fit this new future. In 1865, as the war reached a bloody crescendo, Beecher wrote about the need for expertise in domestic work with even more fervor, penning an essay in *Harper's Magazine* about how to "redeem woman's profession from dishonor." In it, she references the "great emergency in our nation"[50] that has caused thousands of women to be "forever cut off from any homes of their own by marriage."[51] A generation of women now found themselves widows or unable to marry because there were not enough men. In this loss, Catharine Beecher saw an opportunity: she argued for women to be able to set up communal living compounds in which they could pool their domestic labor and adopt orphaned children. Beecher was now using the traditional cult of domesticity to argue for something altogether more radical.

✿

After the Civil War, Catharine moved in with Harriet and her husband to help manage their household. They occupied a farmhouse in the idyllic Nook Farm neighborhood in Hartford, Connecticut. Just a few years after the bloody battles of that war, the Beechers lived a sheltered life, far from the rubble of devastated Southern cities. The sprawling semirural paradise of Nook Farm was populated by the dream houses of the intellectual elite. It was there that Catharine and Harriet would begin writing what would become *The American Woman's Home*. *Uncle Tom's Cabin* had sold millions of copies by that point, and Harriet and her husband joined a neighborhood populated by lawyers, actors, and newspapermen. Each farmhouse was home to a prominent member of the Hartford community, and their dinner tables and backyards were transformed into salons for discussions about suffrage, Reconstruction, and the latest novels. A few short years later, Samuel Clemens would build his home—a nineteen-room manor[52] where he would hold weekly billiards tournaments—a few doors down from the Beecher Stowes in the sprawling rural park. "I think this is the best built and the handsomest town I have ever seen,"[53] Clemens, better known as Mark Twain, announced after settling in. There was a utopic communal nature to Nook Farm. It was ripe for the kind of idealism that would categorize the book the Beecher sisters would write, making it the perfect place for them to dream up their model family structure.

By the time they began work on *The American Woman's Home* in 1868, Harriet Beecher Stowe was arguably one of the most famous women in the United States. While Harriet's name shared the cover, Catharine was the person who wrote an overwhelming majority of the book.[54] As they began drafting their vision of ideal womanhood, that competing model embodied by Elizabeth Cady Stanton was already starting to edge them out. Women's suffrage may still have been fifty years away, but already by 1869 women were conceiving of their role in society outside the home. The same year that the Beecher sisters' book came out, Stanton and Susan B. Anthony founded the National Woman Suffrage Association with the aim of lobbying for women's right to vote. The Beechers' younger half sister, Isabella—a fervent suffragist—even organized the Hartford, Connecticut, convention for Stanton and Anthony's organization.

As people like Stanton—and even their own sister—argued for women's access to the historically male sphere of politics, Catharine and Harriet put forward an alternate future reality for the women of America. When *The American Woman's Home* was released in 1869, it depicted a strikingly similar vision to domestic work that had appeared in *A Treatise on Domestic Economy*—in fact, many of the pages were directly reprinted from Beecher's original work. Interspersed with architectural drawings and illustrations of happy families, the book attempted to expand upon and restore faith in a much earlier vision of family life. It included chapters on sewing, etiquette, and home decoration, as well as much more philosophical passages on building a Christian home and community. Women did not need access to men's work, the book continued to argue. They instead needed training and appreciation for the necessary work of the home—and this book was there to give them both. The introduction read, "It is the aim of this volume to elevate both the honor and the remuneration of all the employments that sustain the many difficult and sacred duties of the family state, and thus to render each department of woman's true profession as much desired and respected as are the most honored professions of men."[55]

If domestic work were a profession, *The American Woman's Home* was its most expert handbook (around 150 pages longer than *A Treatise on Domestic Economy*). *The American Woman's Home* mingled Christian and patriotic duty in order to effectively raise the stakes of domestic life to a moral imperative. Especially after the Civil War, the Beechers contended that a family's health or sickness was a far more symbolic litmus test of the nation's salvation at large. Much like Webster's speller and then his dictionary, *A Treatise on Domestic Economy* had made Catharine Beecher a bestselling author—but *The American Woman's Home* was her crowning ideological achievement. There is no hard data available on just how many copies it sold, but it was both well received in its time and left a lasting legacy: the Library of Congress would name it one of the one hundred most influential books in all of American history.[56]

The book made the case that, more than ever, women's work in the home carried both practical and spiritual value, representing the patriotism and Christianity of the nation. The timing of this message was critical: the Beecher sisters mounted a last stand for the cult of domesticity, making a convincing and rigid blueprint for its endurance at a time when there was less agreement than ever as to what constituted a good American. The book was called *The American Woman's Home*, and it was not just about the best way to do things in the home but about the best *American* way. The word "American" appears seventy-six times as the authors describe the best American table, American home cooking, American-style butter, American manners, and American virtue. The "good cooking" chapter, for instance, focuses mostly on the importance of bread and its connection to republican virtue. "The green, clammy, acrid substance, called biscuit, which many of our worthy republicans are obliged to eat in these days, is wholly unworthy of the men and women of the republic. Good patriots ought not to be put off in that way— they deserve better fare,"[57] reads a passage from this section. Never has the word "republic" been called into play so much in a chapter on bread and butter. In a chapter on decoration written by Harriet Beecher Stowe, she made the case that even draperies and plants were communicating messages about American values. Everything that women did—from what time they got up to which carpets they chose and how they organized their kitchens—became a symbol of their relative virtue, the Beecher sisters argued.

Unifying "one nation under woman,"[58] as Dr. Allison Speicher, vice president of the Harriet Beecher Stowe Society, put it, was a way of bringing a group of heterogenous Americans into the fold, especially after the ways in which the Civil War had violently divided Americans. Regional division was "both a cause and an effect" of the war, Speicher said, one that pushed many northerners, southerners, and westerners alike further into their regional camps. The upheaval of the war had also caused profound changes to the American relationship between food, socioeconomic class, and social structure, and with this book the Beechers attempted to reorganize those ideas in a way that was palatable to women like them. Now that women no longer had enslaved people to cook for them, and the Beechers warned against hiring excessive servants,[59] they needed more than ever to convince women of their class to take on what they saw as vital work. In this way, the class implications of food have always run deeply through the domestic manuals, but those messages about the value of work and cooking became even clearer after the war.

The Beechers delivered the book's message with an intense religiosity—crafting an even more explicitly Protestant vision of homemaking than appeared in *A Treatise on Domestic Economy*. As early as the very first chapter, entitled "The Christian Family," the authors categorize men as mere "outdoor labor[ers],"[60] while women "who train immortal minds are to reap the fruit of their labor through eternal ages."[61] The Beechers go so far as to claim Jesus of Nazareth said, "Whoso will be great shall be your minister, and whoso will be chiefest shall be servant of all."[62] The Beechers' answer to the question of whoso? Women. "The family state then, is the aptest earthly illustration of the heavenly kingdom, and in it woman is its chief minister,"[63] they wrote in this chapter. Even within the context of elevating the role of women in the home, this is fairly radical. In the Beechers' conception of the home, women instead of men were the spiritual and moral leaders, the ministers guiding the family congregation toward a better path. They went so far as to call women "the ministers of home"[64] and "Heaven-appointed ministers of Christ"[65] in an essay leading up to the publication of this book. In *The American Woman's Home*, the Beechers took this idea of the woman as home minister to its most sweeping possible end. The home that the Beechers have designed, depicted in an illustration in the second chapter, entitled "A Christian House,"[66] is part church, part schoolhouse, with a cross hanging over the door. The home itself, then, reached its final, most sweeping end: becoming a microcosm of Christian America, with women its moral leaders. Not only do women form the character of citizens for the good of the nation, according to the book; they form the immortal souls of all Americans.

❀

For the Beechers, home was not just a political statement: in much the same way it is today, home was meant to be a haven. It's a theme that recurs throughout American history: in times of change, economic chaos, or upheaval, people often retreat to their homes and rekindle interest in activities such as baking bread, sewing, and crafting (we need only look to the 2020 coronavirus pandemic to see the ways in which that is still true). "One of the reasons that domestic advice is so important in so many different periods is because it speaks to something you have control over when you don't have control over anything else,"[67] said Dr. Sarah Leavitt, historian and author of the book *From Catharine Beecher to Martha Stewart: A Cultural History of Domestic Advice.* Especially in periods of technological change or political upheaval, the outside world comes to represent a chaotic, dirty threat. Home is still a place you can close the door on all that, Leavitt explained.[68] It becomes a place for self-expression, for plants, colors, and a degree of harmony. And in a way the Beechers likely could never have imagined, the COVID-19 pandemic momentarily pushed women into the many roles described by *The American Woman's Home*. With schools and churches closed and many people sick, mothers transformed into schoolteachers, nurses, and (for the religious families) substitute Sunday school leaders.

The home as haven is just one part of a much broader legacy we inherit from these nineteenth-century domestic manuals— from lingering gender roles to the home as a tool of conformity— that has resurfaced in vastly different cookbooks and moments in history (including the 1940s and *Betty Crocker's Picture Cook Book*). Catharine Beecher has been mostly forgotten by the American public today, superseded by her more famous family members. The contributions of Lydia Maria Child and Sarah Josepha Hale, along with dozens of other authors of domestic manuals, have mostly been lost, too, never the household names of their male writing peers. And yet their stamp on American culture—especially when it came to women's lives and education—was indelible. Beecher's prolific writings on domestic life would teach several generations of women about what kind of Americans they should be. Her dozens of books bridged the gap from the beginning of the cult of domesticity in the Victorian era to the rise of women's education at the end of the nineteenth century. And her activism allowed so many women to become teachers that some scholars even point to Beecher when explaining why K–12 teaching continues to be dominated by women today.[69] Because Beecher was complex, paradoxical, and downright unlikable, her impact on our culture has been grossly minimized.

These women's influence must also be credited to the many women they inspired, those who would pick up domestic philosophy after their deaths and carry on their work in the fields of women's education and homemaking. The turn-of-the-century expansion of women's colleges and the invention of the field of home economics would have been impossible without the tireless work of education pioneers such as Beecher, Emma Willard, Mary Lyon, and other women of this much earlier generation. They serve as a link between Victorian domesticity and what would become the twentieth-century home economics movement. For instance, it's hard to imagine a place for Ellen Swallow Richards, founder of the home economics movement and an MIT-trained chemist (in the 1870s, making her the first American woman to be admitted to a scientific school), without the foundation laid by Beecher and her cohort. Even the later decision to make home economics part of the public school curriculum was a path paved by their activism.

We might like to think of these authors' ideas as solidly from another generation: old, outdated, and certainly not lingering still. And yet this first wave of domestic literature set up a long line of books that would tell women their role was important but not public, that they were uniquely qualified for their duties as wives and mothers, and that their country needed them to stay home. This notion that a woman's value is tied to the tidiness of her home, the appearance of her children, and the quality of her baked goods is arguably something that never went away. Women today might not be confined to her vision of domestic life in the way they once were, but the foundations of Beecher's American home have yet to fully crumble.

CHAPTER SIX

Etiquette in Society, in Business, in Politics and at Home (1922)

After ending an affair with a twentysomething showgirl in the summer of 1905, New York financier Edwin Post received a visit from an editor of the tabloid *Town Topics*. The tabloid ran a healthy side business blackmailing the upper crust of New York City, and the editor offered Post a choice. He could buy one of the paper's forthcoming books for the affordable price of $500[1] (upwards of $13,000 today)—or read a piece on his adulterous dalliance in the next issue of *Town Topics*.

Post refused the blackmail and instead went to the police. He was just one of dozens of New York men from prominent families who had been extorted by the tabloid, and Post—enraged and indignant—decided to take a stand.[2] Or, depending on which version of the story is told, he could not come up with the $500 after suffering a string of financial losses, and he had no other choice.[3] Post would spend the rest of that summer in court, battling the tabloid in a highly public legal fight.

Appearing in court alongside him was his wife, Emily Post. She had long been aware of her husband's affairs over the course of their thirteen-year marriage, but for the sake of appearances, she had suffered in silence. Now her public shame was splashed across headlines in *The New York Times* and every other local paper, which each day breathlessly recounted every sordid detail of Mr. Post's affair. Refusing to slip away to her lavish home in the aptly named Tuxedo Park, Mrs. Post strode into the court-room wearing an exquisitely tailored linen suit with a scarlet hat.[4] She sat tall next to Mr. Post, her Roman nose upturned and her blue eyes clear as a judge recounted all her husband's indiscre-tions with a "fair charmer" fond of "white shoes with red heels and patent leather tips."[5] Of all the ink spilled during the course of that protracted trial, little was devoted to Mr. Post's wife. One reporter would describe the five-foot-nine Mrs. Post only as "small."[6]

Within six months of the end of the trial, the Posts filed for divorce. Edwin, it turned out, was so broke that Emily did not ask him for alimony.[7] Looking for a diversion from her public shame—and faced with the prospect of depending on her mother for the rest of her life—Mrs. Post sought a new stream of income. She'd later write that the only appropriate ways for a woman of her social standing to earn money were portrait painting and writing novels.[8] Having no passion for the former, she turned to fiction. When her marriage had first started to disintegrate, she had begun work on a novel, *The Flight of a Moth*; her second book would appear as the blackmail trial was still underway. The books delved into the social mores and schemes of her class, and marriage was an institution they dissected in particular. She turned her personal tragedy into fiction, penning stories of cheating husbands and the wives who suffered alongside them. Her novels were considered "very spicy" for their day, according to *The New Yorker*,[9] and her work was even compared to the society tales of Edith Wharton.[10] *The Flight of a Moth* was based loosely on a series of letters she wrote home to family during a trip to Europe without her husband, where she was chaperoning a young couple. In real life, that trip was cut short when Edwin grew so jealous of his wife's travels that he faked being sick in order to call her home.[11] When she arrived, she discovered that not only was he in perfect health, but he had purchased a 129-foot yacht without telling her—and she was furious.[12] Emily Price Post and the protagonist of her debut novel shared many similarities—they were both smart, beautiful, and well-bred society ladies—but they had one important difference: her heroine, Grace, was a widow. In the book, Grace writes to a friend: "The French say that the ideal condition for a woman would be to be born a widow; and that is nearly my case, as I am just now starting out upon what I feel to be a new life."[13]

The death of Emily's marriage did indeed signal a rebirth for her—not just in her lifestyle but seemingly in her attitude, too. She took on new adventures, traveled around Europe and America, and took on societal issues of the day, from Prohibition to refugee resettlement. "I would rather be a burnt moth than a crawling worm!"[14] Grace also says in the book. "If I am burnt to a crisp I shall at least have flown to my end, not *crawled*."[15] Emily Post would be someone throughout her life who did anything but crawl. For all the rules of society she would write throughout her life, she was constantly breaking some of the most basic social contracts of her milieu in the early twentieth century: she got divorced; she worked for her money; she even traveled cross-country in a car before women could vote.[16]

Post found her true calling not by writing about the indiscretions of her class but by correcting them. Post would make a name for herself—and a small fortune—with her book on etiquette. Her 1922 tome on the subject outlined rules for everything from courtship to stationery (devoting nearly one hundred pages to proper romantic etiquette). In its numerous examples of how not to behave, she also offered barely veiled references to real-life socialites who had snubbed either her or her Baltimore family since their arrival in New York City almost five decades earlier. The nearly seven-hundred-page volume[17] was a veritable opus to Emily Post's social rivals. She would dedicate her behemoth on what she called "best society" to them, writing, "To You My Friends, whose identity in these pages is veiled in fictional disguise, it is but fitting that I dedicate this book."[18]

Despite addressing the seemingly minuscule audience of Manhattan's elite, Post's book would become an overnight success. It spent approximately a full year on the bestseller list[19] following its publication in 1922, and it had to be reprinted eight times within that period to keep up with demand. Soon she would add a newspaper column to her etiquette platform— syndicated in two hundred newspapers nationwide[20]—a magazine column with 2 million readers, and a radio program starting in 1930 that made her a household name. Post was so much the

gold standard in radio that President Franklin Roosevelt supposedly said the greatest compliment he received on his fireside
chats was "You're as good as Emily Post."[21] By the time she died
in 1960, *Etiquette* would be in its eighty-ninth printing.[22] Post
may have been responding to her own personal crisis, but what
she created resonated with an ever-expanding group of people:
namely, immigrants, the nouveaux riche, and all manner of new
arrivals to urban centers who dreamed of being invited to the
opera or to the Rockefellers' dinner table.

"Why, in a supposedly classless society like America, do so
many people fret about table manners?"[23] asked *New Yorker*
writer Elizabeth Kolbert. It's undeniable that they do indeed
fret about them. For all the United States' pride in being without an aristocracy, rules of social conduct cause huge anxiety for
so many people. Books on American etiquette existed even before the country itself did (a fact that has served as fodder for
ridicule to the many Europeans who insist that Americans have
no manners at all). Perhaps it's exactly because the guidelines
are more ambiguous, and the ruling class in the United States
cannot be defined simply by a noble title, that people yearn even
more for social clarity. Post—not unlike many of her class and
generation—feared that the shifting social values of the 1920s
would lead to chaos, and that the only thing standing between
humans and animals was good etiquette. Meanwhile, people in
the lower and middle classes saw in etiquette a means of social
mobility, a ticket to a better life. The book imposed order on the
turmoil both of her own life and of her time—namely, the
Roaring Twenties. In trying to assuage her own fears and insecurities, her book forged the perfect marriage between the fears

of the upper class and the aspirations of the underclasses, creating a new kind of status quo.

Over time, the book would continue to serve as a guiding hand through the rapidly transforming social landscape of the mid–twentieth century—teaching everything from how to set the perfect dinner table to how to welcome home veterans suffering from post-traumatic stress disorder. Emily Post—a woman who was born during the Reconstruction period and died during John F. Kennedy's presidential campaign—served as a bridge between the nineteenth and twentieth centuries, the cult of domesticity and the modern age. She may have shared Catharine Beecher's penchant for telling women how to behave and for seeking American homogeny through shared codes of conduct, but her book on etiquette represents a real departure from the housewifery books of the 1800s. As women's lives increasingly stretched outside the home—to restaurants, operas, and later, to the workplace—Post's book reflected the shifting contours of society. Hers was a new book for a new century, one that defined not just women's role in the home but women's *and* men's behavior—at work, at home, and just about everywhere else.

❀

Long before she would become Emily Post—not just wife to Edwin but a stand-in for the very idea of etiquette—she was born Emily Price in 1872 in Baltimore to an heiress and an architect. While Post is associated with the distinctly twentieth-century moment of the Roaring Twenties, she was a daughter of a much older generation. The Beecher sisters' *The American Woman's Home* came out just three years before her birthday, with its firmly nineteenth-century vision of women and domesticity firmly intact. Emily grew up in the whimsical playground distinct to the superrich of the Gilded Age. Her youth was a whirl of governesses, debutante balls, tea receptions,[24] and summers in the quaint opulence of her father's Tuxedo Park project, a gated community in New York State and the second country club[25] in the United States. Later, as a young woman, she would attend Mark Twain's seventieth birthday celebration[26] and summer (certainly she must have used the word "summer" as a verb) at the same woodland retreat as Sigmund Freud.[27] As her parents' only surviving child, she was an adult from a very young age, preferring to spend as much time as possible with her architect father. He would take her on-site to client meetings even when she was a little girl, and he set up a drafting table with tools for her so she could "work" alongside him.[28] Most of her family agrees that if she had been born a century later, she likely would have become an architect herself.[29]

Soon the family moved from the suburbs of Baltimore to New York City, and when other kids played in Central Park or hit baseballs in the street, she attended afternoon teas and dress fittings. Sometimes she'd take a boat off the southern tip of Manhattan with her father to visit his friend Francis Hopkinson Smith, a man whom she called Uncle Frank.[30] As the men chatted, the young Emily ran around Uncle Frank's construction project, exploring the "secret" rooms at its core, pretending she was a princess locked in a castle.[31] That construction project—one of the most sought-after government contracts of its era—was the dais of the Statue of Liberty. For weeks, the base of the statue was her personal dollhouse. Uncle Frank toured the structure with her on his tugboat, inspecting support beams and showing the eleven-year-old his sketches. As she came of age, she was constantly striking a balance between being willful and independent and remaining a dutiful daughter of her class. She mostly did what was expected of her, even if she preferred to be working with her father. One of her only faux pas came around Christmastime one year when she was a young girl. Whereas a male relative had received a model train set, the young Emily—being groomed for a lifetime of high teas and garden parties—received a complete child-size porcelain tea set. As soon as she opened it, she scooped it up, ran outside to the garden, and smashed it piece by piece against the rocks.[32]

Despite all her family's wealth and privilege, the Prices were never quite old-money enough for the old-moneyed people of New York City. Of course, she could trace her lineage back to the *Mayflower*,[33] but her family had earned their fortune in coal.[34] To the original families of New York City and their fashionable wives—the so-called Four Hundred—that made the Prices decisively new money. To truly fit into New York society, she would need to marry New York nobility.

Enter Edwin Post, a blond-haired, blue-blooded New Yorker who, as the story goes, caught Emily's eye at her debutante ball as she waltzed by with another partner.[35] She wore a yellow satin dress that brought out her deep blue eyes and the dark color of her softly curled hair. She would describe their meeting—and ensuing first polka together—as something of love at first sight.[36] Edwin was decidedly less romantic about the whole affair,[37] seeing a good match in the young woman who had the figure, face, and perfectly coiffed hair of a Gibson girl. Both sets of parents questioned their child's choice, and Bruce Price in particular saw Edwin as little more than a profiteer, making his living by buying up properties seized in bankruptcy.[38] In return, Edwin's teetotaling mother seemed to view the Prices as downright bohemian, scandalized by the copious wine at their dinner table and a nude statue in their foyer.[39] An engagement party between the two families ended in a screaming match about local politics,[40] but the wedding went forward nevertheless. The marriage, after all, was less about personalities and more about social obligation. It was the perfect match of money and title, what one of Post's descendants would refer to as a "domestic bargain"[41]—more business deal than romantic happy ending.

※

Mrs. Post likely would have spent her life raising children, managing the maids, and hosting elaborate dinner parties for her similarly situated friends if not for the highly public implosion of her marriage. Instead, her divorce sent her on a radically different path. She was divorced in 1906, a time when the idea was about as foreign to people of her social set as the notion of preparing their own food or working for an hourly wage. That initial transgression engendered a kind of chain reaction, allowing her to shake off (at least in part) the yoke that bridled so many women at the turn of the century. Despite early rumblings of first-wave feminism, choices for women during this era remained few. In a city like New York, poor women labored in the downtown factories to make the clothes and decorations purchased by uptown women to wear for an endless stream of frivolous social engagements. Post's son would later describe this era as "the Great Waste," a time when even women of Emily's class received little education beyond finishing schools, their future generally limited to child-rearing and socializing with other mothers of their set. By the time Emily Post began work on what would become *Etiquette* little more than a decade later, few people could have predicted just how drastically their world would have changed.

World War I had wreaked havoc on the United States and on the world—and nearly robbed Post of her firstborn child. Her eldest son, Edwin (Ned) Post Jr., enlisted to fight in the war when he was twenty-three years old. Ned began training as an aviator as soon as he graduated from Harvard, and he soon enlisted and was dispatched to Europe. Early on in his time in France, the plane Ned was piloting caught fire in the air, yet he managed to land the aircraft one-handed, all while gathering the precious equipment with his other hand—escaping from the plane just moments before it was engulfed in flames. Emily must have waited anxiously at home the years he was away at war, keeping an eye on the letter box and the daily news for word of her son or his battalion. In her personal scrapbook, she would cut out and paste more than half a dozen newspaper write-ups of her son's miraculous brush with death, with headlines such as AMERICAN FLYER WHOSE COOLNESS WARMED FRENCH HEARTS.[42] Ned would be one of the lucky ones: his

citations for gallantry from the French and American govern-
ments would not cost him his life. At the end of the war, Ned
returned home to his mother, unlike the millions—more than
one hundred thousand of them American—who would die across
Europe.

By the time Emily was writing *Etiquette* in the early 1920s—
just a few years after the armistice that ended the war—
female Manhattanites could dance in smoke-filled clubs wearing
nothing but short slip dresses over their corsetless bodies. American women had just voted in their first presidential election,
helping elect Warren G. Harding. They might not have been
able to drink gin in public with Prohibition in full swing, but
they could dance, flirt, and enjoy a bit of independence. Some
women even cut their hair short and smoked the same cigarettes
as the men who had returned home from the so-called Great
War. And yet, amid the celebration of the Roaring Twenties, a
sense of loss lingered over the dance halls in Harlem and the
speakeasies scattered across Manhattan. Readers were eager for
stories that showed people grappling with the upheaval that
World War I represented: not just the American lives lost in the
war and the many thousands more who would bury a part of
themselves on the front lines, but a broader splintering of faith in
humanity. In books by John Dos Passos, Ernest Hemingway, and
other writers of their generation, we see the extent to which World
War I had exploded the ruling logic of civilized life. With this war
and its unprecedented carnage, the rules of engagement appeared
shattered. In every sector—politics, literature, and society—we
see an America on the verge. It was on the cusp of something

new, but with that newness also came a fear of chaos, a disintegration of social structure.

Far from any smoke-filled speakeasy or muddy trench, Emily Post was hosting one of her Saturday night dinners for twelve at her Park Avenue apartment one night in 1920.[43] Now a successful novelist in her forties, she surrounded herself not just with the usual society women of her formerly married life but also with agents, editors, and literary types, including the *Vanity Fair* editor Frank Crowninshield. Laments about Prohibition soon turned to a broader discussion of personal liberty and public space. As other guests called for taxis, Crowninshield lingered over dessert and lambasted the growing number of poorly written books on etiquette.[44] Then, as if a lightbulb had suddenly been switched on, he turned to Emily and said, "Why don't you compose a book on how to behave?"[45] Emily found the subject asinine and said she wasn't interested in lecturing people about what fork to use. In the weeks following, Crowninshield would call her again, showering her with compliments to convince her just how much all the war wives, new immigrants, and nouveaux riche desperately needed her advice.[46] After weeks, possibly months, of flattery, Emily Post finally conceded, legend has it. And yet even her descendants Lizzie Post and Daniel Post Senning—who run the Emily Post Institute today—doubt the veracity of that story.[47] Post's biographer Laura Claridge uncovered proof that Emily was interested in etiquette all on her own. A letter she had written nine years earlier to her agent all but betrays her entirely: Mrs. Post had just about begged her agent[48] to find her a gig as a monthly magazine columnist on the topic of etiquette.

The question then lingers as to the real reason why she became interested in etiquette in the first place. It might seem like a natural transition to go from writing fictionalized accounts of manners to writing a how-to guide about them. And yet, nearly everyone close to her—from her agent to her son[49]—thought this project was beneath her and that it might be a sign she was too out of touch with the times. Her passion came from elsewhere, a mix of the personal and the profitable. From the start of her writing career, her work seemed driven by a desire for both clarity and control, and etiquette as a subject offered both. It also served as an opportunity for something she certainly thought about but would not have admitted: she needed money. By the time she began work on the book, she was a successful writer, but her career was cobbled together with magazine articles, the uncertainty of whether a novel would sell, and the occasional architectural models she constructed as a side job. A book about etiquette represented both a way to earn money and the antidote to what she saw as mounting errors of etiquette all around her, an opportunity to put a messy world onto paper in a way that forced it to make sense. Once she started, it was a project she took to with passion, beginning her writing at six thirty a.m. with coffee and toast in bed[50] before quizzing friends and even strangers waiting in taxi lines about best behavior.[51] Her workroom was wallpapered with notes about the book as she thumbtacked cards with titles such as "Traveling," "The Debutante," and "Weddings."[52] She continued that way for the better part of two years, reemerging only for an appearance at Tuxedo Park's clubhouse for lunch or a Sunday visit with her sons.[53] The final product was a more than six-hundred-page manuscript, written in longhand.[54]

When *Etiquette in Society, in Business, in Politics and at Home* came out, her publisher had only modest hopes for a book that sold for $4 a copy (nearly $62 today). That first edition instead went through seventeen printings, making both the author and her book household names far beyond the penthouses of Park Avenue. The book was sold in stores across the nation, from Montana and Nebraska to North Carolina, Ohio, Massachusetts, and New York. Advertisements for it ran in more than one hundred newspapers in forty-three states plus Washington, D.C., reaching a combined circulation of 2,096,447.[55] Post received tens of thousands of letters in the years following its publication, and by 1930 her syndicated column had 2 million readers, most of whom were not from her social class.[56] The opus included everything from rules for organizing a bridal shower to explicit tips on becoming upwardly mobile. What made it a success, too, was that people found it entertaining to read. Dozens of etiquette books from the Gilded Age to the Roaring Twenties had fed popular demand as the migrations toward urban centers began to happen at the turn of the twentieth century. But where many of the earlier etiquette manuals were excruciatingly dry and scolding, Post's book was filled with characters such as the Gildings, the Kindharts, the Tithering... ton de Puysters, and Mrs. Wordly[57] (characters that held an extra layer of salacious appeal to people of Emily's social set, as the real-life people they represented were torn from the families of New York's elite). Despite its hefty price tag, the book was finding its way into the hands of people who were a far cry from Post's milieu. For most of the twentieth century, it was the second most stolen book from the library[58]—just after the Bible. "It's delicious, too, stealing an etiquette book. Could there be a more American phenomenon?"[59] her descendant Daniel Post Senning quipped. In her personal scrapbook, Post cut out close to a dozen different articles in magazines, newspapers, and trade magazines citing her book as one of the most requested books at public libraries.[60] People seemed to read it almost as they would a self-help book, seeing in its pages the road map to a better life, a blueprint for the type of American that an increasing number of people longed to become.

That type of American was not just someone who knew when to remove their gloves and hat but someone who would be comfortable in an increasingly varied number of social and business situations. For those who wanted an entrée into the world that these figures represented—not just a better life, but what Post referred to as "best society"—her book was their golden ticket. "To liken Best Society to a fraternity, with the avoidance of certain seemingly unimportant words as the sign of recognition, is not a fantastic simile,"[61] Post wrote in the book. "People of the fashionable world invariably use certain expressions and instinctively avoid others; therefore when a stranger uses an 'avoided' one he proclaims that he 'does not belong.'"[62] In this way, *Etiquette* shows social success to be a tapestry of subtle clues that move someone either closer to or farther away from acceptance. In a social landscape full of land mines, then, a book like this one becomes an indispensable map. It is not just offering broadstroke advice; it becomes necessary because it includes everything a social climber might need to know. Nineteen twenty-two might have been the year of "modernism"—a term *The New York Times* later described as "the washing of the corpse of tradition"[63]—and for some young people, it may have felt as if the old rules no longer applied. But for those who want to rise through the ranks of society, the rules always apply. We can imagine someone such as F. Scott Fitzgerald's Jay Gatsby reading *Etiquette* to find out how to mime best society. Fitzgerald himself was so fascinated by Post's book that he wanted to write an entire play based on its principles.[64] The people who can successfully break the rules have to first know what they are.

A 1922 advertisement for the book reads, "Manners are telltales: of men—yes, and women, too. As our manners are polite or vulgar, so we are either admitted or denied admittance as an equal."[65] Being a successful American, then, was a question of "admittance as an equal," something that in the eyes of the book could be earned through behavior and not simply bestowed by birth. Post's book offered an everything-you-need-to-know approach to this vision of the American establishment. Now the original manuscript is in the public domain, and anyone with an Internet connection can access its hundreds of pages. This vision of a good American, which seemed destined more for social strivers than for social successes, was increasingly finding its way across the whole of the country. The promise held in *Etiquette* is extraordinary: that we, just like Gatsby, could fool just about anyone into thinking we belong—and all it takes is memorizing several hundred rules and gestures. It may be a lot of work, but it is a question of dedication alone, not of privilege or even of luck, *Etiquette* promises. As Senning explained, "My impression is that it suited the times perfectly. That, at its best, America viewed itself—hopefully continues to view itself—as a meritocracy. And that there is this -ocracy, this cluster some-where, that theoretically anybody with the goodwill and the capacity can achieve."[66] The word "theoretically" is key here: as Post's own later behavior would show, the way America views itself and the way it behaves are often two entirely different things.

❀

Emily Post envisioned the good American as someone who was willing to put in a Herculean effort to change his behavior and at the same time take pains to keep that effort hidden, like the furious paddling of a duck's feet underwater. There's an entire chapter (featured prominently in advertisements for the book) essentially about social climbing entitled "One's Position in the Community."[67] It taught readers such well-kept secrets as "how total strangers acquire social standing"[68] and "the entrance of an outsider."[69] The section totals only a few pages, whereas Post devoted nearly forty pages to how to write and respond to invi-tations.[70] At the same time, another passage warns readers against name-dropping, saying that "evidence of one frantically climb-ing" appears "merely ludicrous"[71] to those who live on the ledges above the social ladder. This is one of the strange elements of *Etiquette*: the book's sections seem designed for completely dif-ferent audiences. People of Emily's social class hardly needed to know what to wear to a restaurant, for instance. And yet the

tone of the book insists that navigating social strata is deceptively simple—with an emphasis on "deceptive." She writes:

> You who are establishing yourself, either as a young hus-
> band or a stranger, would you, if you could have your wish
> granted by a genie, choose to have the populace look upon
> you askance and in awe, because of your wealth and ele-
> gance, or would you wish to be loved, not as a power con-
> ferring favors which belong really to the first picture, but
> as a fellow-being with an understanding heart? The grant-
> ing of either wish is not a bit beyond the possibilities of
> anyone. It is merely a question of depositing securities of
> value in the bank of life.[72]

With good etiquette, good living becomes the "bank of life."
There's something fundamentally transactional about etiquette,
even when it's supposedly motivated by the ethical ideas of
putting people at ease, creating a frictionless society. There's a
calculation to be made that requires strict adherence to the
rules: more conformity than ingenuity is required to make it in
America.

This idea took hold among a growing audience of people who
had just come to urban centers, just come into money, or both.
The unspoken subtext of *Etiquette* was the questions of race and
immigration that were reaching a fever pitch by the middle of
the 1920s. Influxes in immigration caused many Americans—
both naturalized and U.S.-born—to think critically about who
was and who was not American. In a famed speech just a few

years before the publication of *Etiquette*, President Theodore
Roosevelt had argued that there could be no such thing as an
Irish American or a German American. A man was either German or Irish, or he was American, according to Roosevelt. "All
of us, no matter from what land our parents came, no matter in
what way we may severally worship our Creator, must stand
shoulder to shoulder in a united America,"[73] he said. A new way
of defining American identity, then, was the road to national
unity, and that definition might require relinquishing ethnic
identity, according to those in the Roosevelt camp. The Statue of
Liberty where Emily had played as a girl had now waved more
than 14 million immigrants into the United States. New York
City in particular, thrumming with the activity of Italian,
Czech, Irish, and Polish newcomers, was becoming a litmus test
for how well the elements of the supposed melting pot could
work together. At the same time, questions of race, of the many
Black Americans who were not immigrants but were nonetheless treated as outsiders, were coming to the fore. This was the
era of Jim Crow, of eugenics, and of ongoing mob violence
against Black people. The Ku Klux Klan saw a major resurgence
by the middle of the 1920s, with estimates putting its member-
ship somewhere between 3 and 8 million strong. In the summer
of 1925, tens of thousands of Klan members would openly march
up Pennsylvania Avenue in a parade through the center of Washington, D.C., pausing for a picnic not far from the White House.

Within Post's circle, questions of race and ethnicity were
playing out increasingly in terms of social engagements, parties,
and even weddings. Her son Ned was now spending his nights

dancing with friends in the clubs in Harlem,[74] and one of Post's neighbors from Tuxedo Park married a young woman whose father was reportedly "colored." The ensuing scandal of that marriage, dubbed the Rhinelander Affair, reverberated through-out New York society as gossip flared among Post's social set. Over the next two years, the marriage became the fodder for dozens of breathless newspaper stories. After the young Rhine-lander filed for an annulment of his marriage on the grounds of "racial deceit," Post herself wrote a letter in 1925 to the social register, urging them to omit the bride's name from the blue book of society. "For the sake of race, as well as for the decency of society, which you do uphold, please explain,"[75] she wrote. For all her talk of putting people at ease with etiquette, when it came to personal matters Post could wield the rules of behavior as a tool of exclusion. The supposed meritocracy of manners, that democratic vision of etiquette, only applied to people who could physically pass as members of the elite: white people (and only certain kinds of white people). As had been the case for generations, upward social mobility was a selective virtue, one that systematically bypassed Black people and certain immigrant communities based solely on the color of their skin. In the wrong hands, the rules of etiquette can—even now—serve as a pretext for exclusion or a cover for prejudice. Instead of outright saying that someone was not invited to an event because of the color of their skin or the country where their parents were born, so-called best society could simply say that those who were excluded merited their ostracism because they did not know the rules or had not enjoyed the right "education."

In a similar way, gender roles were a blind spot in *Etiquette*. Post was someone who bristled at the injustice of the restrictions imposed on her as a member of her gender. She was herself a workingwoman and a divorcée who hardly if ever addressed the realities of divorce or women working outside the household in her books. This is perhaps understandable for a woman born in the 1870s, but it's slightly less comprehensible for a book that came out in 1922, in the era of the "new woman." Even if the majority of women working outside the home at this point in U.S. history were those in factories or other menial jobs (that is to say, a working-class audience to whom her book was not marketed), it still seems like an oversight. She devoted dozens of pages to proper romantic etiquette, including courtship and marriage.[76] Divorce, however, was a subject that Post barely addressed in her book, despite the fact that nearly 150,000 couples in the United States divorced in 1922.[77] On divorce, one of the few things Post wrote in her book was this:

> As an unhappy wife, her dignity demands that she never show her disapproval of her husband, no matter how publicly he slights or outrages her. If she has been so unfortunate as to have married a man not a gentleman, to draw attention to his behavior would put herself on his level. If it comes actually to the point where she divorces him, she discusses her situation, naturally, with her parents or her brother or whoever are her nearest and wisest relatives, but she shuns publicity and avoids discussing her affairs with any one outside of her immediate family.[78]

Part of the female American ideal, then, continued to require a strong degree of discretion, even secrecy, when it came to unfair treatment. Post may have been someone who broke the rules of gender norms in her own life, but her work in *Etiquette* only served to reinforce those roles around women, money, and public life at a time when many people were actively challenging the guidelines governing all three.

For all that was changing in 1922—and all that has changed since—certain rules remained immutable. The reality is that socioeconomic class and the markers that go with it still exist—and can still determine our social and professional success. Where exclusion was once based on table settings or stationery, now people can exclude others based on tone of voice, dress, or other signals that remain inextricably tied up in our socioeconomic backgrounds. "Class cues that we send are impactful. They affect how job interviews go; they affect the evaluations that we make of one another,"[79] Dr. Andrea Voyer, a sociologist who has studied the relationship between etiquette and inequality, told me. "To some extent we can say we have democratic manners, but it doesn't speak to the reality of the judgments that we're making in our everyday life," she said. Dr. Voyer spent several years exploring how etiquette affects inclusion or exclusion in three supposed democratic spaces: a public school, a church, and a community board. What she found, however, were not inclusive communities but rather different types of exclusion based on subtler clues about class, gender, race, and immigration status. We're all constantly sending these messages about our backgrounds, often in unconscious ways. She explained:

Those mundane expectations can often be part of people's decision rules about who they sit next to, or who they'll support for a position on the board of an organization— baseline decisions about the people who are "Us" and the people who are "not Us" in the social world. . . . It's not okay in the social world to say, "We don't hang with poor people," or "Our friendship network is closed to people of color," but it is legitimate to say, "She seems angry," or "I just don't really think she has time to be part of our organization."[80]

As manners become more democratized, then, they often become simply more varied or complex rather than more inclusive. Some people today may bemoan a supposed lack of manners in American society, but Voyer's research suggests not only that manners continue to exist, but that they have become harder to read while still determining our social success or failure. We may have moved beyond the oyster fork understanding of etiquette, but our contemporary society has still been unable to create the frictionless ideal suggested by *Etiquette*.

The supposedly democratic nature of *Etiquette* appealed to Americans especially, eager for a view of the world that was based on accomplishment, money, and all variety of things that can be earned. And yet, research like Voyer's, and Post's own missteps on questions of race, reveals the hole in the center of etiquette: some people, no matter how hard they work, no matter how many rules they memorize about handshakes and thank-you notes, are simply not going to advance (or at least not to the Emily Post echelon). Maybe because of skin color or gender or the jobs their parents had, their social advancement is capped at a certain level. It's impossible to know whether the woman that Post tried to exclude from the social register knew which fork to use, but I'm certain it would not have mattered if she had. Sometimes conformity can be levied for a better life, but sometimes the markers of difference that kept doors closed in the first place will still keep them forever and firmly shut, good etiquette or not. Perhaps, then, etiquette did not exist as a leg up on the social ladder but instead served simply to put those at the top more at ease.

A review of *Etiquette* in a 1922 issue of the magazine *Town & Country* notes that the book will be useful for "enormous numbers of second generation immigrants"[81] who have money but don't know the rules of social usage. In what can only be described as a tone dripping with blue-blooded condescension, the reviewer writes, "Such a book is a part of the large Americanization process which we, the grandchildren of those who wished foreign immigration upon us, are using as a sop to Cerberus, as an effort to bring back an appreciation of the art of gentleness which was considered a self-evident desirability some forty years ago."[82] The image of Post's book being thrown to calm a three-headed dog guarding the gates to the underworld just about says it all. This review betrays what may not have been Post's intention but was surely part of why the book was popular among the upper crust: they were using *Etiquette* not as a method for putting everyone at ease nor to help others move up but rather as a means of ensuring that their lifestyle would remain unchallenged. In that way, the glitterati became a stand-in for aristocracy in the United States. Often without our knowing, etiquette teaches us simply how to act like rich people do. We inherit rules about behavior that we take to be true; those rules, however, might not come from the best way of doing things but rather from the rich way of doing things. If *Etiquette* truly were a ticket into best society, it would have represented a threat to those already living at the top. That they welcomed it says more about the ways in which the book was functioning in this dual purpose. By situating etiquette as a moral imperative and not a frivolous set of niceties, Post was able to further convince people of its necessity, effectively marrying new ideas of social mobility into the age-old notion of caste. Post, then, was in many ways a bridge, not just between the upper class and those who wanted to become them, but between the Gilded Age of manners and the Roaring Twenties, providing a potent challenge to the rejection of societal norms taking place in the modern era. Katherine Anne Porter, award-winning author of *Ship of Fools*, called Post both "interpreter and apologist"[83] for the upper class, describing her as "an excellent liaison officer between New York society and that great formless indiscriminate welter, the population of the United States of America."[84]

❀

Post was not able to bask in soaring sales figures and glowing reviews for long. In 1927, her younger son, named Bruce for her beloved father, began complaining of a stomachache. She eventually forced him to go to the hospital on February 25.[85] Little did either of them know, his appendix had burst. Within a few hours of being admitted to the hospital, Bruce Price Post was pronounced dead at the age of thirty-two. Out of all of the sorrows that Emily Post had and would endure throughout her eighty-seven-year life—her bitter divorce, her father's cancer, her mother's sudden death when her skull was broken in a car accident—this was the loss that struck her the hardest. Post retreated to her home and for weeks refused to accept that he was in fact dead, according to her eldest son, Edwin.[86] While Emily remained a private person throughout her life and rarely spoke publicly about her own experiences with loss, her passage on grief from the 1922 edition, which remained unchanged throughout her life, offers some insight:

> At no time does solemnity so possess our souls as when we stand deserted at the brink of darkness into which our loved one has gone. And the last place in the world where we would look for comfort at such a time is in the seeming artificiality of etiquette; yet it is in the moment of deepest sorrow that etiquette performs its most vital and real service. All set rules for social observance have for their object the smoothing of personal contacts, and in nothing is smoothness so necessary as in observing the solemn rites accorded our dead. It is the time-worn servitor, Etiquette, who draws the shades, who muffles the bell, who keeps the house quiet, who hushes voices and footsteps and sudden noises; who stands between well-meaning and importunate outsiders and the retirement of the bereaved; who decrees that the last rites shall be performed smoothly and with beauty and gravity, so that the poignancy of grief may in so far as possible be assuaged.[87]

The rules of etiquette, perhaps strangely, were a way of making space for the impolite entry of grief. Etiquette could serve as a buffer between the grieved and those trying—sometimes tactlessly—to comfort them. We may think of the rules for social engagement as a way to conceal our raw thoughts or feelings, but in this instance, they seemed to cushion them. That poignant passage could only have come from someone well versed in that "brink of darkness." Post's words would soothe the grief of many, many readers to come, including famed twentieth-century writer Joan Didion, who credited Post's writings on grief as one of the only texts to allay her suffering after the twin losses of her husband's death and her daughter's illness.[88]

Post would not allow herself to wallow in grief for long, however. As she had often done during difficult times throughout her life, she turned again to writing with a fierceness amid sorrow and chaos. Therein lies one of Emily Post's strongest motivators: control. Long after she had earned more than enough money to live, she continued to write. Her intrinsic motivation seemed to be a desire to organize, to put things in their place and then to put them away. She wrote for the same reason that many of us read: to slowly, piece by piece, try to make sense of a confusing world. The newly revised edition, which included dozens of new pages and new characters, would come out just a few months after Bruce's death.

This intense desire to reassert some kind of control motivated much of her writing and shows up in the personal scrapbooks she kept throughout her life. These scrapbooks (and a garden log) are some of the only personal writing that survived after her death. Each photograph is meticulously dated and titled, and she cut out and saved just about every news item written about herself or her sons, whether in *The New York Times* or *The Pittsburgh Press*. She would go through and circle mistakes, striking out a line about her father designing "one or two" sky-scrapers and writing in the exact number, or correcting the name of a duke (Queen Victoria's son) who traveled with her father, among other small details.[89] The scrapbooks are essentially a correction of her life's record, a red pen scratching out errors in a *New Yorker* profile written about her, annotated with notes about the journalist's "stupid mistakes."[90] She insisted in *Etiquette* that divorced women be referred to with both their maiden names and their formerly married names, and she circled in every single news item where a journalist referred to her as "Mrs. Post" and not "Mrs. Price Post" (there were many, many instances of this particular error). The scrapbooks reveal someone who was both highly concerned with appearances and also meticulous about details, preoccupied many decades before her death with how she would be remembered.

This kind of intense dedication to detail can be seen throughout all the editions that she edited of *Etiquette*, and it certainly pushed her to meet deadlines for that second edition. The revised version of *Etiquette*, released in 1928, was decidedly middle-class in many ways, thanks in part to the continually changing social mores of the 1920s and to the evolving readership of the book. The new version included what would become one of Emily Post's most notable creations: the character of "Mrs. Three-in-One," for the woman who was waitress, cook, and hostess at dinner parties. Where the original *Etiquette* assumed that readers had both a cook and waitstaff, new editions would increasingly take into account the realities of middle-class American life, what Julia Child would later call the "servantless American cook."[91] Mrs. Three-in-One could cook the soufflé and manage to have it on the table before it began to droop, all while keeping guests entertained with her poise and charm. In this way, the middle-class revisions returned to the very roots of etiquette in America: a third path that avoids the extremes of familiarity and pretension, all while acknowledging the challenges inherent in American middle-class life.

❁

From the start, the origins of etiquette in the United States warn above all against affectation. The advice from early American etiquette experts insists on a middle path in all aspects of life, from manners to temperament. Their approach discourages direct contradiction of others and insists on putting everyone at ease (as a step on the way to personal achievement). Even before the Revolutionary era, the etiquette books circulating at the time—many of them imported from England—looked to facilitate social mobility by teaching the marks of a "gentleman" to the middle class, according to one historian of etiquette.[92] The elite in early America may have been determined more by money than by birth, and while society may have been less rigid than it was in Europe, the social order still encouraged social mixing among "equals," which is to say those of a similar socioeconomic class. Markers of one's class therefore become even more important in determining social mobility. In observing the United States in the early nineteenth century, French diplomat Alexis de Tocqueville found that Americans were doing everything within their power to give the impression that there were no differences between people. And yet, the inequalities between different socioeconomic classes had not been erased. "The picture of American society is, if I may put it this way, overlaid with a democratic patina beneath which we see from time to time the former colors of the aristocracy showing through,"[93] he wrote. American manners in that way can be a cruel trick, a milky veil that gives but the illusion of equality.

Etiquette historians point to the election of Andrew Jackson as a turning point in the United States' relationship with social conduct. Soon after Jackson ascended to the White House in 1828, the publication and sale of etiquette books exploded.[94] Jackson had grown up the son of destitute immigrants, and he was the first president who was neither a Virginia landowner nor a Harvard man. As rules requiring land ownership for voting started to disappear, a growing number of people had been able to vote for the first time, leading to Jackson's being dubbed "the people's president." As was the tradition at the time, Jackson held an open house at the White House for his inauguration, attended by many of his rural supporters. As one witness later told the *Chicago Tribune*: "It seemed as though every uncouth backwoodsman and rough-in-country had made a descent upon the capital. Fully half the crowd wore pistols and had their trousers tucked into their boots."[95] The ball grew so rowdy, with glasses smashed and oriental rugs ruined, that the White House staff threw kegs of alcohol onto the lawn to lure the partygoers out of the house itself. A sense of a new era reigned in American society, and amid the breaches in etiquette, the

American people would soon discover a renewed interest in rules for behavior. Dozens of new etiquette books appeared for men and women, and debate over best etiquette practices began to take over an expanding place in a growing number of magazine pages. As historian Arthur Schlesinger put it in his seminal book *Learning How to Behave: A Historical Study of American Etiquette Books*, "The passion for equality, in other words, found expression in the view that all could become gentlemen, not that gentlemen should cease to be."[96]

Manners existed in even the most remote islands and helped define "a self-constituted aristocracy, or fraternity of the best," a middle-aged Ralph Waldo Emerson would argue in an essay entitled "Manners,"[97] little more than a decade after Jackson's inauguration. In this way, etiquette had long since been understood for its highest possible function: a type of democratic social contract. It might not be democratic in the sense that everyone gets an equal say in deciding how to behave but rather in the sense that ordinary people—presidents, not kings; society women, not countesses—would decide the fundamentals of best society. If the Constitution serves as the most basic form of an American social contract, etiquette practices and books expanded on the questions of what we owe one another as people and as citizens. By the mid–nineteenth century, a growing number of Americans or people who wanted to become American were hungrier than ever for a version of etiquette that would be an equalizer of people, a kind of social lubricant to ease all kinds of difference in an increasingly heterogeneous nation. Americans no longer wanted to be "mere imitators of foreign manners, often based on social conditions radically different from our own," as they were in 1856, according to one etiquette writer.[98] They wanted their own kind of etiquette that took into account the specific social conditions of their time and place. Much like Webster looking to take the best forms of European cultural life and make something fundamentally new and uniformly American, etiquette served the same kind of standardizing purpose. It allowed Americans (or at least the Americans at the top) to select the best forms of behavior, ideally in a way that would avoid the pitfalls of European aristocracy.

While Emily Post's *Etiquette* might not have fulfilled the type of middle-class utopia that American etiquette books espoused, there's evidence that she was in fact trying to achieve a similar vision. Her section on conversation has a distinct American egalitarianism, teaching people to avoid both extremes of formality and familiarity in order to encourage a kind of mutual easiness. She cautions against both ignorance and affectation, warning against saying "I done it"[99] just as she does "partook of liquid refreshment."[100] Her list of "never says"[101] includes both ends of this spectrum. She even suggests buying a pronunciation dictionary, for "while affectation is odious, crudeness must be overcome."[102] In this way, too, these authoritative reference books across *Americanon* were almost never standalones, but were rather working in tandem, scaffolding one another in subtle ways. The same person who might have bought Emily Post's *Etiquette* almost certainly would have had *Merriam-Webster's Dictionary*, both for the status it conferred and for the way it could (in theory at least) transform someone's way of speaking. Each of the books in *Americanon* was there to shape new Americans in particular in the image of the best, most American way of doing something—as decided by this handful of people at the top. *Etiquette* reveals this balance that needs to be carefully struck by outsiders, those who are essentially pretending at an easiness that the upper-class people were taught by their mothers and governesses. The warnings against pretension seemed destined less for the old money than for the new, a way of encouraging people to act the way that people in Post's class already did. For all the democratization of manners taking place in the twentieth century, etiquette remained, at least in part, an imitation of gentlemen and their gentlewomen wives.

We cannot entirely blame Post for not revolutionizing etiquette in a way that shattered old ways of doing things: this is a restriction of the form itself. Etiquette authors are not in the position to entirely reinvent the rules; they are rather choosing one way from an already whittled-down number of choices concerning best behavior. The popularity of this book also served as a kind of feedback loop, confirming both to Emily and to readers of the book that information about best society and their behavior was indeed very valuable to have. Her personal authority was amplified by the fact that she was not just any etiquette author; she had quickly become a celebrity in her own right. In 1950, the popular women's magazine *Pageant* named Post the second most influential woman—just after Eleanor Roosevelt.[103] After her death, *Life* magazine would name her one of the most remarkable women in the first two centuries of American history.[104] Even today, when someone spills a glass of red wine on a white couch or blows their nose too loudly, people will jokingly moan, "What would Emily Post say?" Her influence was more than that of an author; she became the mid-twentieth-century version of a lifestyle guru, her face and voice recognizable from TV, radio, and her monthly column. Emily Post was a brand unto herself, guiding social standards for much of the twentieth century, and her book was only one facet of disseminating that message. "Few of the hundreds of etiquette books published in America since the time of Jackson left any more than a thumb-print on American behavior until Emily Post came along in 1922," historian Esther B. Aresty wrote.[105] Where people ask for Kleenex instead of tissues, they started to ask for Emily Post instead of an etiquette book, according to Aresty. That kind of name recognition elevated her book from the level of a bestseller to a part of the canon, something that at once captured and defined a corner of American identity.

If the book managed to strike a surprising resonance among so many readers, it already seemed an anachronism to some critics, who deemed it an artifact of a stuffy, snobby era gone by. It was modern in many ways, addressing things that did not exist when other etiquette books were written, such as elevators, flappers, and telephones, but some writers fully in the modern age did not find it nearly modern enough. Dorothy Parker skewered the second edition of *Etiquette* in a 1927 piece for *The New Yorker*. "Those who have mastered etiquette, who are entirely, impeccably right, would seem to arrive at a point of exquisite dullness. The letters and the conversations of the correct, as quoted by Mrs. Post, seem scarcely worth the striving for," Parker wrote.[106] She took special umbrage at the rules in the conversation section, which included tips such as "talk of something you have been doing or thinking about—planting a garden, planning a journey, contemplating a journey, or similar safe topics."[107] It's understandable coming from Parker, a woman known for acerbic wit and bristling at social norms for women, and she was not alone in finding both Emily Post and her book to be the driest kind of relic.

That conviction was not shared by the millions of Americans who continued to buy and read both Post's books and columns. A flourishing readership of wannabes and social almost-theres continued to grow throughout the mid–twentieth century, as the line between best society and those imitating them grew blurrier in the years following *Etiquette*'s first publication. The "Blue Book" would see another huge boom during the World War II and post–World War II years, thanks in part to a boost from famed war correspondent Ernie Pyle,[108] who mentioned that soldiers who wanted to become officers were reading Emily Post. USO clubs reported as many as sixteen thousand requests in one week[109] for this book, and Emily Post continued to oblige her audience. In the post–World War II years, it was being used increasingly like Dale Carnegie's *How to Win Friends and Influence People*: as a guidebook to the shifting social situations inherent in climbing the corporate ladder. The World War II–era revisions were also thoughtful about issues of shell shock, urging readers to have empathy in welcoming veterans home. Veterans might appear "absent-minded, untalkative or tense,"[110] she warned, but their loved ones must "try to realize what he has been through and be patient."[111] Following Post's original audience of World War I war wives, World War II also created tens of thousands of war wives, just as the GI Bill infused cash and opportunity into the U.S. economy. That potent combination created a fertile audience for *Etiquette* as new-money women navigated the social sphere and their husbands waded through the changing workplace politics of new offices, factories, and postwar industry. Perhaps strangely, people continued to cling to etiquette, consideration, and social niceties even in the face of a Second World War that included genocide. It was an unlikely refuge of civility in the face of unthinkable violence.

Whether in the 1920s, the 1940s, or even today, etiquette exists despite social upheaval—or possibly because of it—offering structure in times of uncertainty. These rules, about everything from dating to death, are handed down systemically without much notice, taken to be truth. While etiquette may evolve to suit the time, and it can be used to make others more comfortable, it is based on an invention: an arbitrary set of rules chosen by a few people. We like to think we have some kind of democracy, but these rules—which most Americans had no say in creating—still govern our ease or discomfort, our inclusion or exclusion, our success or failure. Part of why the book lasted was that Post—and now her descendants—insisted that it would, continually revising the book to ensure its relevance, updating it to follow (and sometimes restrain) the shifting social mores of the twentieth century.

❈

The Emily Post Institute today is located in the hippie enclave of Burlington, Vermont, a city known to New Englanders for fall foliage, Ben & Jerry's ice cream, and pot-smoking skiers. It's

a college town packed with free-trade coffee shops, hemp cloth-
ing, and secondhand bookstores. The institute is located in a
former schoolhouse—which seems about right.

The inheritors of the institute, Lizzie Post and Daniel
Post Senning, are Emily's great-great-grandchildren, both born
more than a decade after her death. They may still feature Post's
signature and her trademark blue on some of their books, but
now they write about everything from Instagram and email etiquette to holiday gift exchanges. Lizzie, who consumes mari-
juana almost daily, wrote a book on pot etiquette.[112] Nearly a
century after *Etiquette*'s original publication, few vestiges of
Emily's white-gloved approach remain. I showed up early in a
button-down shirt and one of two pairs of slacks I owned, trying to remember the small amount of etiquette I had learned in
a social manners class given at my local town hall when I was
nine years old.

Lizzie Post arrived almost a full hour late, wearing a wrin-
kled shirt and her hair pulled back in a messy bun, with a rescue
dog named Jack in tow. She apologized profusely, explaining
that she had driven nearly twenty-four hours to pick up Jack
from a foster home several states away. Her breach in etiquette
was actually a big relief. She and her cousin Dan, who run the
institute together, were casual and fun. I had been prepared for
an excruciating tea complete with judgmental looks about my
hand placement on a teacup. I wasn't expecting pho noodles and
a freewheeling approach. Emily Post's "archives" fill up a handful of cardboard boxes that Lizzie had to pick up at her parents'
house. She and Dan were preparing for a training program, one
of the institute's main functions today, and the office was a mess

of boxes, stacks of paper, and unhung picture frames. One framed magazine article quoted Emily saying this: "I'm interested in what you are. Anyone's greatest asset is charm, and it comes from sincere, kindly impulses. Most of us want to be liked. We want to be graceful and not awkward. We don't want to hurt others. If we follow those impulses, we'll find that charm goes along with them."[113]

The institute's books no longer sell the mega-numbers that they did in Emily's heyday, but that result might be a product more of our era than of anything the current Posts are doing or not doing. There will always be a market for etiquette books, but in a time when an increasing number of how-to questions concerning etiquette practices are available online (as is the first edition of Emily Post's *Etiquette*, which is now in the public domain), people are less likely to buy a book about it for $24.96. The institute instead finds enduring relevance by tapping into contemporary culture: using the books to discuss our polarized political climate or how new technology affects manners. Dan and Lizzie even have a podcast.

Lizzie defined the role of etiquette today first in terms of what it is not. It's not just thank-you notes, or restrictions on what women can wear, or something from her grandmother's era. Both Dan and Lizzie said they envision etiquette today as a different kind of bridge. They seem to be thinking less about the issues of socioeconomic class that drove *Etiquette*'s initial success and instead about the questions of partisanship and incivility that lead social debates now. "It becomes a great equalizer in allowing you to respect and understand the people around you, even though you might not agree with their opinion," Lizzie

Post explained.[114] The goal is to put people at ease with one another, to come together regardless of difference. There is a shift, however subtle, in embracing just how disparate Americans have always been. They say the three principles guiding the institute today are consideration, respect, and honesty. Both Lizzie and Dan insisted on the self-help aspect of their institute's principles. They said that the best uses of etiquette today come not from people interested in litigating who has good or bad etiquette but rather from those who come to their courses hoping to improve the way they interact with friends, colleagues, or even family.

For all the difference between today's institute and Emily's original work, several throughlines remain, especially when it comes to facilitating social ease, creating success along the corporate ladder, and smoothing out the kind of social mobility that first motivated *Etiquette*'s early readers. In flipping through one of the few photo albums that survived from Emily's early life, one book yellowed with age consisted of photos mostly from the end of the nineteenth century. Images showed Emily in a bathing costume at the beach with her children or wearing a hat and floor-length dress, perched on a park bench at the turn of the twentieth century.[115] One of the first images in her 1895 photo album showed Emily's dog, a surprisingly mutt-looking breed, and underneath she had written "Jack." Meanwhile, Lizzie shouted good-naturedly at her dog, "Jack, stop jumping; I don't want to have to say 'jack off' on a tape recorder!"[116]

Like Emily, Lizzie and Dan recognize that etiquette rules need to be continually revised—and sometimes gotten rid of—but that etiquette always survives in some form. It might not follow us from our debutante ball to the grave in quite the same way it did in 1922, but even in an increasingly casual world, rules for behavior do not disappear. "It's about making people feel comfortable. That's the big one. And at the same time, the tiniest bit about preserving tradition,"[117] Lizzie said. "But we don't preserve tradition only for tradition or the past's sake. You know, if it really doesn't fit anymore, we've got to move on."[118]

❀

CHAPTER SEVEN

How to Win Friends and Influence People (1936)

O ne of Dale Carnagey's earliest memories was the smell of
burning hog flesh. Year after year, his parents lost the pigs
of their small farm to cholera, and year after year they were
forced to burn them—the crackling smell piercing his nostrils
as a boy. He watched, too, as the floodwaters of the 102 River
bowled over the cornfields and the hayfields of their Missouri
farm, leaving nothing but refuse in their wake.[1] Six out of seven
years on the farm, the 102 overflowed and ruined their crops.
Despite working sixteen-hour days, the family was drowning in
debt. The seventh year they did well and fed the surplus crops to
the animals, but they still earned less for the livestock than what
they paid for them. "No matter what we did, we lost money,"[2] he
later wrote.

It may have technically been the Gilded Age—Dale was
born little more than fifteen years after Emily Post—but the
spoils of a booming economy barely touched his family's corner
of northwest Missouri, much less Dale's parents. Post's lavish

coming-out party, with its couture evening wear and cases of champagne, took place the year after Carnagey was born to a life of mucking the barn, chopping wood, and just barely scraping by on a struggling farm. The town's first flushing toilet was the kind of thing that made news in the nearby town of Maryville, Missouri.[3] He remembered going into town to try the newfangled toilet and then walking away immediately after the deafening sound of the flush embarrassed him. Far from most major cities, Dale and his schoolmates played across hundreds of acres of pastureland and timberland. That same 102 River that caused his parents so much grief was also the location of some of the "happiest hours of my childhood,"[4] Dale wrote in a letter to his daughter, which doubled as an autobiography, a few years before his death. In the summer, he would spend his days swimming or catching fish with a willow pole and a baited worm in the river before eating ripe fruit from the plump watermelon patches scattered across northwest Missouri. He recounted both the hardships and a beautiful American pastoral quality to his childhood. "As a child, I knew where the robins and the turtledoves nested. I knew the color of their eggs. I knew their songs. . . . The bird songs I heard in our orchard seem in retrospect to have been lovelier than the music of Schumann Heink and Caruso,"[5] he wrote. Despite living in New York City for much of his adult life, Carnagey remained a country boy at heart. When his parents died, he took over their farm, and in 1951 he bought his own eight-hundred-acre farm near Harrisonville, Missouri.[6]

The hardships of life on the farm were many, and Dale's early life was marked by both the mundane grind of poverty and a bizarre string of accidents. There was the daily task of trying to grow enough food and earn enough money to survive on the farm, and as a boy Dale hated all the chores that farming required: churning butter, milking cows, cleaning the henhouse, weeding, and chopping wood.[7] His parents were of an already disappearing breed of American at the turn of the twentieth century: true yeoman farmers who followed the lifestyle of old-school self-reliance. For someone who would write a handbook to corporate America, guiding a generation from farm to office, the young Carnagey had experience almost exclusively with the former. He would spend the first twenty years of his life never far from their corner of Missouri—and throughout his career he never held down any typical office job, working instead as a traveling salesman, an actor, and a teacher. When he was growing up, his family raised livestock, grew crops, made their own clothes, and had a smokehouse for meats.[8] They even rode to town in a wagon to barter for what they could not make or grow themselves.[9] But their daily life was often very far from the idealized version of small farming vaunted by publications like *The Old Farmer's Almanac*. Dale did not know it at the time, but there was a moment when his father was so ashamed of his lack of money and success, when his "spirit was broken at the failure he [was] making of his life,"[10] that he threatened to hang himself from a tree on their property.

Many of his father's hardships came from unavoidable natural disasters, such as floods or disease. Others were just plain bad luck: his father once bought a donkey to help out around the farm. Just moments after the donkey set foot in the barn, it stepped on a loose board, and—like something out of a cartoon—

the board catapulted upward, its exposed nails puncturing the donkey's stomach, killing it on the spot.[11] It was an anecdote Dale would later recount to *The Saturday Evening Post*.[12] Dale, too, was prone to a series of violent mishaps. He was almost shot by a friend while hunting squirrels in the forest at age fourteen.[13] While attempting to mount his horse in freezing weather, the shivering animal bolted when he had only one foot in the stirrup, dragging Dale along the frozen ground in the nearly twenty-below-zero weather.[14] One day, while playing in an abandoned log cabin with his cousins, he tried to jump down from the attic while wearing his mother's wedding band on his left pointer finger. As he fell through the air, the ring caught on a nail and ripped his finger entirely off, stripping it clean of the first two joints. He ran all the way home wailing, his stub of a finger wrapped in a handkerchief. When they arrived at the town doctor's office, the handkerchief clung to the exposed bone. The doctor could not reattach the finger,[15] and Carnagey became a public speaker who could point with only one hand. In many photos after he became famous, he can be seen shielding his left hand, tucking it into his coat or wearing gloves.

Shame, fear, and the kind of anxiety he would spend the rest of his adult life fighting against pervaded much of his early life. He feared his family would not have enough to eat. He worried that they would lose the farm. And for much of his youth, especially in school, he was an awkward boy, self-conscious and suffering from intense anxiety (he would even later write an entire book on how to stop worrying). The books he would write were not born of a care-free philosopher but of a man desperate to survive, whose numerous brushes with failure and death would serve as fodder for a lifetime of motivation.

The moment that gave him his first break—and set him on the path that would win him fame and wealth—came when he was a student. His parents decided to buy a new farm closer to Warrensburg, Missouri, in order to send him to a teaching college because the school had no tuition. Unable to afford the $1 per day room and board, Dale commuted to school on horseback. Wearing threadbare, patched clothes that no longer fit him, he cut a strange figure riding each day to class. His school years were marked by what he described as an "inferiority complex."[16] While standing at the blackboard, he could hardly concentrate, shuddering at the thought of people making fun of his raggedy appearance. Self-conscious of his poverty and lacking in confidence, he joined the speech team as a way of becoming more self-assured. He would practice his speeches, including the Gettysburg Address,[17] on those daily horse rides to college— talking to himself in snow, sleet, and sweaty summers—and soon he became the star speaker of the school, known for his charisma and his magnetic public speaking skills. Shame, especially concerning his own poverty and appearance, had been perhaps the single defining emotion of Dale's formative years. But he had finally found its antidote: charm. Years later, he wrote: "True, clothes don't make the man; but they do make 90% of all we see of the man."[18] The book he would write became a kind of amulet guarding against shame—because if you get other people talking about themselves, they'll be too distracted to notice your flaws (or what you're wearing). His book cleverly put everyone in the position to sidestep the traps of humiliation that had haunted him as a young man.

Throughout his life, Carnagey believed that the skills that had proven most valuable to him had not been learned in a classroom. As a result, autodidacticism and a kind of bootstrap mentality would become central to the philosophy he would go on to preach in his classes and his books. His largely self-taught skill at public speaking rescued him from unpopularity and from shame; he found himself more able to make friends, to talk to girls, and generally to acquire the kind of social status that all young people long for. Carnagey discovered early on that a way with words and a faculty for charming people could be leveraged for a better life. It was that skill that would earn him a living long before he became a bestselling author.

By 1911, Carnagey had moved to New York City in the hopes of working as an actor. Upon his arrival in Manhattan, the thing that shocked him most was just how much money everything cost. Even the cheapest hotels were three times as expensive as the best rooms back in Missouri,[19] and coffee and toast for breakfast could quickly drain him of his meager savings. Carnagey had only learned how bank accounts worked two years prior, at the age of twenty. The man who would become a business guru had been forced to write a letter to his parents, asking, "When I put my money in there how do I know I can ever get it out?"[20] He took up residence in a run-down apartment on West Fifty-Sixth Street. The room he rented was so infested with cockroaches that the insects would scatter every time he went to take a necktie off the wall.[21] Carnagey fought to find acting roles, all while hustling to make ends meet by working as a car salesman.

What would become the basis for his bestseller *How to Win Friends and Influence People* started as a public speaking course he gave at the 125th Street YMCA. The struggling actor ended up there even as several schools and other institutions turned down his offer to teach. Carnagey's main professional experience came from working as a traveling salesman selling soap, bacon, and lard in the Dakotas prior to his arrival in New York City. Even the 125th Street YMCA was not convinced that anyone would be interested in his public speaking classes, so they refused to pay him a fee. Projecting little profit, they offered him 80 percent of the net receipts[22] rather than any upfront payment. In the beginning, the YMCA was proved right: his first lecture in 1912 was certainly not a runaway success. He started off lecturing as a college professor might on "oratory," but within a few short minutes he ran out of material. To stall for time, he asked one of the only five or six attendees to tell the rest of the group about himself.[23] And then he called on another man to do the same while he tried to figure out something to say next. He never finished that initial lecture he had begun, and instead he began formulating his conviction about how much people enjoy talking about themselves. "A lot of the methods I used were desperation methods,"[24] he later wrote. Desperation drove Carnagey to work harder, to try everything when it came to teaching, to working, and to surviving.

He revamped the class to focus on participation, steering students toward talking about any subject that they were passionate about, and he quickly discovered that two of his students' favorite subjects were themselves and the things that made them angry. The class focused on self-confidence, salesmanship, and communication. The next year, his enrollment tripled, and he soon expanded to teaching at a Brooklyn YMCA. Enthusiasm steadily built, attracting more attention from other nearby YMCAs. Within a few years of that first lecture, he was earning between $30 and $40 a night (between $750 and $1,000 in today's currency).[25] By the end of 1914, Carnagey was teaching in New York, Philadelphia, and Delaware, pulling in $500 a month.[26] The YMCA had a hit public speaking course on its hands, and Carnagey finally had a commodity. Students all over the Northeast flocked to his classes, eager to acquire Carnagey's way with words. With his steady income from public speaking courses, Carnagey decided to rent an office space. The location he selected—and whose auditorium he would later fill on multiple occasions—was Carnegie Hall. There are myriad theories as to why "Carnagey" became "Carnegie" within the next decade—ease of pronunciation, a dissociation from his origins, or a closer link with steel baron Andrew Carnegie—and there seems to be at least some truth in many of these hypotheses. Perhaps above all, Dale was a skilled showman and self-promoter, someone who simply could not turn down the clout that the "Carnegie" name conferred.

The crux of those public speaking courses—self-confidence, developing personality, and an interest in others—would become the basis for his 1936 bestseller, *How to Win Friends and Influence People*. The smell of manure and damp hay, the sound of sniggering schoolmates—they may have been distant memories by the time Carnegie started work on his book more than twenty years after that first YMCA course. But the lessons he learned from those early failures would become the cornerstone of a philosophy that reached tens of millions of people, earning him the moniker of "the father of the self-help movement."

❀

The book that would influence over 30 million people was almost never written. In 1934, Leon Shimkin, a rising star at Simon & Schuster, happened to be invited to a course for young executives given by Dale Carnegie.[27] By that point, Carnegie was making a comfortable living through his courses on public speaking, drawing crowds of businessmen each week. After just briefly watching Carnegie work his personal brand of magic—teaching people positivity and confidence—Shimkin was hooked. He approached Carnegie that very night with an offer to write a book.[28] As soon as Shimkin mentioned his employer's name, Carnegie flat-out declined. The publishing house had already rejected two prior manuscripts he had submitted, and anyway he was "too busy,"[29] Carnegie told him. Shimkin, seeing the potential after just one course, persisted. He pursued Carnegie aggressively and even convinced him that a stenographer could write up some of his letters and submit them as a rough draft. After seeing his own work compiled in such a way, Carnegie was just as mesmerized by his own power and agreed to write the book.

Carnegie's book and the context of the Great Depression are like two sides of the same coin—impossible to separate from each other. The book seems to represent the advice he wished someone had given him[30] when he, like millions of Americans, saw much of his hard-earned money evaporate. With the stock market crash in 1929 and the ensuing Great Depression, not only did people lose their savings; they lost their pride and sense of control. That is exactly what Carnegie gave them back, for the low price of $1.96. The 1920s, with its flappers, booming economy, and growing cities, was an age of optimism, brought to a sharp end by the 1929 stock market crash. Soon, Americans would be less interested in Emily Post's rules for giving a debutante ball and more desperately in need of tips on how to survive food shortages and mass layoffs. In October 1929, the New York Stock Exchange tumbled, causing losses that totaled hundreds of billions of dollars in today's currency. It wasn't just rich investors who lost their money. An increasing number of working-class people had been trying their hand at playing the stocks. As *Time* magazine wrote at the time of the crash, "For so many months so many people had saved money and borrowed money and borrowed on their borrowings to possess themselves of the little pieces of paper by virtue of which they became partners in U. S. Industry. Now they were trying to get rid of them even more frantically than they had tried to get them."[31] Carnegie himself had not been immune to the effects of Black Thursday, and like so many other Americans, he had lost much of his savings in the crash. He would later write in a letter, "When I think of my record in the stock market, it seems a joke for me to be giving anybody financial advice on anything."[32]

In 1935, as Carnegie was finishing his book, the majority of the United States was still in a blackout at night,[33] as most people could not pay for electricity. Unemployment had peaked at nearly 25 percent in 1933, and—even after the New Deal—it still hovered at around 20 percent in 1935. It wasn't just the struggles of daily life that challenged average Americans. The effects of so much fiscal damage had given way to psychological despair, feelings of worthlessness, and even clinical depression. By 1932, the suicide rate had soared—growing by more than a fifth of what it had been in 1928. The Depression forever altered people's habits and caused lingering psychological effects even as the results of the New Deal were starting to change people's financial situations. At its core, *How to Win Friends and Influence People* promised a different kind of commodity than its practical lessons; it also offered people hope, a balm for the trauma of so much loss. Carnegie would tell readers that they already had the keys to their own survival; they simply needed to change the way they thought about their own lives. "It isn't what you have or who you are or where you are or what you are doing that makes you happy or unhappy. It is what you think about it,"[34] he would write in *How to Win Friends and Influence People*.

Carnegie worked on the book over the course of 1935 and 1936 but turning in the manuscript was still something of a sprint. He did not have time to write the last chapter, and as Simon & Schuster moved the book to production, they realized that the title, *How to Make Friends and Influence People*, did not fit comfortably on the cover of a book. Carnegie suggested the change from "make" friends to "win," which was the title he used in his courses. Shimkin was wary of the swap, but in a desire to get the book out as quickly as possible, he sent *How to Win Friends and Influence People* to press.[35]

Carnegie's book came out in the fall of 1936, part self-help book and part blueprint for climbing the ladder of corporate success—a potent combination that made it a near-instant bestseller. *How to Win Friends and Influence People* is often seen as a departure from the more traditional American manuals and how-to books that came before it, signaling a new kind of advice book based on personality. And yet, much like Emily Post's *Etiquette*, Carnegie's book was a bridge between older visions of American success and our contemporary understanding of self-help and self-made men. *How to Win Friends and Influence People* can even be understood partially as an etiquette book for business relationships and friendships, offering rules for behavior. Despite being born on opposite ends of the socioeconomic spectrum, Carnegie and Post both created books meant to help readers climb the social ladder. The book that Carnegie wrote would serve so many different functions for the American public: an etiquette book but also a self-help book and a get-rich-quick book—a book that taught you how to get over social anxiety and also how to keep your job. *How to Win Friends and Influence People* draws together so many different aspects of the books across *Americanon*: it took significant cues from earlier advice literature, mixing Franklin-era wisdom with modern psychology. At the same time, *How to Win Friends and Influence People* incorporated these aspects of the traditional work ethic, setting into motion a new American story, one about attitude and personality.

Carnegie may have been picking up on an existing national fascination with charismatic figures, but he captured it, distilled it, and put it to use in average Americans' lives in a way that had never quite been done before. The book included six ways to make other people like you, twelve ways to win others to your way of thinking, and seven rules for making your home life happier, among myriad other tips and tricks for becoming a more likable, more successful person. It combined the wisdom he had gleaned from a career as a public speaker and his research on celebrities in a range of fields, from presidents to movie stars. Its central tenet was that a nonconfrontational personality and a keen interest in others were the keys to success. "My popularity, my happiness and my income depend to no small extent upon my skill in dealing with people,"[36] Carnegie asks his readers to repeat aloud to themselves from the first chapter. His philosophy taught readers that a combination of positive thinking and charisma could bring others around to their way of thinking much more easily than criticism or disagreement. It was a guidebook to business acumen that focused on friendliness: if people like you, Carnegie told readers, they'll give you what you want. In the years following the Great Depression, this message resonated on a huge scale: the book was so popular that only the Bible outpaced its sales. It went through dozens of editions before 1940, and it has sold more than 30 million copies since its release. Even more remarkably, *How to Win Friends and Influence People* kept its place on bookshelves long after its Depression-era context drew to a close. In 2016 alone, eighty years after the book first appeared, it sold a staggering three hundred thousand copies as it continued to show up on the reading lists of businessmen, salesmen, and all sorts of striving Americans (many of them men) who longed to become the kind of person Carnegie embodied.

Just what kind of person he represented varies widely depending on whom you ask. For acolytes of his books, he preached a William James–inflected philosophy of positivity, curiosity about others, and a spirit of community. For his detractors, he served as a stand-in for a calculating individualism, corporate interests, and the manipulation of others for personal gain. Regardless of where you fall, Carnegie's influence is undeniable, restoring faith in the self-made man and the American project at a time when both seemed on the verge of crumbling. The book reinforced old ideals about self-reliance while mixing in new ones about the role of appearance, self-promotion, and personality. On another level, the story he told was just as much about determination, failure, and grit as it was about charm. Much like those of Benjamin Franklin and a choice few self-made men, Carnegie's traumas and insecurities would come to shape Americans' understanding of success and social behavior for decades to come.

Many of the first millions of people who read Carnegie's book were either looking to get a job or trying simply not to be fired. The country was in survival mode in 1936, and this book represented a guide to that approach to American life, whether Carnegie intended it that way or not. Part of what sold those millions of books was not just a desire to succeed but a true fear of failure. Widespread business collapse and increasing poverty created a mire of desperation for millions of Americans. Carnegie's book was there to usher them back to a feeling of safety. *The Saturday Evening Post* declared in a 1937 profile of Carnegie, "The secret of the book's success seems fairly simple. Every man or woman who buys it is instantly handed, for the sum of

$1.96, the information that he, or she, is potentially as powerful, brilliant, rich and successful as anybody in the world, and perhaps a good deal more so than most. Like the beauty doctors and the professors of charm, Dale Carnegie sells people what most of them desperately need. He sells them hope."[37] The book imbued the American optimistic spirit with fresh energy, obscuring the bleak reality of Depression scarcity. It also made the same promise that self-help books and get-rich-quick books would assure Americans with over the following century: that every single reader was capable of success. All it took to reach their potential was a good attitude and a positive outlook. Self-help is a forward-looking genre: especially when the present feels unbearably bleak, it invokes a future in which things could get better.

Positivity was the foundation of Carnegie's philosophy just as it had long been a bedrock of the American ethos, one that endures even in contexts—such as the Great Depression—in which it seems a mismatch. Many people associate the power of positivity with a distinctly twentieth-century outlook, but it arguably goes back far earlier. It is so fundamental to our national culture that, as writer Barbara Ehrenreich explained, "Positivity is not so much our condition or our mood as it is part of our ideology—the way we explain the world and think we ought to function within it."[38] Carnegie's book both exemplified and came to define a kind of magical thinking that took root early in American culture. Much of what *How to Win Friends and Influence People* preaches is that one need not be exceptionally talented or smart in order to succeed in America—in fact, those features might even be detriments. Instead of changing actions or acquiring new skills, all you really need to do is cultivate a better attitude. In an almost religious way, Carnegie puts the emphasis on belief over everything else. Things may be going terribly, but you can still control how you think, and your capacity to effectively change your thinking is what will define your future success or failure. Almost like the New Age philosophy of later books such as *The Secret* and *You Can Heal Your Life*—and even the current trend toward mindfulness and manifestation—the emphasis was on a mental change that would in turn bring about tangible results. Much of the advice that Carnegie gives on positivity has become so entrenched in the cultural lexicon that it's understood as an "American" habit today: smiling, repeating people's names, cultivating a "genuine interest" in others. While Carnegie certainly is not solely responsible for millions of smiling Americans, his book was instrumental in instilling the idea that positivity—more than expertise—was the most important ingredient in a successful person.

His book is considered the grandfather of the self-help books that would explode in popularity in the twentieth century. But given its influence on everyone from Warren Buffett and Lee Iacocca to President Lyndon Johnson and Pope John Paul II,[39] it did more than that: it laid out some of the unlikely dualities that have come to define the American psyche, especially the idea that being liked is a requirement of true success, just as actual achievement is. Early promotional material for Carnegie's classes focused on popularity over anything directly related to business success. In a flyer entitled "17 Things This Training Will Help

You Do," the first three things have nothing to do with money. Instead, the class promises social capital, guaranteeing attendees that they will be able to:

1. Make friends quickly and easily.
2. Increase your popularity.
3. Win people to your way of thinking.[40]

So much of *How to Win Friends and Influence People*, as well as Carnegie's other books and his speeches, uses the language of love (How do I become popular, liked, loved?) as opposed to the language of success (How do I earn more? Go further? Get more acclaim?). This notion has lingered in our cultural DNA in ways that researchers have actually been able to quantify. Carnegie was correct in believing that in the United States, likability—more than knowledge or expertise—often matters more than anything else in determining our accomplishments. In one study, researchers found that when participants evaluated a speaker on a videoconference, they were more influenced by how much they liked him than by the content of what he said.[41] That measuring stick translates to the highest office in the land: likability has remained one of the most important determining factors in nearly every U.S. presidential election in recent history. Being likable could even save your life. Another study found that doctors spent more, potentially lifesaving time with patients they found likable.[42] Carnegie's book seems to have been the first to so explicitly recognize this near-universal truth about American success: being well-liked is more important than knowing what the hell you're doing.

The notion of likability and personality addressed this collision between the American mythology of the self-made man—who worked hard and reaped the rewards of his labor—and the daily reality of surviving in Depression-era America. The Great Depression served as an existential challenge both to American optimism and to the idea that hard work could be leveraged for a better life, showing the extent to which even the most powerful stood on a precarious foundation. A life of hard work was not always enough to stave off bankruptcy—and that magical mixture of striving and thrift that had defined generations of self-made American men was suddenly shown to be insufficient, vulnerable to forces outside their control. His book came up with new answers to the question: What does it take to make it in America? Thanks to Carnegie, a new kind of self-made man, one who valued his interpersonal skills—his way with people and his power of persuasion—emerged over a more old-fashioned archetype that had endured for a century and a half. Where the Protestant work ethic had once preached the importance of morality and discipline as a prerequisite to success, Carnegie added in a new layer: personality and public relations. As Carnegie wrote in a letter to his parents after they sold land for a profit: "Now you see how money is made. It is not by hard work."[43]

The irony in Carnegie's quip to his parents was that he did work hard throughout his life; there is a gap between the story he's telling the reader and the life he led. Like many of the authors throughout *Americanon*—whether a childless Catharine Beecher preaching republican motherhood or Emily Post, the rule-breaking divorcée writing about societal guidelines—Carnegie defined the rule while living the exception. In that way, he was not so different from Benjamin Franklin, another American who led an exceptional life that he credited to small, achievable changes. Carnegie wrote a book about personality and smiling, but the narrative of his own life was one of grit, perseverance, and a stubborn willingness to fail and fail again so that he might one day succeed. Carnegie was admirable in his willingness to fail spectacularly—whether as an actor in that cockroach-infested apartment or on that first night in front of a handful of students at the YMCA. His true secret to success, one that appears only subtly in the book, lies not in his relentless positivity but in his resilience. Those who cynically dismiss his ethos as mere manipulation miss its hearty core: that he, like so many others, was just trying to survive. The many stumbling blocks that Carnegie encountered along the way did not prevent him from becoming the man he was; those were the very things that made him the successful person he became. Carnegie was impressive in his ability to learn from his mistakes and to bounce back stronger. As he instructed readers within the first few pages of the book, the only thing they needed to succeed was "a deep, driving desire to learn" and "a vigorous determination."[44] His philosophy was not based on pure, unwavering positivity in the face of hardship; it was rooted in a different kind of fortitude: the book he wrote came out of his own survivorship.

⚜

For all the criticism *How to Win Friends and Influence People* has received over the years, there's at least some evidence that the people drawn to its philosophy are not master manipulators but are instead socially awkward.[45] Carnegie wrote often of his own crippling anxiety—he even wrote another book, entitled *How to Stop Worrying and Start Living*—about ten years later. Anxiety is a constant theme in his books and in his own life. Whether worrying about the precarity of his parents' farm or feeling self-conscious about his raggedy clothes while standing at the blackboard, anxiety shaped much of Carnegie's early life. An almost doglike affability was part of Carnegie's solution for the anxiety that plagued many of his readers, and he called dogs "the greatest winner of friends the world has ever known."[46] It's easy to see Carnegie's philosophy embodied in man's best friend, its tail wagging so that it might be fed instead of slapped away. According to one profile, Carnegie maintained some of that awkwardness throughout his life. A writer from *The Saturday Evening Post* had this to say about him after an interview in 1937: "Carnegie talks like that—in quotations, along with the qualifying phrases, mostly from his book, which he knows by heart. It gives his conversation a curiously stilted quality."[47] At the same time, both Carnegie's own story and the narrative of the book show the extent to which courage and fear, bravery and social awkwardness, do not have to be at odds. Much like Franklin and his fake-it-till-you-make-it philosophy, Carnegie's courage lay in his ability not to live without fear but to continue on anyway.

Perhaps that's why Carnegie gravitated toward the personable easiness that emanates from certain beloved celebrities. In *How to Win Friends and Influence People*, celebrity becomes the twentieth-century embodiment of individualism. Unlike Franklin's *Autobiography*, for instance, Carnegie draws not on his own rags-to-riches story but on the lessons gleaned by those ultimate success stories: celebrities. Carnegie urged readers to emulate the personal charm of famous people, integrating the spice of a celebrity profile with more traditional elements of self-help literature. In an era of talkies and tabloids, this was a winning strategy. What's more, by weaving examples of traveling salesmen and bank tellers alongside Mary Pickford and Clark Gable, he constructed the idea that people could be the celebrities in their own towns—and they might even become model success stories for others to emulate. Carnegie made the case that individuals with the right attitude could still be successful anywhere in America (especially if they read his book or took his classes). This line of thinking would become a major trope in the twentieth century as celebrity worship ballooned, with many actors and musicians even writing their own self-help books or penning autobiographies that recounted their personal rags-to-riches stories. His book foreshadowed the way that actors and sports stars are now held up not just as entertainers but as leaders.

Carnegie would soon experience his first taste of the power of celebrity. Around the time the book came out, he decided to go on a European cruise to celebrate the accomplishment. On his return, as the ship pulled into harbor, the dock was packed with people shouting. Shocked by the number of onlookers waiting onshore, he assumed he must be sharing the ship with some famous person. Carnegie lore has it that he turned to his companion and asked, "Who's on this boat?" It wasn't until he listened closer that he discerned the word they were chanting was "Car-ne-gie! Car-ne-gie!"[48]

Thanks to a wildly successful advertising campaign—and the rise of mass-market paperbacks—Carnegie's brand of optimism had reached an enormous audience. While Carnegie was well-known from his public speaking courses, he was hardly a household name, and his publishers initially had modest expectations for the book. There was a demand for self-help literature in the 1930s, but the market was already crowded by 1936. People might have had fewer resources than ever before, but an expanding number of competitively priced books promised that the only resource Americans needed was themselves—or a better version of themselves they could buy for a couple of dollars. Guidebooks and pamphlets, on everything from penny-pinching to cooking with less, grew popular around this era. Napoleon Hill's *Think and Grow Rich*, a remarkably similar book that drew on magical thinking and the power of positivity, came out just one year later, in 1937. It, too, would go on to sell tens of millions of copies. The publishing company designed a full-page advertisement for Carnegie's book—much like the one that launched *Etiquette*—to run in several newspapers in major cities across the country. This book will "mean more to you than ANY book that you have ever read,"[49] the advertisement assured readers. They priced the book at just $1.96 plus a few cents in postage for the mail-in orders, and the coupon included in the advertisement allowed readers to return it after five days if they didn't like it. Three weeks after its initial publication, the book had sold seventy thousand copies. Simon & Schuster expanded the ad to thirty-six newspapers and magazines across the country. Just a few years later, Robert de Graff, founder of the mass-market paperback giant Pocket Books, convinced Simon & Schuster that paperback books would not detract from hardcover sales. He started selling *How to Win Friends and Influence People* in all sorts of nonbook venues, such as drugstores and other shops. Hardcover sales remained unaffected, demonstrating that his paperbacks were reaching a new market. Both strategies proved crucial in stirring buzz among neighbors, coworkers, and families—and just two years after being published, the book had sold 1 million copies. When Carnegie's first royalty check landed on his secretary's desk, it clocked in at $90,000[50] (well over $1 million in today's currency).

The American people found reassurance in Carnegie's vision of the world as a winnable place. The sheer number of people buying his books and writing testimonials about how it changed their lives spoke to the ways the book served as a haven from the current chaos, telling them something they needed to hear. "I wouldn't sell it at any price. The contents are priceless," wrote one reader.[51] The popular success of the book stood in contrast to decidedly mixed reviews from the press. As *The New York Times* wrote in 1937, "There is a subtle cynicism, to be sure, in directions which depend so largely upon flattering the other man's egotism. But Mr. Carnegie disclaims flattery, and calls egotism by a sweeter name."[52] The criticism from newspapers and magazines did not deter the millions of people who would buy the book in stores, order it in the mail, or borrow it from their local library. Even in 2020, it remained on the list of the most frequently borrowed books from the New York Public Library of all time, being borrowed at least 284,524 times since its first publication—making it more frequently borrowed than *Harry Potter and the Sorcerer's Stone*.[53] The book so quickly entered into popular culture that just one year later, a satire book based on it—*How to Lose Friends and Alienate People*—came out. The number of people enrolling in Carnegie's courses also reflected just how deeply his message was resonating. By the 1940s, Carnegie was enrolling fifteen thousand people per year in his courses. Just ten years later, seventy thousand people reportedly paid $150 for fourteen-week courses given by Dale Carnegie & Associates.[54]

Part of the magic of the classes—and of Carnegie's philosophy—was the very same driving force behind effective group therapy. Carnegie discovered the power in group catharsis and recognized that the best way to learn was through the cumulative experience of a community. It is not a coincidence that Alcoholics Anonymous launched just a year before Carnegie's book and would publish its guide, *The Big Book*, by 1939 (this book, too, would sell tens of millions of copies). Both philosophies, borne of their Depression-era context, drew on the power of community and the necessity of learning from one another's successes and failures. For all Carnegie's triumph in reestablishing the power of the individual, the group therapy principles in his classes were a key factor in his success. The book is remembered for restoring faith in individualism, or even for creating a new, toxic brand of "me versus the world," but his philosophy was grounded in the power of the group. He wrote of his public speaking courses: "They come to our classes for one purpose only; to solve their problems and do it quickly. They want to overcome an inferiority complex, timidity, shyness and fear. They want to develop courage and self-confidence, and I know of no other way outside of developing a deep religious faith, that will so quickly help men to develop an abounding courage and self-confidence as will sensible, practical training and practice in speaking effectively before a group of adult men and women."[55]

Part of what appealed to people about his classes and later his book was this element of shared purpose. There's both comfort and catharsis in releasing mutual pain and feeling less alone in any problem. Bonds between people in a group were essential to Carnegie's philosophy because much of what *How to Win Friends and Influence People* accomplishes is teaching people how to be better communicators. Many of Carnegie's principles in the book revolved around interpersonal skills, learning how to better express yourself—and how to better listen. "The essence of his philosophy was around relationships, and the essence of that was really about understanding the person," Joe Hart, the current CEO of Dale Carnegie & Associates, told me. "His intention in this was to give people a new way of life: a life of courage, of relationships, and of confidence,"[56] Hart said.

Carnegie's beliefs concerning the individual and the group can be summed up in one word: "charisma." Charisma embodies the kind of soft power that he personified, whose authority comes from the ability not to instill fear in others but to make them feel valued. Much like Carnegie's philosophy, charisma has little to do with expertise. And yet overwhelming research has shown its powerful effects. One study, led by a psychologist and a business administration expert, even theorized that at the heart of charisma is the ability to convince others that you are the best person for uniting the interests of a large group.[57] There is even an element of magic to people's beliefs about charisma: another study found that people preferred a hug from a charismatic person rather than someone who had been described as competent, as if some of their power could rub off on them.[58] "Charisma" has become a shorthand for a whole host of qualities—the ability to inspire, a strength in public speaking, even likability—but the word has been used in a secular context for fewer than one hundred years. Up until around 1922,[59] "charisma" was used strictly in a religious sense, for someone with special power from the Holy Spirit to be used for the good of the church. A word that used to mean a gift from God has transformed to mean a gift from the individual, a "personal magic."[60]

Charismatic people have come to stand in for religious leaders in American culture, just as the books across *Americanon* function as secular bibles. As people moved away from their hometown churches, many people longed for the element of community that religious worship carried with it. A movie star, a president, a boss—or a particularly charismatic teacher at the YMCA—became a substitute for the preachers that had always been central to American cultural life, doling out advice and inspiration. These leaders provided some human element that was missing from the new, corporate way of life. Even more than any concrete wisdom, charismatic leaders seem to have the same kind of magnetism as an effective preacher, a way of reassuring us that everything will be all right. This is what draws us to celebrities, or to especially charismatic presidential candidates: it's less about an eagerness to follow and more about a deep-seated need for leadership, a desire to put our faith somewhere outside of ourselves. That need becomes even greater at times of change or upheaval, when we may have lost that belief in ourselves and require an outside example to regain it.

Carnegie's earliest lessons in both charisma and public

speaking—the basis of a philosophy that would teach millions of Americans how to succeed—came not from business school but from the religious revival tents of his childhood. His mother, Amanda Harbison Carnagey, frequently attended revival meetings, rocking back and forth as traveling preachers shouted the word of God. She was a talented speaker herself, and her church group even raised money for her to travel the revival circuit to preach.[61] There's something infectious, egalitarian, and seemingly organic about revival meetings: people being moved by a force outside themselves to talk, not studying oratory in an expensive university. Dale would later write, "I have taken courses in Columbia University and New York University and various other institutions of learning. I can honestly say that in none of these institutions did I find even one professor who had as much contagious enthusiasm as did my mother."[62] Enthusiasm is what revival culture is built on, just as it would become the cornerstone of Carnegie's own philosophy. Amanda Carnagey was perhaps the single most influential figure in Dale's early life. She formed his moral character and instilled in him a love of performance from a young age. When he moved out of his home and went on the road as a traveling salesman, the person to whom he wrote letter after letter was not his brother or a childhood sweetheart but his mother. God was Amanda Carnagey's whole life, and when she wasn't at revival meetings, she read the Bible or religious treatises against dancing, such as *From the Ball-Room to Hell*.[63] On Sundays, the family hitched up the wagon; even in winter they drove over frozen roads to Maryville and the Methodist church where she taught Sunday school. In her classroom, she kept a plaque on the wall that read: "Good, better, best. Never let it rest. Till your good is better. And your better, best."[64] Even if Dale did not share the dogmatic religious beliefs of his mother, an unwavering faith finds its way into *How to Win Friends and Influence People*. Carnegie promised his readers a kind of secular faith in the self.

Moral renewal and an almost religious devotion to self-improvement were two ideas Carnegie found in another source beyond the Bible: *The Autobiography of Benjamin Franklin*. Franklin's book was so seminal for Carnegie that he would later require all his employees to read it before their first day of work.[65] At the Carnegie archive in Long Island, Dale Carnegie & Associates have preserved his well-worn copy of *The Autobiography*. For how different their lives and legacies turned out to be, the similarities between the two men are striking. They both grew up poor and were mostly self-taught. They were both known as magnetic charmers (and popular with women). And they both wrote bestselling books that served as guideposts for so many striving Americans. Like Franklin's *Autobiography*, *How to Win Friends and Influence People* both reinforced and at times reinvented cultural norms around the self-made man. Both existed within a broader feedback loop: the books were popular because they took some train of thought—in this case, American meritocracy—that people already believed in, and they codified it, blowing it up to bigger proportions. Then the specifics of these authors' visions entered into popular culture and people's beliefs about themselves. In that way, Carnegie built his platform on the bricks that Franklin had laid. And then Carnegie's ideas became the bricks for later generations of bestselling authors and self-made men.

Carnegie encouraged readers to constantly refer back to the chapters, to check their progress much as Franklin urged with his thirteen virtues section. Their insistence that the books be read over and over again, referred to in an almost biblical sense, pushed both books beyond the ranks of bestseller and into the echelon of entrenched popular culture. Carnegie may be remembered for showmanship, whereas Franklin was remembered for substance, but Franklin, too, was a master of public relations, a world-class performer whose success came from his versatility. Their books also shared a fundamental tenet that ostensibly grew falser over time: the idea that anyone can succeed with the right attitude. Carnegie's context of corporate America in the late 1930s and early 1940s was more of a zero-sum game than Franklin's eighteenth-century Philadelphia was. As Dr. Trysh Travis, a cultural historian studying self-help, described the Depression-era United States: "Each job I get is a job you don't get."[66]

This is the dark side of the self-made-man mythos, especially in *How to Win Friends and Influence People*: it may be a great motivator for generations of strivers, creators, and ingenues looking to make it in America, but it can also work against our collective best interest. Dr. Travis told me: "There's nothing in American culture to have created the expectation that there is something larger than the self. On the one hand, that's what makes America great: we are this nation of free individuals. And it is also what makes the U.S. a frightening, cold, often mean-spirited place, because we have no hope for help or assistance from anyone outside our own person or perhaps our immediate circle of friends. One result of our singularity is that we are always thinking: 'There has to be a personal solution, and if I can't find it, then that's my own fault.'"[67]

The power of outside influences—generational poverty, institutional racism, or even just bad luck—is suppressed by the Carnegie vision of America. Because if we're in control of our destinies, then those who fail must merit their failure. Carnegie's book was there at once to reassure people that the right attitude could be leveraged for a better life, all while subtly hinting that struggling people might merit their problems through their own poor attitude. "Happiness doesn't depend on outward conditions. It depends on inner conditions," he wrote.[68] Even—or perhaps especially—at moments when the American dream is challenged, people cling to it even more desperately. Where the challenges of the Great Depression could very well have led to an overthrow of the American status quo, many people became only more resolute in their belief that the system was not at fault—they were.

Carnegie's ideas first took root in this Depression context, but they would flourish after World War II as people increasingly worked in bigger corporate structures. Rising through the ranks in a large corporation requires that same kind of faith in the system that defined the American response to the Great Depression. Many Americans were increasingly flung into a sea of skyscrapers and thousand-person corporations. In a workplace where you no longer know all your colleagues and bosses personally, a degree of faith is required: faith that hard work will be rewarded, that a promotion is within reach, or that a company might provide financial security. The early twentieth century had seen a migration from country to city and the accompanying shift from small entrepreneurs to corporations. The mid–twentieth century then saw its own kind of exodus: from the city to the suburbs. The book ended up preparing businessmen for all these social practices in corporate America: conferences, dinner parties with the local manager, and cocktail parties with colleagues. Carnegie's book in that way can be seen almost as a companion to Emily Post's book on etiquette, guiding a generation of Americans from farm to middle management.

Over the years, the book has maintained steadily high sales, even after Carnegie's death. Much like Robb Sagendorph did for *The Old Farmer's Almanac*, or the Merriam brothers did for *Webster's Dictionary*, part of the lasting history of Carnegie's book needs to be credited to those who worked for decades to preserve his legacy. In this case it was his wife, Dorothy Carnegie, who took over the business after Dale died in 1955 at just sixty-six years old. She commissioned frequent rewrites of the book in order to ensure that it would never become obsolete. Ironically, Dorothy had written a book discouraging women from working so that they might better support the careers of their husbands (her book came out around the same time she took over her husband's business during his illness). And yet Dorothy "had all the business acumen [Dale] lacked,"[69] according to J. Oliver Crom, her son-in-law and later president of Dale Carnegie & Associates. By the 1970s and 1980s, books preaching an opposite message to Carnegie's grew in popularity. Aggression and the ability to take charge were what was needed in business, not a cheerful affability, these books argued. Robert

Ringer's books such as *Winning Through Intimidation* and *Looking Out for #1* became bestsellers. They never became classics, however, failing to reach the same fever-pitch popularity as *How to Win Friends and Influence People*. Meanwhile, the classes at Dale Carnegie & Associates only expanded, and by 1986, 2.5 million people had graduated from a Carnegie training. Some four hundred out of five hundred Fortune 500 companies had taken classes from Carnegie & Associates (including IBM and three of the biggest automotive companies). Today, the company has 224 offices across eighty countries. *How to Win Friends and Influence People* would outlive its Depression context, fitting into a much longer tradition of capitalism, individuality, and self-help that both preceded and survived long after Carnegie.

It should be at least a little surprising how popular the book has remained, given just how much the landscape of working life has shifted in the eighty-five years since *How to Win Friends and Influence People* was first published. Demographic changes—such as an increasing number of women and especially women of color joining the workforce[70]—have created a fundamental shift in the average American worker. The way people work is changing, too: increasingly fewer Americans are employed within a corporate structure, for instance. About 36 percent of U.S. workers received at least a portion of their income from freelance sources in 2017, and that number is expected to jump to as much as 50 percent of the population by 2027.[71] It's hard to imagine how Carnegie's guide to corporate life might apply to teachers, writers, and independent entrepreneurs. Many of Carnegie's suggestions, too, seem especially unhelpful to people who might be marginalized at work. Directives to smile, agree, and not talk too much are now the opposite of the advice given to people of color and workingwomen everywhere. Trysh Travis suggested that part of what the book did then—and perhaps still does now—is to teach men the kind of soft skills that women are already socialized to have, such as listening and not criticizing.[72]

Nearly a century later, Carnegie lingers in the new, self-promotional lifestyle that dominates social media, technology, and the way we live now. At a time when "influencer" is now a career path, it seems Carnegie's nearly one-hundred-year-old philosophy is never far from the zeitgeist. I'm not sure how many social media influencers have read Carnegie's hit book, but their very existence seems a testament to the ways in which influencing people remains a highly coveted skill—and a lucrative one. During my visit to the headquarters on Long Island, leadership from Dale Carnegie & Associates described him as an adept self-promoter, someone who would have loved Instagram. His philosophy seems prescient for our world in other ways he could never have predicted. In 2020, the United States saw the highest levels of unemployment since the 1930s. A similar level of uncertainty, fear, and desperation marked daily life. The coronavirus pandemic that brought economic disaster along with disease suddenly made the Great Depression feel eerily relevant once more. We may not respond to this economic crisis with Carnegie's brand of positivity, but it's clear that once again the American self-made-man mythology is proving itself to be insufficient.

Much like Benjamin Franklin, Dale Carnegie thought he was telling one story—about Americans, work, and what it takes to survive—but the book he wrote was actually doing something else. It was a story of fake-it-till-you-make-it, maybe even one of manipulation, but it was also a narrative of resilience. His book remains the perfect parable for twentieth-century America: a tale not of moral perfection but of failure, recovery—and a healthy dose of public relations. Carnegie's hit book reveals the extent to which our beliefs about American-made success are not a slow development of right or wrong ideas over time; they are forged in this crucible of personal and national trauma, fashioned into a survival guide. In responding to the trauma of his era and his own life experiences, he set into motion new success archetypes destined to be picked up and refashioned by others. As with Franklin's legacy, we see in Carnegie what we see in our country: whether we view him as manipulative or openhearted—an optimist or a cynic—might say less about Carnegie and more about how we understand the current state of the American dream.

CHAPTER EIGHT

Betty Crocker's
Picture Cook Book (1950)

In the turmoil of World War II, alongside Rosie the Riveter, women were given another feminine ideal to look up to: Betty Crocker. As men jumped off boats in Normandy or parachuted into Italy, women in apartments in New York City, on ranches in Lansing, and in duplexes in Detroit tuned in to one radio show: *Our Nation's Rations.* When women struggled to cope with war rations, rising food prices, and shortages of basic supplies, their trusted friend and neighbor offered advice on everything from recipes to blood drives. With the home-front war effort in full swing, she reminded her listeners that the job they were doing was not mere drudgery; it was vital to victory. She spoke directly to the women of America, telling them, "You have saved and saved—and gone without. Upon you have fallen the brunt of these routine, daily, humdrum activities. They don't bring medals or parades with cheering crowds—but there is no greater patriotism—there is no truer greatness—than giving of yourself constantly, day after day, in these simple inglorious tasks."[1] The stakes were high, and just as men had a role to play, so, too, did the women at home. If women carried out their jobs properly, Betty told them, they could raise and love the type of men who were fighting for freedom overseas. She elevated homemaking to something that did more than ensure the stability of one's family: it safeguarded the fate of a nation.

Already by 1940, nine out of ten housewives knew Betty Crocker's name,[2] and millions had purchased her recipe pamphlets. During the war years, Betty received more letters than the average Hollywood starlet. In 1945, Betty Crocker was named the second most influential woman in America by *Fortune* magazine[3]—just behind Eleanor Roosevelt. By the time Crocker's comprehensive cookbook was published in 1950, she had been a national sensation for nearly three decades. She would guide women through the Great Depression and the Second World War, alongside all the more mundane challenges of daily life in supporting their families at home. When that cookbook finally came out, it would fly off shelves in a way that surpassed nearly every nonfiction book that had come before it. People around the country would clamor for *Betty Crocker's Picture Cook Book*. Seven decades after its first publication, the book has now sold 75 million copies, making it the bestselling U.S. cookbook of all time.

How did Betty Crocker manage to do it all? She was an invention—maintained by a staff of about forty home economists. The ideal woman, as it turned out, was a fiction created by a flour company. And yet, she exerted a very real influence over the vision of American womanhood in the mid–twentieth century. Much like Catharine Beecher's domestic guides had done almost one hundred years earlier, *Betty Crocker's Picture Cook Book* elevated women's work in the home, setting up the women of America as gatekeepers of virtue. Like Beecher's too, this book also served as a vehicle for conformity, upholding a uniform vision of American women through decades of change. *Betty Crocker's Picture Cook Book* offered a veritable everything-you-need-to-know approach to cooking, just as it served as an everything-you-need-to-know approach to American women's duties. Betty's message was a complex mix of consumerism and empowerment: part of why she was so popular was that she provided a real service to millions of women who were hungry for recognition of their work's value.

Betty Crocker offered a ready-made mold for women of the day to step into, giving them the recipes for dinner and for a successful home life—all they had to do was heed her directions without deviation. Not only did the book's sales nearly close in on those of the Bible, but many people across the country treated it in the same kind of authoritative way. Mothers passed it down to their daughters, and some daughters started using it as soon as they could read. With the 449-page book (and its 2,161 recipes), cooking and cleaning became "homemaking," which in turn became an "art," according to the book's very first page.[4] The book reestablished the connection between goodness and good homemaking in a way that has lingered in our American DNA even as the cult of domesticity has faded over time. More than just offering recipes, Betty and her book reconstructed and cemented core national values, from optimism, self-reliance, and thrift—to the enduringly central role of the American mother.

❀

Betty Crocker was "born" in the 1920s to the Washburn-Crosby Company, which would soon become General Mills through a merger with several other milling companies. In an advertisement for their signature product, Gold Medal flour, Washburn-Crosby included a puzzle that readers could solve and send in for a prize. Much to the surprise of the all-male advertising team, thousands of women included all sorts of questions alongside their completed puzzles,[5] asking why their dough was lumpy or how to make their cakes rise. The male employees were loath to sign their names to any letters in response, and so they invented a new name—Crocker for William G. Crocker, a recently retired executive, and Betty because they thought it sounded wholesome.[6] After an informal contest among the women of the office to sign the letters, secretary Florence Lindberg's signature was chosen. With that, a handful of businessmen selling flour invented a fictional homemaker—and the perfect woman for the first half of the twentieth century was born.

Betty Crocker emerged at around the same time as the heyday of radio, and it quickly skyrocketed her to fame. By 1924, Betty had her first radio program, broadcast locally in Minneapolis, where Washburn-Crosby and then General Mills were located. Blanche Ingersoll of the Home Service Department became the first Betty Crocker radio voice,[7] and that same year saw the first *Betty Crocker Cooking School of the Air*, in which women could follow along and complete recipes and activities to "graduate" from the radio cooking program. In Minneapolis alone, two thousand women tuned in to the show and 239 completed the cooking school.[8] The program quickly expanded to Buffalo, New York, and then a dozen stations across the country,[9] all with different local Betty Crockers (as radio did not yet have the capacity to broadcast one voice nationally). By the 1930s, the newly incorporated General Mills had distributed the first Betty Crocker recipe pamphlets through grocery stores: a record-breaking 4 million copies were demanded.[10] As General Mills widened its product line, Betty was there to incorporate new must-have items into her repertoire of recipes. She might have begun by helping sell Gold Medal flour, but soon she was plugging Bisquick, Softasilk flour, and later, boxed cake mixes. After General Mills' 1933 invention of Bisquick, her pamphlet of Bisquick recipes sold a staggering 731,000 copies at 25 cents each.[11] By distributing through grocery stores and tapping into the power of mail-in orders, General Mills was able to reach people who might never have purchased her literature through traditional outlets. Much like the unorthodox campaign to put Dale Carnegie's *How to Win Friends and Influence People* in drugstores and other nontraditional sales points, Betty Crocker's recipes first became successful being sold anywhere but a bookstore (her recipes were even included in sacks of Gold Medal flour themselves).

From the start, part of what made Betty Crocker and her products so successful was that she effectively raised the stakes of homemaking to life-or-death levels. A good meal was no longer a simple pleasure to be enjoyed; it was the difference between a happy husband and a violent one; good, Christian children or sickly, immoral ones; a powerful nation and a weak one. In her very first radio broadcast in 1924, she warned listeners, "If you load a man's stomach with soggy boiled cabbage, greasy fried potatoes, or leaden biscuit, can you wonder that he wants to start a fight, or go out and commit a crime? We should be grateful that he does nothing worse than display a lot of temper."[12] This sentiment—which she repeated constantly throughout more than three decades of broadcasting—claimed that women were responsible for the fate of their families, perhaps even more than men were. It was a great power but also a hefty responsibility. Much like Catharine Beecher's in the nineteenth century, a fundamental facet of Betty Crocker's message was that a good home was what made for a good country. The vision she presented of the ideal American woman was someone who cheerfully and dutifully cultivated her home for the greater good, crafting a better nation from the warmth of her own kitchen.

Arguably no one understood Betty Crocker's pivotal role in women's lives as much as Marjorie Child Husted did. Husted was the guiding hand over Betty Crocker for more than twenty years, joining Washburn-Crosby in 1924 and going on to serve as the director of home service for Washburn-Crosby and then for General Mills from 1924 to 1946,[13] taking the lead in shaping Betty's role in women's lives and even voicing Crocker for many years when the program went national. Like the many women over the decades who would popularize Betty Crocker and her products, Husted's own life diverged from Betty's message in myriad ways. Throughout her nearly one-hundred-year life, Husted would have likely never listed "homemaker" on her

tax return. She would reach a rung on the corporate ladder reserved for a rarefied minority of men—much less women. Born
in Minneapolis in 1892, she graduated from the University of
Minnesota in 1913—seven years before women had the right to
vote and nearly sixty years before women would be accepted into
universities en masse. Early in her career in the 1920s, Husted
lobbied for the need to maintain personal correspondence with
consumers, leading the charge to respond to every letter Betty
received.[14] She's the one who designed the radio programs, who
spearheaded the Depression-era and World War II–era initia-
tives, and who would lead the team for *Betty Crocker's Picture
Cook Book*. From the start, her mission became to elevate the role
of women's work. "Here were millions of them staying at home
alone, doing a job with children, cooking, cleaning on minimal
budgets—the whole depressing mess of it. They needed someone to remind them that they had value,"[15] she once said.

Thanks in part to Husted, Betty Crocker pamphlets and
radio programs soon had a direct line from General Mills in
Minnesota to ranches, islands, and rural regions across America. Many of the thousands of daily letters that poured in to
Betty Crocker arrived from women living in some of the most
far-flung places in the United States. Within little more than a
decade after the invention of Betty Crocker, women working on
ranches in the West or living on Chappaquiddick off the coast
of Massachusetts (an island that has fewer than two hundred
residents today) wrote in to Betty to join her cooking school.[16]
These women often thanked Betty and told her how the radio
programs and recipes made them feel as if they had neighbors
living close by. From the earliest years, Betty Crocker filled a

real need beyond cooking tips: she felt like a friend. A home-maker living on an isolated Pennsylvania farm in the 1940s went as far as to write that each sack of Gold Medal flour brought "a world of friendship, that hands out to all members of the family—drama, entertainment, prayerful communion with our Divine Lord daily."[17] As this woman and her friends listened to the Betty Crocker radio programs on their farms, they had the feeling that "we need never feel alone, no matter what we are doing."[18] Betty Crocker took an active role in women's lives, far beyond the scope of the radio show itself: in many of the letters, women describe trying to follow her advice to a tee in all areas of their lives. When Betty did an episode on "what men want in the women they marry," many listeners wrote in to say they were trying to emulate her wisdom in the way they conducted them-selves not just as home cooks but as women, being more patient with their husbands and "smiling always."[19] By the mid-1930s, Betty Crocker was receiving thousands of similarly ardent let-ters every single day. General Mills soon had multiple staff members responding to the Betty Crocker letters.

The first major test for Betty Crocker and her mission for American women came fewer than ten years after that Washburn-Crosby secretary signed the first Betty Crocker letter. With the arrival of the Great Depression in the 1930s, families across America faced increasing strain as unemployment soared, and salary cuts for the remaining employees were prevalent. Espe-cially for families with children, a hefty portion of their reduced income went toward grocery bills. Women, who had long been responsible for shopping, cooking, and planning meals, found those tasks to be increasingly fraught. Betty was there to help, with radio broadcasts, free pamphlets, a friendly letter, or tips for cooking on a budget. The fleet of women writing as Betty Crocker responded to the flood of letters about money troubles and unemployment with a firm but caring maternal voice. Betty spoke to her fans like a kindly neighbor, someone looking out for them when they felt that no one else cared. "Won't you let me know how you get along? I'll be so anxious to hear. . . . I'm always here and happy to help you in any way I can,"[20] she wrote in one letter to a listener. It's no wonder that people thought she was real. Much as Dale Carnegie provided hope for the millions of unemployed men in the wake of the 1929 crash, Betty Crocker served to reassure women with a similar spirit of American optimism. Americans could still get by with some belt-tightening, hope, and a handful of practical tips, and Betty was there to make all three a little easier. She updated American values that had often been associated with men—self-reliance, thrift, and hard work—and applied them to women's work in the home. The Great Depression solidified Betty Crocker as someone who was doing much more than selling products: she was both a practical and an emotional support for women, even in lean times.

For Betty Crocker—and the women she spoke to—the Depression was barely drawing to a close by the time the Second World War broke out in Europe. It would be World War II that would skyrocket Betty to the peak of her popularity as she took on war work alongside the rest of the country. This moment of wartime uncertainty solidified Betty Crocker's voice and message to millions of women. And in convincing women of the value of their work, General Mills set in motion lasting ideas about the connection between virtue, women's work in the home, and national prosperity. General Mills would distribute millions of pamphlets on rationing and home-front war work, while Betty's broadcasts reached an increasing number of listeners. Letter after letter after letter rolled into General Mills, and soon Betty's mail jumped from four thousand to five thousand letters per day.[21] Companies like General Mills became instrumental in giving women the motivation and the know-how to participate enthusiastically in home-front war efforts. As quickly as February 1942—just two months after the United States entered World War II—General Mills distributed its first war pamphlets to millions of households. In a way that is strikingly reminiscent of Beecher's work, the pamphlets—and Betty Crocker's message at large—made the case that it was women's work that would determine the nation's future. As General Mills president Donald D. Davis wrote in the introduction to that first pamphlet, entitled *War Work: A Daybook for the Home*: "You will contribute to victory if you have the same goal in your home as people in the armed forces, in factories and on farms; to *win the war*. You homemakers, however, have an additional job. We look to you to preserve, in spite of the war's challenge, those spiritual ideas that have always characterized the American home."[22] Women's role was not simply a practical one: they were being tasked with maintaining some kind of American story. Their work in the home was taking on an explicitly spiritual, even mythological quality—much like republican motherhood did in the nineteenth century.

The insistence on maintaining the "American spirit" during the war was a way of staving off fear. Even with all their optimism, there was a somber quality to both the 1942 and 1943 editions of *War Work*, a recognition that behind the smiling women tilling victory gardens lurked a real threat of annihilation. The 1942 *War Work* pamphlet even offered some tips on how to survive a bombardment.[23] Advice included lying down to lessen the effect of a bomb or using a "fine spray"[24] of water to put out an incendiary bomb. By 1943, as many of the service flags in the windows turned from blue stars (for an active serviceman) to gold (for killed in the line of duty), the human cost of the war became a daily reality for an increasing number of Americans. A section from the 1943 edition of *War Work* urged women to "watch your words!"[25] The pamphlet told women not to ask where their neighbor's son was stationed[26] or what their best friend was making down at the ammunition factory. And they must not share any negative feelings about the United States' allies in the war. This was the way to be a "good citizen" who did not "aid the enemy."[27] The pamphlets continued to emphasize a particular brand of American optimism, a belief that with communal hard work and a good attitude, things could be made to come out right. If that optimism could not be maintained, however, silence was second best.

This message of positivity, patriotism, and a bit of grit resonated with women across the war effort: many of the millions of women working in defense plants wrote letters to Betty Crocker, just as young fiancées waiting for their servicemen at home did. If there is any through line across the hundreds of thousands of letters that Betty received during wartime, it was a sense of vulnerability. The women confided in Betty, sharing their anxieties and even their secret fears that they did not dare tell their friends. One woman in 1944 wrote in to tell Betty how disappointed she was that she could not listen to the radio program anymore, but "I got myself a job in a defense plant to help end this thing."[28] A woman in San Diego working in a defense job thanked Crocker for a low-sugar ginger cookie recipe that allowed her to bring a treat in her lunch pail at the plant. "I haven't seen my husband for two years and six months but he is still safe + well and someday, soon I hope, he'll be coming home and reaching for the cookie jar and I'm doing my best to keep it full,"[29] that same woman wrote. Another homemaker told Betty how she still managed to use Gold Medal flour and Betty Crocker recipes to send cookies to her husband overseas in the army air forces, all while taking care of a pair of twin boys who had yet to meet their father.[30] Betty also served as a comfort to the many women who were new war wives—or about to become them. An Oregon woman wrote in 1944 to ask for a recipe, saying, "I'm just another girl married to a Navy man and I want to make a happy home for him when he returns. He's a great big lug—six feet tall and weighs two hundred pounds, and what he loves to do most is *eat*."[31] An eighteen-year-old in Illinois wrote in at the same time to tell Betty of her fiancé in the navy. As he was off fighting, she spent an increasing amount of time with her soon-to-be mother-in-law. "Miss Crocker, if my fiancé is used to eating his mother's cooking I'll really have to get started and learn how to cook and bake as well as she does,"[32] she said. Women shared their lives with Betty Crocker: their work, their husbands, their families, their worries, and their hopes. The letters they wrote are full of warmth and life, a rich tapestry of the U.S. home front that included both terrible loss and the simple pleasures of a favorite cookie. And the fleet of General Mills staff, all writing as Betty, was there to respond to each letter. They encouraged the women in war plants, assuaged the insecurities of the young navy wives, and reassured them all that the work they were doing was bringing the United States one day closer to victory.

Part of the success of General Mills and of Betty Crocker at this time was that both took women seriously. Betty may have sometimes told women what to do, and she was certainly selling a product, but she did not pander to her audience. One pamphlet encouraged women to read newspapers and magazines about the war so that they could remain informed and forge their own opinions. Maybe they could even brainstorm legislation for peacetime, the pamphlet suggested.[33] The literature, radio programs, and letters from Betty were not just patriotic propaganda; they recognized the real sacrifice of an effective home-front effort and offered concrete tips for making that sacrifice easier. Women needed to buy in advance and at times when the store was less crowded, store uncooked food properly to avoid waste, grow crops, preserve extra vegetables and fruits through canning, and of course check every outlet, gas, water pipe, and electric device to make sure they were not wasting anything.[34] General Mills recommended that women save cauliflower leaves for a soup, scrub vegetables instead of wasting precious food by peeling, collect dandelions and other wild greens, or use carrot and radish tops for garnish.[35] This work was incredibly time-consuming, especially on top of defense work or raising children. The victory gardens alone were an enormous undertaking: an estimated 40 percent of the nation's fresh vegetables during the war were grown in some 20 million gardens nationwide. The recipes General Mills provided of course incorporated General Mills products, such as Bisquick (which contained its own sugar, allowing women to avoid using their precious sugar rations). There was "Plentiful Pot Pie" made with Bisquick, and "Emergency Steak," comprised of ground beef, milk, one cup of Wheaties, pepper, and onion and patted into the shape of a T-bone steak.[36] It would be easy to cynically dismiss General Mills' participation in the war effort as a way to directly market their products to women, and the war certainly increased women's reliance on Betty Crocker, General Mills, and their products. At the same time, the pamphlets, radio programs, and personal letters offered women a real service: not just in reassuring them that their work was important but in helping ease the difficulties of that work.

Looking for new ways to keep up wartime morale, Marjorie Child Husted, now director of a forty-person department, added a new element to Betty Crocker's repertoire in 1944: "the Home Legion."[37] The war had forced Husted to stop development on what would become *Betty Crocker's Picture Cook Book*, but she found a new way to further build the Betty Crocker brand into women's lives. The Home Legion was designed to valorize and professionalize homemaking, encouraging women to dedicate their lives to "Good Homemaking for a Better World."[38] The program was symbolic: women could sign up for free through the mail and in turn receive the "Homemakers Creed," meant to hang on refrigerators across America. An excerpt from the Homemakers Creed reads:

> I believe a homemaker must be true to the highest ideals of love, loyalty, service and religion.
>
> I believe a home must be an influence for good in the neighborhood, the community, the country.[39]

Despite the heavy burden of shouldering the community through "love, loyalty, service, and religion," the very idea that women could change the world from their kitchens resonated on a large scale. Within just one year, seventy thousand women had signed on[40] to Betty Crocker's Home Legion.

After four years of saving, recycling, planting victory gardens, and working in munitions factories, the end of the summer of 1945 brought the end of the war. As many as 75 million people—more than four hundred thousand of them Americans—were dead. Following the war, Betty Crocker's role in the war effort would become so well recognized that even J. Edgar Hoover wrote a letter thanking her for her service. In it, the director of the FBI showed no sign of knowing that Betty Crocker was not a real person, and he seemed just as convinced as the women of America. "It is my earnest hope that our activities will continue to merit your confidence and I trust you will feel free to call upon us whenever we might be of further service,"[41] Hoover wrote in 1945. Millions of surviving troops were finally coming home to the United States, and in turn several million women would be forced to leave their wartime jobs and return home, too. The end of the war also brought a new beginning for General Mills. The company had been developing what would become *Betty Crocker's Picture Cook Book* in 1941 before the United States entered the battle fray, and now they could resume work on it.

৹৹

As General Mills finished developing the recipes for *Betty Crocker's Picture Cook Book*, the postwar economy was back to a boom. Just as Betty had been there to guide some 6 million women[42] into the workforce during wartime, she was there to usher them right back into the home after the war was over. World War II had brought fresh appreciation for women's work in the home, but it had also taught women that they were capable of work that had been traditionally reserved for men. For the millions of women who had taken work outside the home, leaving their jobs could be a fraught transition. In a January 1946 broadcast, Betty did a segment on the radio about a woman in Ohio who had clerked in a grocery store while her husband was at war. When the soldier returned home, the woman quit her job but struggled to readjust to full-time homemaking. The fights between this woman and her husband were constant, until she got help from a good neighbor, who was of course a listener of Betty Crocker's show. In Betty's view, women needed to adjust their attitude, not their situation. Instead of suggesting part-time work or some other kind of compromise, she told listeners:

We know that millions of men returning from service
have a new appreciation of home and a new image of happiness. To them happiness means the simple, fundamental homey things that they hold so much dearer after
months or years away. And can the girls they marry understand this yearning? Many of them are pretty young
and they haven't had these same maturing experiences. . . .
If we can only help realize that their future success and
happiness depends on the way they meet the challenge of
homemaking! If they will think of it as a noble and challenging career—as an art requiring many different skills,
and a great privilege—I am sure they will also strive to
make life pleasanter for their dear ones.[43]

A good home had once been the tool for fighting the war, and
now it was the reward for victory. Much like Catharine Beecher's,
Betty's goal in making homemaking a "career" was a way of convincing women that keeping a home was something still worth
doing. In this aim, Betty could be restrictive and even scolding,
with lines like these heaping culpability on women who longed for
something more, or just something different than homemaking.
Betty's steady hand was there to guide women back into the home,
to convince them of the "privilege" and "art" of homemaking. It
would take several years of development and recipe testing (after
ten years of planning), led by Marjorie Child Husted, before the
full-length book was ready for press, but in the meantime, Betty
never abandoned her central role in so many women's lives.

When *Betty Crocker's Picture Cook Book* appeared in 1950, it
was an instant sensation. *The New York Times* estimated that the

book was selling eighteen thousand copies per week following its release (for reference, Ernest Hemingway—who was topping the fiction bestseller list in late 1950—was selling approximately 3,500 copies per week of his latest novel).[44] It remains the best-selling cookbook in American history, ranking well above *The Fannie Farmer Cookbook*, *Joy of Cooking*, and Julia Child's *Mastering the Art of French Cooking*, among many other bestsellers. With 75 million copies sold since its first publication, *Betty Crocker's Picture Cook Book* is also one of the bestselling nonfiction books across any genre. The book was mass marketed, made available to the public in ways that many other cookbooks were not. At the same time, it beat out a flood of competition: the 1950s saw a huge number of cookbooks hit the market. In the spring of 1952 alone, some forty new cookbooks appeared in bookstores.[45] The success of *Betty Crocker's Picture Cook Book* was due at least in part to the fact that for many of the millions of women who first purchased it, it was more than a book: it was a promise of community, friendship, and the kind of expertise that makes homemaking an art. And the imaginary woman selling it to them was not an unknown author or even a famous chef. She was the friendly neighbor who had guided them through some of the most challenging moments in the second quarter of the century.

The book included everything a woman might need to know about cooking (including a very thorough culinary dictionary), as well as everything she might need to know about being a successful American housewife. The first edition clocks in at a whopping 449 pages. The book, popular especially with young wives and the daughters of immigrants, offered lesson after lesson on American cuisine, food culture, and dining habits. The

American homemaker, according to *Betty Crocker's Picture Cook Book*, was a Renaissance woman. The book shows her as scientist, nutritionist, artist, and chef. One page even refers to her as a "mathematician" for doubling or halving recipes as needed. The Betty Crocker woman was a professional. The photographs show women in white coats carefully working as if in a laboratory. "Measure as exactly as a Druggist follows a doctor's prescription!" reads one piece of advice, with a side-by-side illustration of a homemaker and a man in a lab coat with beakers.[46]

Much like nineteenth-century domestic manuals, the book showed homemaking as a profession that required expertise and training, and a textbook to achieve both. As the book told readers, "Smart homemakers say: 'Planning, preparing, and serving meals is an *art* which develops through inspiration and thought.'"[47] In the pages of *Betty Crocker's Picture Cook Book*, homemaking was a profession meant to provide fulfillment to women. And perfection in homemaking—much as it had during the war—required a gargantuan effort, from spotless linen, sparkling glassware, and a neat table to meals that had all five Betty Crocker qualities (appropriateness, appearance, satisfaction, nutrition, and cost).[48] The book promised to transform women from housewives into experts.

Throughout the book, Betty Crocker only expanded on her message that food was a signpost of virtue in a good home. Small gestures in the kitchen became representative of the most important moments in life, and baking determined whether those moments would be happy or disappointing. Cakes, for instance became a "symbol of home life"[49] that played "an important role in the most significant moments in our lives."[50]

And cookies came to stand in for a mother's love. "Some of the sweetest memories of Home are bound up with Mother's Cooky Jar. Long after the spicy fragrance of her ginger cookies baking has faded into the years . . . the thought of that ample cooky jar on the shelf will bring back vividly the old-time peace . . . and comfort . . . and security of Home,"[51] read the introduction to a section on cookies. The pages of the cookbook rendered each bite rife with symbolism, a litmus test of success—or failure—not just as a cook but also as a wife, a mother, and a woman.

General Mills was far from being the only entity in 1950s America thinking about a homogeneous vision of home life that married domesticity, cooking, and some version of American values. Images of happy housewives appeared in advertisements in magazines and on TV for just about every home product, while beloved television characters from June Cleaver to Donna Stone (played by Donna Reed) projected images of domestic bliss each week. What made Betty Crocker especially powerful was that General Mills put those ideas directly into the hands of tens of millions of women, in a book so complete as to be singular, *the one book needed*, something to be consulted every day. And woven throughout that book were these core values alongside all General Mills' most popular products, integrated seamlessly: Gold Medal flour, Softasilk, Kix, Cheerios, and Wheaties. Every single time a recipe calls for flour in the book, it's either Gold Medal or Softasilk. It was a cooking bible—one that sold ad space.

The sense of comfort, abundance, homogeneity, and prosperity painted by *Betty Crocker's Picture Cook Book*—and reinforced across other forms of media—ignored a more complex picture.

As with many of the books in this collection, *Betty Crocker's Picture Cook Book* put forward an idealized vision of the United States that ignored huge swaths of the population. Yes, many women were housewives in the 1950s, and the ideology of domesticity was omnipresent in popular culture, but other options were starting to emerge. By the mid-1950s, married women's employment grew by 42 percent—rising fastest among middle-class women.[52] Legislation in 1954 would for the first time make childcare tax-deductible, enabling more women to work outside the home. And even though some of the top universities would not go coed until the late 1960s, some women were still managing to get college degrees. In the immediate postwar period, for instance, the rate of Black women pursuing college degrees was higher than that of white women or Black men.[53] Much like Emily Post's *Etiquette* or even the McGuffey Readers, *Betty Crocker's Picture Cook Book* was at once representing aspects of American life that were real while at the same time shaping and transforming them into an idealized vision of American identity that could only exist within the confines of its pages.

Race is another major blind spot in the vision we inherit of 1950s domesticity. Just as the wartime American story ignored the fact that the United States fought against eugenic violence in Europe with segregated battalions, the postwar period turned a blind eye to mounting inequity at home. The GI Bill—legislation that had allowed so many thousands of veterans to get an education, move to the suburbs with their new wives, and buy a Frigidaire—did not extend to Black veterans. Black families were also systematically turned away from the suburban lifestyle embraced by *Betty Crocker's Picture Cook Book*. Levit-town, for instance—the nation's first planned suburb—explicitly forbade the sale of homes to Black people. Popular conceptions of postwar domesticity ignore the trailblazers, too. By 1948, Freda De Knight, the first food editor for *Ebony* magazine, had published *A Date with a Dish: A Cook Book of American Negro Recipes*. It quickly became a bestseller. The book was a celebration of the rich diversity among Black cooks. As she wrote in the preface, "It is a fallacy, long disproved, that Negro cooks, chefs, caterers and housewives can adapt themselves only to the standard Southern dishes, such as fried chicken, greens, corn pone, hot breads, and so forth. Like other Americans living in various sections of the country they have naturally shown a desire to branch out in all directions and become versatile in the preparation of any dish, whether it be Spanish in origin, Italian, French, Balinese or East Indian."[54] Her book aimed to raise the expectations of what Black cooks were capable of, and she included recipes for everything from old-fashioned suet dumplings and oyster turnovers to hazelnut torte and "grandmother's feathercake."

Betty Crocker's Picture Cook Book achieves a sort of paradox, putting a similar emphasis on homemakers being able to make foods from around the world, all while maintaining an undeviating image of the American cook. The Betty Crocker woman measured exactly and followed the recipes faithfully, just like her neighbors, building American cuisine on precision and standardization. This is a central irony in *Betty Crocker's Picture Cook Book*, just as it is in many American cookbooks: the book was predicated on uniformity, but our cuisine has always been hugely varied. American food incorporates contributions made by vastly different regional cultures that were themselves built on Indigenous, African, Caribbean, and various European influences. There are the New York bagels, brought by Jewish immigrants from Poland, and New England apple pie, which is actually a mix of Dutch, English, and possibly French recipes. Fried chicken is one of the prime examples of a food that has been claimed by some people as "all-American" when it incorporates Scottish or British batter with spices brought to the United States by enslaved cooks from West Africa. U.S. cooking has long varied so strongly by region and ethnicity that for many generations, dinners in Boston and in New Orleans may have had no common denominator. Cookbooks changed that to some extent, especially as they were mass marketed in the twentieth century. It's only when these recipes are somewhat arbitrarily connected within the pages of a bestselling cookbook that they become national cuisine. The true origins of American food are complex, bringing together both the worst and the best parts of our history: from the food stolen by colonization and slavery to the food given freely by generations of diverse immigrant groups. The story of American food is the story of America itself—but American cookbooks do not always reflect that reality.

❧

One of the millions of women who found more than recipes in Betty Crocker was Marion Schmidt, who worked at General

Mills in the late 1940s and early 1950s. I first met Schmidt seventy years later, when she traveled to General Mills' headquarters in Golden Valley, Minnesota, to speak with me. We met in the company's private archive, a facility that resembles a small-scale university library, stocked with rows of gray folio boxes and rolling racks of books. But instead of classics of literature or philosophy, it is packed with General Mills artifacts, including nearly every Betty Crocker pamphlet, recipe book, and advertisement since the invention of Betty nearly one hundred years ago. Schmidt, now ninety years old, walked with a cane through the corridors of the archive, passing under every portrait of Betty Crocker. There was the first official portrait, from 1936, which blended features of home service employees into a hazel-eyed Betty with tightly pursed lips, coiffed with a classic Greta Garbo wave in her hair. Hung nearby was the painting executed closer to Schmidt's time at General Mills in the 1950s: Betty with a wide smile and an open face, graying hair around her temples. Nearly a dozen Betty Crockers hung on the walls, forever frozen in time at an "ageless thirty-two." Wandering through the aisles, Schmidt was brought back to her first days at General Mills when she was just eighteen years old.

Schmidt, née Stocco, grew up in Minneapolis in the 1930s, the daughter of Italian immigrants. She remembers the sound of tomatoes simmering constantly on her mother's stove, the smell of smoked herring, and the sight of damp hazelnuts her father picked in the countryside and laid out to dry on their basement floor. Their garden was ripe with zucchini and radicchio. Some nights, her father would get together with friends in the basement to make salami, grinding the meat, filling the casings,

and hanging the links from the ceiling to dry. On special occa-
sions, he brought home live chickens for her mother, a woman
whom Marion described as "a farm girl from the old country."[55] In
just a few hours, her mother could wring a chicken's neck, pluck it,
and have it on the table by dinnertime. Instead of meat loaf or
hamburgers or barbecue, her mother made spaghetti sauce from
scratch, handmade potato gnocchi, and polenta that she'd cut
with a string and serve under tomato sauce. Her mother couldn't
read English to use American cookbooks, and it would take several years of living in the United States before her mother could
speak some broken English.[56]

By the time Marion got married in the late 1940s, she did
not know how to make any of the food that her German American husband enjoyed. Her mother never baked cookies (they
always ate fruit for dessert), and she certainly had never made
sauerkraut or any of the other dishes that her mother-in-law had
cooked for her husband when he was a boy. During the first
years of her marriage, Schmidt had access to some of the best-
loved American recipes in the country, coming out of the Betty
Crocker test kitchen at General Mills. From 1948 to 1951, she
worked at General Mills, doing secretarial work and testing
recipes. Some of the first cakes she baked as a young bride were
made with the cake mixes being developed by the Betty Crocker
team. Schmidt herself tested some of those mixes before they
hit the market. They had not even been packaged for the public
yet, and she would grab a loose bag to take home for testing,
back when there were only three flavors: white, chocolate, and
spice. As time went on, Betty Crocker products—and especially
Betty Crocker's Picture Cook Book—became essential to Marion's

daily life with her husband. When the cookbook came out in 1950, she consulted it almost every single day, looking to it for basics such as making pancakes, baking cookies, or trussing a roast. "There was so much I didn't know. I did not know how to make hash or stew or anything else like that," she said. Even now, some seventy years after she first opened that red-and-white volume, she spoke about it in reverential terms. "The cookbook—that was my bible,"[57] she told me. "I tell you, if it wasn't for *The Betty Crocker Cook Book*, I wouldn't have been able to do a lot of these things."[58]

Schmidt recalled those first recipes from the cookbook while huddled around a conference table with her granddaughter, Kateri Lukkes, who now works at General Mills herself. Kateri and Marion, whom the former calls "Noni," have the same almond-shaped eyes and warm smile. Marion is a petite, no-nonsense woman and a natural storyteller, especially when her family is the subject. Under the fluorescent lights of the company's sprawling office park, the atmosphere was more corporate than cozy mid-century kitchen, but a passion for food was not what brought Marion to General Mills in the first place. She was more practical than that: when I asked her if a love of cooking drew her to the company, she said no—it was a job, and it was a job that paid better than many others out there. When I asked if she enjoyed being a homemaker, she looked surprised. "What else was I going to be?"[59] she responded. Schmidt left her job in 1951 because she was six months pregnant, and like many corporations, General Mills had a rule that no visibly pregnant women could work there. After she left, she would continue to use *Betty Crocker's Picture Cook Book* for just about everything. When she herself raised four daughters, she says she did not teach them how to make her mother's polenta or sauce; she taught them the American stuff that they had grown up on. She would later gift her well-worn, dog-eared copy of *Betty Crocker's Picture Cook Book* to Kateri.

⚜

For many women like Marion Schmidt, *Betty Crocker's Picture Cook Book* was much more than a book: it was the authority they turned to for all kinds of cooking questions, sometimes more so than to their own families. Especially for second-generation immigrants or new arrivals to the United States, the cookbook did more than teach them how to be wives: it taught a disparate group of people how to be Americans. There were instructions on American eating habits, American food traditions, and American dinner parties. In that way, it bears traces of Emily Post's *Etiquette*, teaching new immigrants, new wives, and new money a certain way to behave. *Betty Crocker's Picture Cook Book* even has a trace of Noah Webster's spelling projects in that it, too, was an Americanizing tool. At the same time, General Mills seems to have made attempts to create a cookbook that was for everyone, appealing to the broadest possible audience. As Marjorie Child Husted would say in a speech several years after the publication of the cookbook, the successful business "must consider all kinds of women,—the educated and uneducated, the rich and poor,—the idle and the overworked."[60]

The book—much like the Betty Crocker persona—served as a companion to millions of Americans. Many of the women who were homemakers in the 1950s did so because they felt that was the only choice available to them, and some women described feeling unappreciated, unchallenged, and bored. Anxiety—and even hopelessness—shows through in many of the letters Betty Crocker received. More than a decade before Betty Friedan would write *The Feminine Mystique*,[61] documenting the quiet desperation of dissatisfied housewives, many women expressed those same feelings in their letters to Betty Crocker. Whether in cities, in suburbs, or on farms, what seemed to unite many of the women writing in those years was both a feeling of isolation and an anxiety over their role in the household and in the world. One letter, for instance, came from a woman living outside Pittsburgh. Married for nearly ten years and with two children, she tried hard to be happy and to follow all of Betty's instructions.[62] Despite her efforts, she felt an enduring sense of loneliness. She was planning on seeing a doctor for "feeling blue," but she decided that Betty and her listeners would have better advice than any physician,[63] she told Betty at the start of her letter. As a wife and mother, she was active in her church, always trying new recipes and spending time with her children, but she felt empty. She struggled to accept a husband who had never been her companion and was, rather, "nothing more than a provider and a boarder in [her] home."[64] Even writing the letter to Betty felt like yet another failure, and she admits, "I tried to write several times and finally became disgusted with myself for being such a baby."[65] The note is like a confession. As the letter writer confides to Betty, "Some things just can't be told, even to one's best friend."[66] The author of the letter asked Betty for some low-cost recipes, but that request seemed more like a pretext. She wanted help, some kind of reassurance or direction to solve a much larger existential problem than a grocery budget. These same themes show up in so many of the letters that Betty Crocker received from women who felt tired and alone, unappreciated or simply unnoticed, sending off a secret letter like a message in a bottle in between meals, housework, and raising children. It is remarkable that women felt comfortable sharing their most intimate thoughts and experiences with this fictional woman. That they trusted her to this extent speaks to just how much she had come to feel not just like a real person but like a close friend to so many women.

Letters like this one reveal Betty's mission: far more than making women's lives easier with a recipe or a nudge of encouragement, she was there to give them purpose. As she told women in one postwar broadcast, "I believe what women want can be summed up in that one word—happiness. That's what I see as I read the fascinating letters that come to me from homemakers all over our county. Those letters reveal many things. They reveal not only hopes and joys, but secret heartaches. Often they show bewilderment and discouragement. Sometimes they admit unhappiness."[67]

Her advice for overcoming unhappiness was a mixture of Protestant work ethic and self-reliance—all updated for women in 1950s America. Part of what Betty accomplished, then, was taking typical American success tropes and repackaging them for women. If self-made-man lore told men that they needed simply to readjust their attitudes and their work ethics to be successful, then the same could now be said for women. As with the self-made-man ethos, we are both the problem and the solution for our future happiness. Everything could be made more bearable by putting additional energy into a clean home, a freshly baked cake, and a bit of stoicism. In a response to that long-suffering woman from Pittsburgh, Betty Crocker suggested that she look to herself in finding the solution to her problems. The young mother should work harder at the task of happiness, Betty told her. And she should ask herself whether she might in fact be responsible for the bickering at home or the disinterest of her husband. "Have you always shown him your love, and do you praise him for the things he does do?"[68] Betty Crocker asked. Her response showed the harsh, sometimes cold side of what was expected of women: a vision of domesticity with no room for fallibility.

General Mills is not solely responsible for the idea that women were uniquely suited to the work of the home, but keeping women at home was an integral part of General Mills' bottom line. Marjorie Child Husted, the creative force behind Betty Crocker for more than two decades, gave copywriters this piece of advice in a speech that was then turned into a pamphlet: "No matter what their age group—income level—educational advantage—and marital status, WOMEN'S CHIEF ROLE IN LIFE IS HOMEMAKING. . . . This fundamental interest of all women is a vulnerable point for advertising"[69] (Husted's emphasis). That vulnerability was something that both Husted and General Mills were able to capitalize on in an increasingly sprawling corporate landscape. In that same speech, Husted urged the General Mills copywriters to "turn the barrage of our advertising on the target of making women feel that a homemaking heart gives her more appeal than cosmetics."[70] It's clear that for General Mills, the cult of domesticity was not just a national or moral imperative; it was simply good business. It was in their interest for women to remain homemakers, spending their days buying General Mills products, cooking with General Mills recipes, and listening to General Mills radio programs.

The mid–twentieth century would see many other corporate characters (some real and some invented), from Aunt Jenny to Ann Pillsbury, that had neither the name recognition nor the longevity of Betty Crocker. Crocker was able to strike a chord more successfully with women of this generation than other characters, speaking to their anxieties, their hopes, their insecurities, and their secret desires. In doing so, she put a human face on a corporation, making her brand indispensable to women. That personal connection became even more important as people moved away from shopping from a local grocer, baker, or butcher and toward big chains. Betty Crocker's success in the postwar years cannot be separated from the rise of grocery stores. She put a friendly face inside suburban American sprawl—and the expanding leviathans of grocery stores. The first supermarkets had cropped up in the 1930s and 1940s, but both the Great Depression and World War II slowed their growth. By the 1950s, however, food shopping in America had shifted solidly toward the enormous supermarket chains that dominate the landscape today, where an average supermarket now contains forty to fifty thousand items.[71] Already in the 1950s, large supermarkets carried as many as ten thousand items. In this rapidly developing landscape, brand loyalty became of the utmost importance—and *Betty Crocker's Picture Cook Book* was key to building that reliance not just on a product but on a brand. Market research conducted by General Mills in the 1950s found that some 99 percent of housewives recognized Betty Crocker,[72] and the vast majority associated her with General Mills products. One in three women surveyed even went so far as to say they were "definitely influenced by Betty Crocker"[73] in their choice of products in the supermarket. This type of brand loyalty has a value that extends far beyond one woman or her household. People often felt such a strong connection to Betty Crocker, or to products like Gold Medal flour, that they would only buy that brand—something that both the research and anecdotal evidence from Schmidt and dozens of letters attest to. As one of the authors of the research reported, "The name Betty Crocker has two meanings. It implies a product in a carton and, also, implies a female figure. The housewife being interviewed does not make this distinction with any real care."[74] In that way, General Mills set an example for how marketing in the next half century would become increasingly personalized, incorporating product placement and corporate characters—even foreshadowing the age of influencers and integrated advertising.

Women saw themselves in Betty Crocker, which was part of why so many thought she was real. They attributed different qualities to her based on how they saw themselves, market research found.[75] Women who were homemakers were more likely to imagine that she was, too; those who were career women were more likely to think Betty Crocker was an employed dietician.[76] As the report concluded, "The more use that can be made of her reality, the more effective Betty Crocker will become for General Mills. Women find in Betty Crocker, whether a person or a role, the satisfaction of many important psychological needs. . . . Emotionally, women need to think that Betty Crocker is real."[77] The best corporate characters feel human; they make mistakes and have both good days and bad days. General Mills found that women in fact did not want a Betty Crocker who was totally infallible and would therefore make them feel bad about their own mistakes.[78] She instead served this role of friend, neighbor, sometimes even mother, showing women the "value and dignity"[79] in homemaking. And General Mills was dedicated to keeping the illusion of Betty Crocker's reality alive: an internal document distributed to women working in the Betty Crocker department urged them to safeguard the brand. If asked whether she was real, they were instructed to say something along the lines of "we feel there is a Betty Crocker because she is a symbol of service to you."[80]

By the 1950s, it had reportedly cost $50 million to create Betty Crocker—and it required a staff of forty-five people, including twenty-four home economists,[81] to keep her going. Much like a childless Catharine Beecher preaching the utmost importance of motherhood, there was a disconnect between some of the women behind Betty Crocker and the message they created. Adelaide Hawley Cumming, for instance, the woman who would play Betty on radio and TV in the 1950s, was a divorcée who "hated cooking."[82] Cumming would go on to teach at the college level and earn a Ph.D. from New York University.[83] Jean Wade Rindlaub, born on a Pennsylvania farm in 1904, would become one of the first American women to work as a major advertising executive.[84] By the age of eleven, she could type fifty words per minute, and as a young woman she quickly worked her way up from secretary to copywriter, eventually running her advertising group from a Madison Avenue office.[85] Rindlaub designed the mid-century Betty Crocker cake mix advertisements—complete with smiling children and a tagline urging women to bake "cake after cake, after cake"[86]—that would take General Mills' lagging cake mix sales and surge them ahead of both Duncan Hines's and Pillsbury's.[87]

General Mills and the women who helped create Betty Crocker had recognized both a need and a lucrative opportunity in mid-twentieth-century America. After all, what better way is there to sell cake mixes or soup mixes or books than to make them a moral imperative? In Betty Crocker, General Mills created the perfect marriage of old-fashioned American values and consumerism, selling the American public hope in lean times—and just about everything else in times of abundance. They were able to solve problems of Depression-era and wartime scarcity with optimism, self-reliance, and a promise of glory to come. One company's brilliant marketing strategy put the archetype of the perfect housewife—a woman who literally did not exist—into the kitchens of millions of homes across America. Betty Crocker and General Mills are not singlehandedly responsible for the revival of the cult of domesticity in midcentury America, but their efforts served as one of its most potent symbols, shaping American feminine ideals over the course of several decades.

At the same time, it would be wrong to entirely dismiss what Husted and others at General Mills accomplished in the service of homemakers. Betty Crocker gave women recognition for the sheer amount of work that goes into cooking, cleaning, and raising children. Many women felt unprepared, overwhelmed, or even trapped in their home life, and Betty offered them relief. Some of these women who bought the books and listened to her radio shows had a relationship with Betty Crocker that lasted as long as—if not longer than—their marriages. Betty Crocker accompanied some women throughout their entire lives: one woman wrote to her of her thirteen-year marriage, mentioning how Betty sent her special recipes after she found out her infant daughter was allergic to honey, and now that daughter was eleven years old and winning blue ribbons at competitions thanks to Betty Crocker's recipes. While many women today may know her only as a name on a cake mix, for many millions more she was that trusted friend: "America's First Lady of Foods."[88]

✾

CHAPTER NINE

*Everything You Always
Wanted to Know About Sex**
(*But Were Afraid to Ask)
(1969)

B arbara Reuben rearranged her simple cotton dress as she
spoke about her passions: tending her vegetable garden and
trying out new recipes to feed her growing family. Any moment
that was not spent caring for her young son was devoted to sewing or reading. Mrs. Reuben may have earned a bachelor's degree in radio and television and a master's in education, but she
says her true calling in life was to support her husband, Dr.
David Reuben. "When we married, David had the insight and
I had the desire to learn from him," she told *The New York Times*
in 1971,[1] adding, "We agree on everything."

The interview took place not long after the publication of her
husband's sexual-revolution-era manual, *Everything You Always
Wanted to Know About Sex (*But Were Afraid to Ask)*. As Mrs.
Reuben discussed the bestselling book with the *Times* reporter,

she paused to wait for her husband's approval, speaking of the joys of marriage and dismissing the burgeoning women's liberation movement as superfluous.[2] Just as Mrs. Reuben found her life's work in her marriage, so, too, did Dr. Reuben. In the acknowledgments of his book, Reuben would thank Barbara specifically, writing, "Only her modesty prevents me from naming her as co-author."[3] The sex manual that made Dr. Reuben a household name took its inspiration not from the muddy Woodstock festivities of 1969 or even the general spirit of free love of the late 1960s. His philosophy around sex and sexuality located itself firmly in the institution of traditional marriage. What on the surface appeared to be a fun, judgment-free, hippie-era guide had less in common with *Sex and the Single Girl* and shared much more with turn-of-the-century marriage manuals. The psychiatrist assured his readers that he would guide their sexual organs into "the Space Age," a place where orgasms were plentiful and Coca-Cola was the best vaginal douche. The latter piece of advice—like much of the book—turned out to be medically unsound. The conversational, quippy guide—which became one of the bestselling books on sex in U.S. history—sorted sexual behavior into good and bad, healthy and aberrant. Both interracial and same-sex relationships were either frowned upon or dismissed outright as sheer animal lust. At a time when people were starting to shake off some of the yoke of 1950s domesticity, Reuben's bestselling smash hit helped guide them back into the old boxes of procreation and traditional marriage, with a shiny new veneer.

Reuben's book—much like nearly every book of sex advice literature—was about much more than sex. It was a book about anxiety and uncertainty within the shifting social expectations of its time, namely, the late 1960s and early 1970s. In the pages of *Everything You Always Wanted to Know About Sex*, Reuben addresses nearly every form of upheaval in the United States during the sixties and seventies, from women's liberation to civil rights to the burgeoning push for LGBTQ rights. If these movements represented a seismic shift in American identity, Reuben's book was a full-throated defense of the status quo. In responding to—and attempting to assuage—an intense anxiety experienced by a portion of the population who felt that too much was changing, Reuben smuggled in old ways of thinking through this most intimate vehicle. With the rise of a specifically American brand of sex advice literature in this era, being a good American became no longer just a public endeavor but a private one—and Reuben codified the idea that your public worth was a reflection of your intimate home life (and vice versa).

In reflecting and responding to social change, he shored up old institutions, reaffirming the American nuclear family as a cultural battleground. His book defended keeping things as they were, maintaining hierarchies between men and women, doctor and patient, the healthy and the sick. His book was not unique in that way: sex advice can function similarly to etiquette books, instructing people about their responsibilities as individuals in a much larger system. Reuben may not have been thinking about a national project or the ideal American in the ways that someone such as Noah Webster was, but what he created served a similar purpose: shaping an understanding of "American" that was predicated on uniformity. At the same time, he set into motion a new type of authority in American culture: the sexpert. Reuben was one of the first in a very long line of contemporary celebrity sex gurus that stretches up to the present day, advice givers who wield immense authority pertaining to issues not just about sex but about marriage, careers, gender roles, and much more.

❀

Very little is known about Reuben's life, and he has only become more shrouded in mystery in recent years. The doctor turned sex guru turned American icon absconded to Costa Rica in the 1990s to live on a 250-acre farm with his family, citing his children's allergies.[4] Since then, he has churned out many less successful—and often bizarre—books about everything from honeymoon sex to high-fiber dieting. A 2014 book was titled *Psychiatric Hospital: Where Insanity Meets Reality . . . and Reality Is Insane*. Reuben has not given an interview to a major newspaper since the 1990s, when he released a completely revamped thirtieth-anniversary edition of *Everything You Always Wanted to Know About Sex*. Now in his eighties, he had his most recent interview with a local Costa Rican television station. He has proved impossible to locate.

Before he became a sex guru to Americans across the country, Reuben was born and raised in 1930s Chicago, where he would later complete his residency in psychiatry at Cook County Hospital.[5] He served as a medic in the air force before opening his private psychiatric practice in San Diego. It was in that private practice, in a surfer town in Southern California, that he became inspired to write the book that would become *Every-*

thing You Always Wanted to Know About Sex. Reuben treated
many patients with sexual problems, and he said the book had
originally been intended as a pamphlet for them, but he soon
decided that all of America needed access to medical information about sex and sexual problems. Publishers disagreed, and
his manuscript was rejected twenty-three times before finding a
home. One editor included a brief note with his rejection: "Funny
books about sex close on Saturday night." Reuben would later
frame that note alongside *The New York Times* bestseller list that
showed his book at the top for fifty-five weeks.[6] Reuben was
correct in recognizing that there was a dearth of reliable medical information about sex even as Americans started to dis-
cuss sex in magazines and an increasing number of bestselling
books. As he explained within the first few pages of the book:
"Most people have more sexual freedom than they know how to
handle."[7]

Everything You Always Wanted to Know About Sex came out in
1969. That same year, tens of thousands of people went to the
Woodstock musical festival to drop acid, roll around in the
mud, and listen to the music of Janis Joplin and Jimi Hendrix.
In June 1969, in the West Village of Manhattan, a police raid of
Stonewall, the now famous gay bar, would turn into a multiple-
day uprising, credited with igniting the modern LGBTQ rights
movement. In retrospect, it can be easy to see 1969 as a turning
point, or a free-for-all of love, sex, and individual liberty. And
in some ways it was, as people rejected not just societal expectations about sex but expectations about patriotism and duty. Separate from the free love movement and the hippie movement
was the student protest movement, with hundreds of thousands

of young people demonstrating against the war in Vietnam. The existential crisis created by the Cold War and the Vietnam War was felt by all Americans to some extent. At the same time, what many Americans perceived as "upheaval" coming in the form of the civil rights movements and liberation movements was in fact an increasingly loud demand for inclusion, a long-overdue call to expand the category of "American" that so many of the books across this collection had defined and refined. Some historians have gone so far as to compare the divisive nature of the 1960s to a civil war.[8] It still seemed unclear what, if anything, would replace that sense of cohesion that reigned, however briefly, in the years following World War II.

For many Americans, all the changes happening, especially on a social level—from desegregation to sex—seemed to create a sense of fear rather than freedom. And for Americans outside large urban centers, it may have felt like if a sexual revolution was happening, it was taking place very far away. Increased access to the birth control pill and abortions may have made premarital sex more available to many Americans, but change occurring in San Francisco or New York City likely felt very foreign to couples in smaller cities and towns across America, the so-called revolution relegated to the pages of *Time* magazine or images on TV. "The sexual revolution that we want to mythologize was far less sweeping than many remember. The idea that 'free love' remade a generation was exaggerated. Monogamy and marriage remained prevailing touchstones of American life. And society's celebration of heterosexual norms—even with watershed events like Stonewall and the rise of the gay liberation movement—

went unquestioned by most,"[9] explained Dr. Joshua Clark Davis, a historian who wrote a book on 1960s and 1970s social movements. The seeds of thought planted in this period would take several generations to come to fruition (and arguably even today have not reached all corners of the country). After all, Americans who were eighteen in 1969 would have been born in 1951. They may have even been raised on *The Betty Crocker Picture Cook Book*, with its perfect fusion of mass consumer culture and domestic bliss. They grew up in the postwar optimism of suburbs and economic growth, and while many young Americans in 1969 vocally rejected the status quo, many more accepted it to some degree. The fact that Richard Nixon would cruise to an easy victory just three years later on a conservative platform speaks to how many Americans were uneasy with all this change. Many middle-class Americans longed for a salve for their anxiety, and the bespectacled Dr. Reuben with his penchant for puns was the approachable voice for doing so.

Everything You Always Wanted to Know About Sex is written in a question-and-answer format, with chapters on everything from masturbation to sex work. The very first question of the book asks: "How big is the normal penis?"[10] From there, Reuben goes on to address hundreds of similarly fear-based questions, covering topics from impotence, menopause, and heart attacks during sex to whether pornography leads to sex crimes.[11] Underneath nearly all the questions in the book lurked much more fundamental queries: "What is normal?" and "Am I normal?" Many Americans seem to view sex as scary, messy, and weird. It seems universal, even in sex advice today, that people long to be assured that *they themselves* are not scary, messy, or weird. For his part, Dr. Reuben was there to reassure a certain type of white, middle-class American that they were normal—all while titillating them with dramatic tales of the other people he deemed abnormal, even deviant. In doing so, he reaffirmed old ideas of who the good American was, all while adding in this new layer of who he was not, both inside and outside the bedroom.

Reuben was the perfect interlocutor for millions of middle-class Americans, young couples, and even conservatives, and they snapped up his book by the millions. It's not as if Reuben did not have any competition: by the early seventies, there were dozens of other books about sex and sexuality on the market, many of them available at the public library. That this book—arguably one of the most conservative and moralizing of the bunch—became the biggest seller is telling. Many people who first purchased the book were looking to see if they were "normal" in their feelings or behaviors around sex. As one bookstore shopper told *The New York Times* while purchasing another best-selling sex manual: "I wanted to see how I rate."[12] That same motivation drove the tens of millions of people who would purchase *Everything You Always Wanted to Know About Sex*. Across the pages of the book was reflected a sense of fear, shame, and anxiety among Reuben's readers, a longing to see how they measured up. The subtitle of the book even has the word "afraid" in it.

By 1970, the book was selling a staggering five thousand copies per day, according to *The New York Times*.[13] "It is just possible that this book does explain everything you always wanted to know about sex,"[14] wrote *The Times* in its review of Reuben's book. The very fact that *The Times* reviewed it at all began to normalize sex literature for a broader, mainstream audience. That review, coupled with another in *Life* magazine, was enough to launch the book to bestseller status, according to Reuben's publisher. "Once those two said it was okay to read it—the rest is history. We didn't need to advertise," Carolyn Anthony, then the publicity director for Reuben's publisher, told the *Chicago Tribune*.[15] That may have been true for the hardback, but Reuben's paperback release saw one of the most expensive advertising campaigns of the era. Where even big literary books might have seen a $10,000 campaign, Reuben's publishers put $200,000 into promoting the book's paperback edition,[16] sending him on a multicity book tour that included frequent television and radio appearances in the early 1970s. As was the case for many of the books across *Americanon*, the success of Reuben's book was a mix of the author's charisma, the book's resonance with average Americans at the right place and the right time—and a clever and intentional publicity campaign. By 1990, the book had reportedly reached 100 million readers.[17]

The book did not receive unequivocal praise, however, especially from those who recognized its inaccuracy and bigotry. Famed writer Gore Vidal skewered both Reuben and his book in an essay for *The New York Review of Books* in 1970, writing, "Essentially he is not a man of science but a moderately swinging rabbi who buttresses his prejudices with pious quotations from the Old Testament."[18] Vidal, who was openly bisexual, took particular issue with the book's portrayal of gay men and Reuben's claim that they were rabidly sexual deviants, incapable of love. Like many psychiatrists of the mid-century, Reuben displayed a deep-seated homophobia, something that may have endeared him to a conservative audience. Psychiatry was a relatively new field, one that was often riddled with superstition and prejudice rather than science. "Homosexuality" would remain a mental disorder in the *DSM* until 1973. Vidal was not the only one to take note of both Reuben's traditional bent and his frequent references to the Old Testament. Another article in *The New York Times* noted, "The result is a zingy, colloquial book, laced with humor (some of it unintended), which sounds a little like a cross between Sigmund Freud and a young, with-it Reform rabbi."[19] The errors and downright misinformation in the book were so apparent that even *Playboy* joined in in criticizing *Everything You Always Wanted to Know About Sex*. In 1972, the magazine ran an article detailing what it claimed were approximately one hundred factual errors in the book.

Despite some criticism, the book became a fame vehicle not just for Reuben's ideas but for the doctor himself. And Reuben remained unapologetic about the content of *Everything You Always Wanted to Know About Sex*. "I wrote a book on human sexuality, I wasn't running for Miss America,"[20] he would tell the *Chicago Tribune* thirty years later. "My goal was to tell the facts as directly as I could in a way that was interesting and entertaining and useful for the reader. It wasn't a popularity contest."[21] The fact that "useful" comes after "interesting and entertaining" seems telling—science might not have been Reuben's top priority. Reuben might not have been running for Miss America, but soon he was making more media appearances than the average beauty queen. By 1970, his face was on the cover of *Newsweek*, and the young doctor made appearances on *The Dick Cavett Show*, *The Merv Griffin Show*, and *The Tonight Show*— often bringing spikes in ratings.[22] *Everything You Always Wanted to Know About Sex* was not the first mainstream sex book to see such widespread popularity, but what set it apart was Reuben's publicly facing persona and his status as the sexpert archetype for the modern age. Alfred Kinsey might have sold hundreds of thousands of books, but he did not make the rounds on the late-night television circuit. Reuben was neither Sigmund Freud nor a San Francisco hippie, making him the perfect sex guru for a public that was still deeply ill at ease with sex. Behind his thick glasses, he still looked like someone's nerdy small-town doctor, but he breezed onto late-night television shows, chatting with Johnny Carson and Rob Reiner as if he had been doing it all his life. Reuben was genuinely funny, and his lighthearted way of talking about sex seemed to disarm anyone who was bracing for a serious medical manual. Reuben was there to field sex questions on anything inside or outside the book—which is to say, everything.

Reuben's perfect mix of doctor-speak and dad jokes allowed much of America to dip a toe into the pool of sexual freedom from the safety of their own homes. For all the book's traditionalism, it did push boundaries when it came to certain types of sexual experimentation. He reassured couples that they could try oral sex[23] (previously considered out of the bounds of acceptable sexual behavior), and he encouraged older couples to find sexual reawakening in their twilight years.[24] He even wrote that masturbation—both for boys and for girls—was natural. While that idea may not seem revolutionary, back in the 1960s masturbation was still far from being accepted. As recently as 1959, a survey of senior medical students found that 50 percent of them believed that masturbation caused insanity.[25] Many of their professors shared the same belief.[26]

Part of what sold all those copies of *Everything You Always Wanted to Know About Sex* was that it was titillating. Reuben went into depth about Peeping Toms, exhibitionists, and shoe fetishists. He discussed how some people masturbated by sticking hair pins inside their urethras, and he pondered whether nuns should have access to the birth control pill. He even dedicated a full page to slang he claimed was used by sex workers, including "slam-bam-thanky-ma'am" ("a fast two-oh")[27] and "balling" ("the same as turning a trick").[28] It's unclear where Reuben would have been able to learn this lingo, much less why it would have been valuable information for his audience to have. Perhaps part of what the book was offering was a safe window into how "the other half" had sex.

That kind of titillation showcased the way that sex advice reflected not just a personal anxiety but a fear of difference: both "Am I part of the normal?" and "Are *those people* part of the normal?" Nowhere was that fear more explicitly felt than in Reuben's offensive and outdated chapter on gay men. Reuben wrote that most gay men "don women's clothes, wear makeup, adopt feminine mannerisms, and occasionally even try to rearrange their bodies along feminine lines."[29] He even offered justification for what is now known as conversion therapy, arguing that psychiatrists can cure people of being gay.[30] He wrote that gay men "thrive on danger,"[31] with many of them embracing sado-masochism. For that reason, he went so far as to claim that many of the men in the Gestapo and the SS were gay sadomas-ochists.[32] A gay liberation movement was already starting to form by the late 1960s, but Reuben dismissed that activism as simply an attempt by gay people to explain away their "prob-lem." *Everything You Always Wanted to Know About Sex*, one of the most widely read sex books in American history, painted all LGBTQ people with the same demeaning brush. The book de-scribed gay men in particular as sex-crazed lunatics driven by a love of danger, so voracious for sex that they masturbated with fruits, vegetables, and flashlights.[33] It's hard to overstate just how damaging this writing was, especially given its huge audi-ence and Reuben's position as a medical expert. The man who would write *the* book on sex demeaned a large swath of Ameri-cans while encouraging the rest of the population to fear them. The book served as a violent standardizing tool, much like some of the other books in this collection, penned by an author ob-sessed with ridding the country of difference. Reuben seemed to be reassuring his straight, often married, middle-class audience that not only was theirs the best way of doing things—it was the only way. So much of sex advice literature returns again and again to the idea that there is a right and a wrong way to do everything, from flirting to blow jobs. For Reuben and arguably much of his audience, gay people were part of the wrong way, and his book made that argument with violent verve.

Sex advice literature can serve as a hidden litmus test of who is generally conceived of as "us" and who is "not us" in American society. The "us" shifts very slowly over time, mirroring broader social movements, whether for single women, people of color, or LGBTQ people. For Reuben, the "not us" resoundingly included not only gay people but Black people (two groups that he saw as intimately connected). Without citing any studies or statistics, Reuben claimed that venereal disease was more prevalent among the Black population. His theory—rather than decreased access to medical care, for instance—was that because gay men were "capable of prodigious promiscuity," a Black gay man was likely to sleep with a white gay man at some point, thereby spreading venereal disease to other white people.[34] He went on to warn against sex between Black and white people, saying, "Sexual intercourse between whites and blacks is relatively rare in this country. If it increases, the incidence of underground infections can also be expected to increase among white people, too."[35] In connecting Black people to sexually transmitted infections, he pointed to Haiti, making another unfounded guess that 90 percent of Haitians had some kind of venereal disease.[36] By drawing a link between Black people and venereal diseases, he sent a dangerous message that encouraged white people to fear their Black neighbors as a public health threat. He warned that the most intimate form of integration could lead to consequences as dire as disease and even death. By the end of the 1960s, many white Americans may have nominally accepted Black Americans into their schools, neighborhoods, and lunch counters, but the bedroom was an intimate frontier. And Reuben's hugely popular book served to stoke these fears, reaffirming racist beliefs under the guise of so-called science.

Interracial relationships have long lagged behind other forms of integration. The landmark *Loving v. Virginia* Supreme Court case, for instance—which struck down miscegenation laws in seventeen states in the United States—was decided in 1967, just two years before Reuben's book came out. Until that time, miscegenation, or the joining of people of two different ethnic groups in marriage, was illegal in nearly one in three states. Mildred and Richard Loving's nearly decade-long saga had begun in the late 1950s, when they were woken up by flashlights in their eyes in the middle of the night. Police had entered their home and were demanding to know what the two were doing in bed together. The Virginia couple had been married in neighboring Washington, D.C., but their union was illegal in the state of Virginia because Mildred was Black and Richard was white. They were thrown in jail and later convicted of miscegenation. A judge told the Lovings that they could not return home to Virginia for twenty-five years. Multiple appeals upheld the ruling, and one judge told the couple, "Almighty God created the races white, black, yellow, malay and red, and he placed them on separate continents. And but for the interference with his arrangement there would be no cause for such marriages. The fact that he separated the races shows that he did not intend for the races to mix."[37]

After years of legal battles, the Lovings' case reached the Supreme Court in 1967. It had taken nine years, multiple appeals, and a plea to Attorney General Robert F. Kennedy, but the Supreme Court eventually heard their case and ruled in their favor—striking down similar laws in some sixteen other states. That victory was bittersweet: after all, the case had only ended up in the Supreme Court because so many other people, from police to judges, agreed that their marriage was indeed a crime. And that Supreme Court ruling did not mean that public opinion was suddenly on their side. In 1967, just 3 percent of newlyweds in the United States were married to a spouse of a different race or ethnicity.[38] The separate-but-equal philosophy continued to endure even as legal battles combating institutionalized racism were won. As recently as 1990, more than half of non-Black Americans said they would be opposed to a close relative marrying a nonwhite person.[39] Public opinion has often lagged behind the law, and Reuben was there to offer a pseudoscientific explanation of why those unions should not be allowed to occur, even if they were legal.

It would be easy to brand Reuben as a bigot and move on, but the more unsettling truth is that so many sex books of the era included similar prejudices. Reuben represents a systemic problem as well as an individual one. Alex Comfort, the British doctor whose book *The Joy of Sex* sold millions of copies on both sides of the Atlantic, played into racial stereotypes across the book. He even decided to name a sex position in which a man takes a woman from behind "la négresse." His son Nick Comfort would go on to claim that this was simply a widely used term, and he refused to update it when assisting with a revised version published as recently as 2002.[40] As Black feminists such as Angela Davis and bell hooks pointed out, even progressive feminist books of the era, such as the seminal book on rape culture, *Against Our Will*, promulgated dangerous stereotypes[41] about Black men as rapists. And this was not just a 1960s and 1970s problem. From the very start, the history of sex advice in America cannot be unwoven from some of the most violent forms of prejudice, discrimination, and pseudoscience.

⚘

Long before Dr. David Reuben, there was Paul Popenoe, best known as the "father of marriage counseling." Marriage had been Popenoe's bread and butter since he opened his clinic, the American Institute of Family Relations, in 1930. By the mid-century, he had a radio program, a syndicated column, and a feature in *Ladies' Home Journal* called "Can This Marriage Be Saved?" In that recurring feature, both a husband and a wife would give their version of their marital problems, and Popenoe weighed in. It was so popular that it ran for decades, and *The Atlantic* called it "perhaps the most widely known column"[42] in the history of magazines. At the height of his clinic, Popenoe counseled as many as a thousand couples per year on issues ranging from adultery to sexual "frigidity."[43] He wrote and printed dozens of "marriage manuals," the forerunner to sex manuals, which gave advice about sex and sexual pleasure within marriage.

Popenoe's calling to save American marriages was born out of his initial research passion: eugenics. While studying biology at Stanford in the early 1900s, he became close to one of his professors, David Starr Jordan, one of the earliest leading advocates of eugenics. Jordan would later tap Popenoe in 1913 to study the progress of California's forced sterilization project, when the state would sterilize some twenty thousand people it had deemed mentally unfit over the course of the first half of the twentieth century.[44] It was then that Popenoe's devotion to eugenics seems to have truly taken hold. As he traveled to asylums across the state, Popenoe envisioned a much vaster plan for eliminating unfit citizens. The thousands of recommended sterilizations were far too few, he thought, suggesting instead that 10 million Americans should be sterilized.[45] By 1918, he would cowrite *Applied Eugenics*, the number one assigned college textbook on the topic in the United States, which would later be translated into German.[46]

His 1925 marriage manual, *Modern Marriage: A Handbook*, was the other side of the same eugenics coin. Just as he wanted to prevent certain Americans—Italian Americans, Polish Americans, and Black Americans, among many other groups—from procreating, he wanted to encourage what he called "Nordic" Americans to make more babies. Like many of the marriage manuals of the day, it was essentially a how-to book about sex— reserved only for a swath of the population that had been deemed fit. Popenoe was unabashed about his goals. As he wrote in the preface to the book, "The book is, therefore, written from the biological point of view. It takes man as it finds him, and tries to make clear how he can fit himself into the American civilization of the twentieth century in such a way as to provide for his own greatest satisfaction and the progressive evolution of the race."[47]

The man who would counsel thousands of couples throughout his decades-long career—who left his thumbprint on marriage counseling so deeply that he was dubbed "Mr. Marriage"—was a dedicated eugenicist. Even in the 1940s, as he prepared to launch his feature for *Ladies' Home Journal*, he continued to write favorably about sterilization in articles that were later reprinted in a German journal.[48] Few people would have suspected that behind that popular *Ladies' Home Journal* columnist lurked a pseudoscientist who deeply admired *Mein Kampf* and described Adolf Hitler warmly as a "convinced advocate of race betterment."⁴⁹ Support for eugenics in the United States had been widespread in the first decades of the twentieth century—proponents included everyone from Theodore Roosevelt and Henry Ford to Jack London and Margaret Sanger—but that changed after the Holocaust. Following World War II, as eugenics fell precipitously out of fashion, Popenoe shifted his language to talk about marriage between equals or the preservation of the American family. But he never disavowed his earliest beliefs. And Popenoe is not an outlier. He was representative of a far larger movement in which sex, sex advice, and eugenics were deeply intertwined.

The publication of marriage manuals had exploded in the United States in the 1920s, often being given to patients by doctors. There was *The Companionate Marriage* (1927), *Sane Sex Life and Sane Sex Living* (1919), and *Ideal Marriage: Its Physiology and Technique* (1928), among many others—all written by avowed eugenicists. In doing my research, I actually found it difficult to find a marriage manual from this period that was *not* written by a eugenicist. *Ideal Marriage: Its Physiology and Technique*, for instance, was written by Theodoor H. van de Velde, a Dutch doctor who was interested in eugenics. The book was translated into English and became such a huge bestseller that it had to be reprinted dozens of times in the United States. In a way that is eerily reminiscent of Reuben's opening lines, Van de Velde writes early on about the lack of good scientific information around sex and the need to give couples basic information about sex and orgasm.[50] He longed to show patients how to let the "bridal honeymoon . . . blossom into the perfect flower of ideal marriage."[51]

Part of what drove the publication of those early marriage manuals was both a fear of immigrants and people of color as well as a fear of women's burgeoning power. The period from 1880 to 1920 is sometimes even referred to as "the first Sexual Revolution"[52] by historians. Especially in the 1910s and the 1920s, as women started to slowly gain ground in a hard-fought battle for autonomy—in the form of suffrage and increasing personal freedoms—marriage manuals suddenly started appearing in all corners of the nation. As people challenged gender roles and social norms, the so-called experts were there to channel their desires into white, procreative marriage. Many of the leading thinkers on this front spoke specifically about women's sexual desire in a way that might seem surprising for the early twentieth century, going into detail about clitoral stimulation and orgasm, but it was all in service of what they saw as the preservation of the ideal American: white, Protestant, and physically and mentally fit. Much like the sexual revolution of the 1960s, this first revolution was straight and patriarchal by nature, encouraging sexual pleasure but only within strict confines. When it came to other types of gender role rejection, the manuals were clear, too. Reuben's claim that some lesbians with elongated clitorises were "in great demand"[53] is an idea that originated in this period. Multiple physicians in the 1920s and 1930s wrote that lesbians—and Black lesbians in particular— had larger clitorises because they were more masculine.[54] In that way, anti-queerness and anti-Blackness were inextricably connected—a theme that shows up in Reuben, too.

For these early marriage crusaders in the twentieth century, then, the problems of women, immigration, Black people, gay people, and the mentally unfit could all be solved through the unifying banner of white marriage and family values. And these pamphlets and books were there to set the right Americans on the path toward that goal. If white people could learn how to have sex the *proper* way (heterosexual, procreative sex), according to these authors, then white, Protestant America could be saved. In this way, the earliest sex manuals in the United States were explicitly focused on a national project. Those seemingly scientific pamphlets on how to have sex were—much like Noah Webster or William Holmes McGuffey—trying to create a future United States that was populated by only a certain type of American.

Sex advice literature has long been inextricably linked to discrimination and the shifting politics of American prejudices. Not only did these reference books determine who was good; they served as potentially dangerous exclusionary texts that reinforced one another's authority. Sex advice literature has sometimes served as a potent tool for marginalization: doling out judgment as to who was (and, more important, who was not) part of "us." At the heart of it is a fear of mixing and a desire to keep different types of people separate. Sex manuals filled this unlikely purpose, serving as a salve for fears about demographic changes in American society and often concretizing old prejudices with new justifications. The early connection between sex

advice and eugenics—as well as the enduring prejudices in books
like Reuben's—are evidence to the contrary of one of our favorite American stories: the melting pot. We tell a story about
acceptance and assimilation, but when it comes to the most intimate forms of integration, true equality has been frowned upon
at best and severely criminalized at worst. Sex advice can seem
on the surface a benign discussion of 101 sex positions, but it's
also deeply political: a tool that can either restrict or expand our
definitions of American identity, accepted behavior, and social
norms.

Between the marriage manual period and the 1960s, bestselling books about sex started to slowly take a scientific attitude, one that began to shake off some of the pseudoscience of
early forays into sex research. The middle of the century saw
scientist Alfred Kinsey publish his extensive research on sex
with the books *Sexual Behavior in the Human Male* (1948) and
Sexual Behavior in the Human Female (1953). The books, sum-
marizing years of research, started to normalize many previously taboo subjects, from premarital sex to gay and lesbian
sex. Despite being somewhat dryly written research findings,
together Kinsey's two books sold several hundred thousand
copies. Then came William H. Masters and Virginia E. Johnson, the scientific-research-partner (and sex-partner) pair known
for their pioneering research on sexual response in the late 1950s
and early 1960s. The results of their research, published in the
late 1960s and early 1970s, would also go on to achieve bestselling numbers.

Being a doctor, a psychiatrist, or a scientist had long been a
prerequisite for doling out sex advice. But by the late 1960s,

expectations began to shift, and experts like Dr. Reuben were already becoming part of the old guard. As Americans increasingly questioned various types of authority, expertise was suddenly something of a liability.[55] After all, Dr. Comfort went so far as to pretend that *The Joy of Sex* had actually been written by a couple he knew, claiming that he was simply an editor. This suspicion of expertise did not just come from people who were on the margins and feared they were being left out of the conversation. A distrust of experts is well documented across American culture. For a country whose heroes are small farmers and autodidacts, it should be unsurprising that expertise is often regarded with suspicion. A whopping 20 to 25 percent of Americans[56] do not trust experts and may even be repelled by them, one researcher found.[57] This tendency plays a role in who is chosen to give sex advice, too, especially as young people challenged the status quo in so many different aspects of social life in the 1960s and 1970s. Shere Hite, for instance, who had begun a doctorate but never finished it, conducted survey research to bridge the gap between authority and the individual. Reacting in part to the fact that books about sex at the time only understood women's sexuality through men's sexuality, she tried to put women back on their own terms. Her 1976 collection of that research, *The Hite Report*, has sold tens of millions of copies worldwide. The feminist answer to a sex manual, the Boston Women's Health Book Collective's *Our Bodies, Ourselves*—written by activists and not experts—has sold more than 4 million copies[58] since its 1970 release.

Much of what made Reuben such a successful sex guru therefore had nothing to do with his qualifications as a doctor. He had the same talents as any good entertainer: he was funny and charming and had an affable confidence. With these assets and a no-nonsense approach to talking about sex, he set up an archetype for the sexpert that lingers today: someone with a mixture of curiosity and candor. Those two qualities have become more important than just about anything else when it comes to becoming a sexpert. Many contemporary advice givers, such as Esther Perel and Dr. Ruth, still have a medical background, but they also tend to be frank, funny, or even a touch mystical. Much like more traditional self-help gurus, the most successful sexperts have this ability to make people feel more powerful, actualized not just in terms of sex but in terms of the self. We have come to make space in American culture for a specific type of guru, especially when it comes to sex: someone who might not always have the answers but is asking the right questions. It is the model that has fueled nearly every sex advice columnist, real or fictional, from *Sex and the City*'s Carrie Bradshaw to Dan Savage. Their authority does not necessarily need to come from anywhere but their own experience. While this change can be liberating, it also carries with it a risk: when we take advice from someone based on their charisma, it's easier for quackery to slip in. As books and columns about sex became more democratic over time, they grew more similar to other advice books in American history. Whether *How to Win Friends and Influence People* or *The Autobiography of Benjamin Franklin*, many of the most popular how-to or advice books come from people who have figured out some kernel of wisdom through their own experience—not from the so-called expertise of people like Reuben.

❀

Since the 1970s, sex advice has seen an even more dramatic de-mocratization process than occurred in Reuben's era. Long gone are the good doctors doling out judgment on what married cou-ples should do in the bedroom. Just fifty years ago, Dr. Reuben dismissed all non-straight sex as deviant. Now even *Teen Vogue* publishes articles such as "How to Navigate Gender Dysphoria During Sex." The sex guru for the twenty-first century is open-minded, experienced, and definitely not an expert. At least, not in the traditional sense.

Unlike the authors of some of the books across *Americanon*, Reuben does not have a generational legacy keeper in the way that Noah Webster or Emily Post does. There is no David Reu-ben Institute carrying on his ideology. After his 1999 rewrite of *Everything You Always Wanted to Know About Sex*, he has mostly disappeared from the public eye. And the people carrying on his legacy in some sense—contemporary sex advice givers—often represent something nearly opposite from what he stood for. They increasingly prize inclusion and ambiguity over exclusion and certainty.

Karley Sciortino, known for her hugely popular website and television show—both named "Slutever"—epitomizes this shift away from the Reuben era of sex advice. With platinum-blond hair, pinup style, and a slightly disheveled quality, Sciortino looks like Veronica Lake crossed with Courtney Love—if both of them read a lot of Camille Paglia. One magazine described

Sciortino as a "slutty, post-woke Carrie Bradshaw."[59] When I interviewed her via video call in the spring of 2020, she had just woken up in Los Angeles (it was eleven a.m. her time). She is easy to talk to, like a cool sister—a compliment she gets a lot. "People don't care that much anymore if their sex advice is coming from someone who's qualified to give advice," she told me. "It felt like a natural extension of writing about my own sex life."[60]

Sciortino has been writing about sex in some capacity since 2007, when she started a blog chronicling her own dating and sex experiences while living in an artist's squat in London. She continued writing after she moved to New York City three years later, earning money to support her writing by working as a sugar baby and as the assistant to a popular Manhattan dominatrix. Within a few years, she started giving advice through her blog, in a section she called "Ask Slutever." In the past ten years, she has turned her blog into a veritable empire, with a show on Vice, a book deal, and a sex column for *Vogue*. Her column draws in a wide readership, and the first episode of her show, focusing on the world's first male sex doll, garnered more than 67 million views on YouTube. Part of her appeal as an advice giver is her willingness to experiment, and she seems ready to try almost anything at least once: she had sex with that same doll, rented a boyfriend, and had her vagina examined by a masturbation expert.

Maybe it's precisely because she does not pretend to have expertise that people want to hear what she has to say. When she started answering sex questions, her responses were playful, framed through the lens of "questionable life advice," she says.

But that is why it worked: she's open-minded and judgment-free. She doesn't pander to her readers, mostly because she is not so different from them. Even if she does not always get it right—and especially in the early years, she fumbled in finding her voice around issues such as feminism—she seems to be figuring it out along with many of her readers, taking them with her for the ride.

Even just in her lifetime, Sciortino says the landscape of sex advice has transformed. As a girl sneaking issues of *Cosmopolitan*, which her Catholic mother would not allow, she noticed how much of the sex advice out there seemed performative and unrealistic. In just the past fifteen years, magazines like *Cosmopolitan* have gone from suggesting women give their boyfriends a massage with their breasts to engaging with trans issues and even institutional racism. "The world has changed so fast," Sciortino told me, noting the seismic social and cultural shifts much of the United States has witnessed in just the past ten years, particularly when it comes to female pleasure and LGBTQ sex. "When I talk about it, I feel like I'm talking about it as an eighty-year-old from my childhood, but I'm literally talking about seven years ago," she said.

The landscape of sex advice remains imperfect, but it has advanced in leaps and bounds. In a similar way to the late 1960s, the past five years have been defined by a feverish amount of social and political division in the United States. And yet our sex advice has responded in almost the opposite way than Dr. Reuben did. Where *Everything You Always Wanted to Know About Sex* reinserted old narratives about traditional marriage, sex advice today has seen a slow questioning of the entire idea of "normal." The pages of *Cosmopolitan* or Sciortino's column in *Vogue* might not represent the views of the entire country when it comes to trans people, sadomasochism, or "sluttiness," but the very fact that those ideas appear in the pages of such main-stream publications is an enormous shift.

What ties past and present is the scaffolding that Reuben built in the seventies and on which most sexperts today still stand: the idea that what you do when no one's watching is somehow still a reflection of who you are, both as a person and, to a degree, as an American. The most popular sex advice books brought American bedrock beliefs laid out by earlier books—such as autodidacticism, the power of the individual, and the importance of self-improvement—into the bedroom. Like so many debates throughout American history, sex has always been a negotiation between the private and the public, the individual and the whole—even the religious and the secular. In a surprising way, sex highlights this constant tension in American cultural life between a devotion to personal freedom and a fear of diverging from the norm. For Dr. Reuben, it was about right and wrong kinds of sex between the right kinds of people. In the intervening years, sex advice—especially online—has developed a much broader range, but it's still often populated with articles about right and wrong ways of doing things: how to give the "perfect" blow job or how to "be better" in bed.

Sex advice, then, becomes part of the quest for our "best selves"[61] that has dominated so much popular literature of the past fifty years. At its best, it can be an exploration of intimacy or desire, or a form of self-expression. At its most practical and calculating level, however, especially in Reuben's era, it can seem far more transactional. As he wrote in the book, "Success in the outside world breeds success in the inside world of sex. . . . Conversely, the more potent a man becomes in the bedroom, the more potent he is in business."[62] In sex manuals—as in self-help writ large—the quest for self-development becomes about not just improving a skill but improving the commodity that is ourselves.

CHAPTER TEN

Surviving the Eighties

In the years following the publication of *Everything You Always Wanted to Know About Sex*, advice books would undergo something of a makeover themselves. While Reuben's book and others that preceded it—such as *How to Win Friends and Influence People*—contained elements of what we now think of as self-help, the ensuing decades would see an enormous uptick in the publication of self-help books. Literary historians often trace the origins of "self-help" to Scottish writer Samuel Smiles's book of the same name in 1859, but the genre arguably began its American heyday in the final quarter of the twentieth century. Between 1972 and 2000, the number of self-help books more than doubled, quickly becoming an industry that generated hundreds of millions of dollars annually.[1]

Part of the rise of self-help in this era was a product of its time: the 1980s and early 1990s might be remembered for economic prosperity and relative peace—spawning the birth of the "yuppie"—but that rosy vision hardly applied to everyone. Those years in particular brought a huge amount of precarity to middle-class and working-class people, who saw stagnant wages, an eroded social safety net,[2] and very few drips from trickle-down economics. As many Americans felt stuck or powerless, books about self-empowerment and self-improvement garnered enormous audiences. Readers could purchase books about everything from dieting and fitness to financial planning and building confidence at work. When uncertainty reigned, Americans turned to the unambiguous promise inherent in self-help: a better life, one that they could take control of themselves. Americans may not have been able to prevent themselves from falling prey to the latest round of layoffs, but they could find solace, however illusory or fleeting, in a positive philosophy book, a personal finance book, or even a diet book.

While there was a wide range in these books, two trends started to emerge in the bestselling advice books of this era. The first was books that fell into the wide umbrella category of the New Age—with authors such as Wayne Dyer, Eckhart Tolle, and Louise Hay, who focused on a metaphysical approach, promising a new life via a new attitude. Louise Hay exemplified this movement: her 1984 book, *You Can Heal Your Life*, alone sold more than 40 million copies, and her seminars and public speaking events would garner consistently massive audiences. I've chosen to focus on Hay because of her sales numbers and the influence of her publishing house, but if the guiding measure were sales alone, I could have just as easily chosen Dyer. The fact that multiple authors were selling tens of millions of copies each, writing about similar ideas, speaks to just how powerful this movement was. The second thread was business or management books—from

Zig Ziglar to Tony Robbins—which also saw a boom during this period. According to sales figures and longevity, this second trend was perhaps best exemplified by Dr. Stephen Covey and *The 7 Habits of Highly Effective People*, which has sold more than 40 million copies since its release in 1989. He, too, built an empire on lectures, seminars, and a slew of other bestselling books that extended far beyond a single bestseller. Much like Catharine Beecher, these authors were both hugely influential on their own and part of a broader trend. Despite their many differences—including the prominent role of Mormonism in Covey's worldview—both of their philosophies offered a reprieve from a whole host of 1980s anxieties about everything from money and success to love and health. Louise Hay responded to that feeling of coming up short with warmth, love, and self-acceptance. Covey offered a vision of Americans as "proactive" people who could "carry their own weather."[3]

Contemporary self-help is the natural culmination of the mythmaking across the books in this collection, because it explicitly spells out both the dreams and the anxieties that earlier reference books only hinted at. Where a dictionary or a sex book made overtures to the kind of nation their authors wanted, self-help unabashedly puts into words exactly what the American dream has promised and how to get it. At the same time, self-help expresses a vulnerability. It says the thing that so many Americans cannot say: that they fear they're never going to become a Renaissance man like Benjamin Franklin or a very influential person like Dale Carnegie. This is the central paradox within the genre: readers feel that they are not enough, but they can imagine a world in which they have confidence, wealth, and success. It's why self-help—like the self-made-man archetype—is self-perpetuating: that anxiety of not being enough never really goes away, but it can be temporarily sated with more books, more improvement, and more achievement. Some people feel embarrassed reading this type of book because it represents this brazen longing: to be prettier, richer, or more in love. These books both recognize that yearning for more and assuage those feelings of powerlessness. These self-help books share many of the same core values as the earlier books in *Americanon*—such as meritocracy, work ethic, and individualism—but they also add this layer of vulnerability, recognizing the fragility of complete self-reliance.

❀

Trauma shaped all the authors in *Americanon*, but perhaps none more than Louise Hay. She experienced innumerable personal traumas in her young life—rape, child abuse, poverty, and teen pregnancy—all before the age of eighteen. Born Helen Vera Lunney in 1926 in Los Angeles, she grew up poor in the Depression years. As she recalls in a chapter of her book *You Can Heal Your Life*, her parents separated when she was a baby. Her mother made ends meet working as a maid, barely scraping by. Lunney's mother soon married, moving in with a man who would physically and sexually abuse Helen throughout her childhood.[4] At around age five, she was raped by an alcoholic neighbor. The man was sentenced to fifteen years in prison, but she was told repeatedly that the rape was her fault, she says. She grew up with the conviction that she was worthless, she would later write.[5]

When she was fifteen years old, she could not stand the sexual abuse any longer, so she dropped out of high school and ran away from home. Only a short while later, she became pregnant. Young and broke, she gave the baby up for adoption just a few days after her sixteenth birthday. Later, she moved to New York City, changed her name to "Louise," and worked as a fashion model, but she continued to struggle with low self-esteem. A marriage to an English businessman named Andrew Hay offered a brief fourteen years of happiness, but her life was once again broken apart when her husband left her for another woman. That heartbreak would send her on the spiritual journey that made her a metaphysical guru to millions of Americans. Both her difficult past—and her path to healing—became the selling point of her philosophy, all of it recounted in a chapter of *You Can Heal Your Life*. Her trauma would serve as a kind of calling card, her life living proof of just how much suffering could be overcome by the power of one's own thoughts.

After her divorce, Hay found solace in the philosophy that would make her a millionaire: positive thinking. In the late 1960s, she joined the First Church of Religious Science on Forty-Eighth Street in Manhattan. Founded by Ernest Holmes in the first half of the twentieth century, the movement preached that positive thinking could literally heal your body. Much like Christian Science, the doctrine of Religious Science taught that your mind created your reality, including changes in your physical body. As she later explained to *The New York Times Magazine*, "I heard somebody say there, 'If you're willing to change your thinking, you can change your life.'"[6] That moment was a turning point for Hay. "My jaw dropped. I said, '*Really?*' And I, who had never been a student, became an avid reader."[7] Hay devoured metaphysical texts by the likes of Florence Scovel Shinn, as well as twentieth-century mysticism, and she was particularly inspired by Norman Vincent Peale. Peale's book *The Power of Positive Thinking* sold several million copies after its release in 1952, arguing that positive thinking could give people both confidence and control over their lives. Hay immersed herself in writings on metaphysics and healing, and within a few years she became a practitioner of the First Church of Religious Science, traveling around the country giving classes and leading self-affirmation sessions.

Hay's beliefs were put to the test when she was diagnosed with cervical cancer in the late 1970s. Hay had come to believe in a strong mind-body connection whereby past traumas could manifest in a physical ailment, and she immediately blamed her cancer on her history of sexual abuse. "With my background of being raped at five and having been a battered child, it was no wonder I manifested cancer in the vaginal area,"[8] she would later write. She decided to delay the surgery recommended by doctors and first try to treat herself through alternative methods, including a steady diet of positive thoughts, foot reflexology, therapy to process her childhood, good eating, and enemas three times a week.[9] She claims that six months later she was cured. With this supposed proof in hand, that her regimen of healing through positivity worked, she would soon lay out her philosophy around health and wellness in her 1984 book, *You Can Heal Your Life*.

While some of her beliefs—including the idea that positivity could help cure cancer—were far-fetched, much of the book fits into a far older tradition of American magical thinking. *You Can Heal Your Life* included many of the same themes as earlier American how-to books, including personal responsibility and the power of optimism. It also touches on the same problems that plague people today, from feelings of worthlessness and imposter syndrome to a sense of being stuck in old patterns of negative thinking. *You Can Heal Your Life* laid out a road map for becoming a happier, more fulfilled individual. The goal was not just self-acceptance but self-love, and Hay's solutions for accomplishing that included self-affirmations, positive thinking, and visualization of the future. The book is structured as a journey of self-discovery, from diagnosis of problems any reader might be facing, to a path to change, and finally to ongoing maintenance of this new, positive outlook.

In reframing her own trauma as part of the path to enlightenment, Hay crafted a structure for others to do the same, creating this metaphysical update of the doctrine of positivity. Many of the books across these chapters were forged in their authors' suffering, but Hay's philosophy explicitly addressed the pain that she and so many of her readers—women, in particular—had experienced. She helped bring the kind of trauma usually hidden away, from sexual violence to child abuse, out into the open. It's one aspect that sets her book apart from earlier American optimism, this embrace of the darkness in order to move toward the light. In that way, self-help books can serve an important social purpose, dispelling shame around some of the taboo topics that plague millions of Americans. It should be unsurprising, then, that Hay first earned national recognition for her work around one of the most taboo topics of the 1980s: HIV/AIDS.

❀

On many Wednesday nights throughout the 1980s, hundreds of people packed into a West Hollywood auditorium. Often, the space was so crowded that attendees spilled out into the lobby. The audience was comprised mostly of young gay men, a few family members, and what one attendee called "the worried well."[10] The worried well were friends or lovers who were not yet sick but lived in dread of a cough, a fever, or a lesion on their skin that would confirm what they all feared: AIDS.[11] Most of the men present were in their twenties or thirties, but some were so emaciated by the disease that they looked like old men.[12] They came from across the Los Angeles area for a "Hayride"—the chance to see Louise Hay speak.

It was Mark S. King's brother's boyfriend's idea to go see Hay one Wednesday in the late eighties, and King was reluctant. King had been diagnosed with HIV in 1985, as soon as the first tests came out. At the Hayride that night, he was wary of the massage tables, the crystals, and the hippie spirituality of Hay's New Age message of self-love, but he was willing to try just about anything once, he said.[13] Especially in the years before AZT was first used as a treatment, AIDS was a death sentence—and a quick one at that. Seemingly overnight, King had gone from spending his weekends dancing in L.A. nightclubs to holding a friend's hand in the ICU while he died. Suddenly, tens of thousands of young people in the United States saw their adult lives condensed into a year or two. Between 1980 and 2000, more than 1 million Americans would be infected with HIV.[14] With his diagnosis hanging over his head, King felt a longing both for meaning and for comfort. He sought answers to life's big questions but was unable to explore the traditional channels of major religions, as many churches shunned gay people more violently than ever before. "Living during that time meant facing all of these very deep, important questions about life and death and mortality and God,"[15] he told me.

King has trouble recalling exactly what Hay said that night, but he does remember how it made him feel: accepted and loved. Hay, middle-aged and wearing a flowing outfit with a scarf knotted around her neck, looked like everyone's estranged mom, he said. And she was there telling them, "You are loved." Sometimes it was one of the last things the men in that room heard. "Many of those guys in wheelchairs going to a Louise Hayride could take comfort in that, internalize it, and believe it before they died," he said. King went to several Hayrides, but he never became a Hay devotee. Some attendees there had read every one of her books, and others still were active skeptics. King would not learn of some of her more bizarre and damaging views— including the idea that gay men might contract AIDS because they did not love themselves enough—until much later in life.

Despite some of her fringe beliefs, Hay's influence as "Queen of the New Age"[16] was undeniable. Some have credited her with changing the spiritual landscape of the United States,[17] and her New Age books about positive thinking and self-love attracted an audience far broader than gay men in Los Angeles. The Hayrides led to her being invited onto both Oprah Winfrey's show and Phil Donahue's show in the same week in 1988. After those two television interviews, *You Can Heal Your Life* immediately became a *New York Times* bestseller. It would stay on *The New York Times* bestseller list for several months. Those interviews launched her from a small-time guru in Carlsbad, California, to a national phenom in the course of a few days. Within the next several years, she created a vast empire whose lectures, seminars, and other products grossed $100 million annually by 2007.[18] The New Age in the 1960s may have been anti-capitalist, but by the 1980s it had fully embraced consumerism, becoming a multimillion-dollar industry. Fellow New Age practitioner Wayne Dyer rivaled Hay in sales with his earlier book *Your Erroneous Zones*, but what set Hay apart was the publishing company she founded, Hay House. That publisher would go on to launch or shape the careers of some of the most famous and bestselling self-help gurus of the twentieth century—including Dyer himself—along with Eckhart Tolle, Deepak Chopra, Marianne Williamson, and even Suze Orman. Hay House still produces multiple bestselling books nearly every year. Hay's influence extended beyond her own accomplishments and spidered out into the lives of the many other bestselling authors she would inspire and publish.

Part of what resonated with so many Americans in Hay's philosophy—and those like hers—was the power of positive thinking. While her take on the idea was much more metaphysical than, say, Dale Carnegie's, the underpinning was similar: you might not be able to control what happens to you, but you can control how you think about it. Hay arguably took Carnegie's brand of positivity one step further by arguing that not only can you make your present more bearable with positivity; your thoughts can metaphysically attract good things to you in the future. Her book encouraged readers to do self-affirmations in the mirror, designed to ingrain the habit of self-love and self-acceptance. A new way of living is planted in the seeds of affirmations, Hay wrote, and "you let the sunshine of positive thoughts beam on it. You weed the garden by pulling out the negative thoughts that come up."[19] Hay is sometimes credited with making affirmations a widespread practice, and even *Saturday Night Live* skewered the practice of mirror affirmations in a parody sketch series. Oprah would note how the directive to "love yourself" was so omnipresent that it became a part of 1980s pop culture. Hay's book brought traditional American ideas about optimism into the 1980s context, responding to the corporatization of America with metaphysical spirituality. At the same time, the roots of Hay's philosophy represented a contemporary update of much older ideas about optimism and the importance of self-fulfillment—what other nation includes "the pursuit of happiness" in its founding document? Where the positive thinker of the early twentieth century carried on in the face of adversity, the new self-made man was all-powerful, almost godlike. Hay's solution to the loneliness of 1970s and 1980s individualism—the "Me Generation"—popularized the idea of an interconnected and benevolent universe, the perfect response to a world that could feel increasingly corporate and lonely.

At the center of her vision—and many New Age philosophies like it—was a thoroughly refreshed version of individualism. The self-made man became a self that could be not only slowly improved but mastered. Throughout the book, Hay returns often to the idea of personal power. "We are each responsible for all of our experiences,"[20] she writes within the first few pages of the book. The idea of personal responsibility resurfaces in nearly every American self-help book—from *The Autobiography of Benjamin Franklin* to *How to Win Friends and Influence People*—but Hay pushed the limits of that notion. Hay's book made explicit what earlier advice books only suggested: that all Americans deserved what they got because there was nothing more powerful than the self. Everything about the New Age—and about self-help in general—situates the individual as the site of power. The glorification of the individual is so omnipresent in New Age books from this era that some religious critics even accused followers of the movement of essentially praying to the self, engaging in a form of individualism so extreme that it became a form of self-idolatry. If the individual was all-powerful, capable of curing even their own cancer, were they not claiming to be a kind of god? That latter belief, while seemingly bizarre and potentially harmful, is essentially American meritocracy taken to its most extreme possible end.

You Can Heal Your Life renewed belief in the American success story and the power of the individual, but it held on to the same traps that had always been endemic to both. The promise made by New Age thinking is essentially the same as that of the United States: that anyone can transcend the circumstances into which they were born. The dark side of that belief is the same shadow that has hung over every book promising to deliver readers into their self-made-man success stories: those who fail must be responsible for their failures. There is nothing outside the self, so the self is the root of any problem, from poverty to cancer. Hay in particular could wade into disturbing territory, sometimes appearing to blame people for the violence or disease that caused their suffering. Even this metaphysical understanding of individualism remained limited by the same constraints, causing Americans to feel culpable for everything that happened to them—good or bad.

The undercurrent of individualism was just one aspect of many that made New Age thinking not a fringe element to American culture but the embodiment of some of its core beliefs. "There is something about the freedom of the individual, the expansiveness, the idea of renewal, a kind of favored nation thing that does start to bubble away in the American context,"[21] said Dr. Steven Sutcliffe, a senior lecturer in the study of religion at the University of Edinburgh and author of several books on New Age social history. New Age thinking encompasses a wide umbrella of people and teachings, but they tend to share a few core principles, many of which echo existing American mythology. There was the democratic underpinning: many of the books and teachings are based on personal experience, not hierarchical expertise. The gurus are not trained professionals such as imams and priests, and their function is not to dictate to people but to guide them to their own personal path of self-discovery. The New Age can be understood as a pop spirituality, built not by any singular institution but by the people and for the people. Another New Age expert described it as a kind of "broad folk religion."[22] New Age philosophy offered a very American update of religion, clearing out old hierarchies in favor of something more grassroots.

New Age believers, with their crystals and vision boards, are often dismissed out of hand by cynics, but belief in metaphysical religion has been central to American spiritual life from the very start.[23] Throughout our history, many Americans—from Ralph Waldo Emerson to William James—have found wisdom and comfort in metaphysical beliefs. William James, for instance, the "father of American psychology," believed in the "mind-cure," or the healing power of positivity. Transcendentalism, with its emphasis on intuition and individual potential, was New Agey, too. New Age philosophy is the culmination of all these alternative spiritualities throughout the course of American history, one historian argued. "All the pieces of American metaphysical history came together in the New Age—Transcendentalism and spiritualism, mesmerism and Swedenborgianism, Christian Science and New Thought, Theosophy and its ubiquitous spinoffs,"[24] wrote Catherine L. Albanese, an expert in American religious history. Those beliefs were simply adapted to the particular type of precarity that defined the lives of many Americans in the 1980s and 1990s. New Age responds very much to its time, but it also comes out of this long tradition in American thought of rebelling against existing religious practices and believing in the expansive power of the self.

New Age beliefs started to take shape around the 1950s—although back then they tended to be focused on UFO sightings—but they went from being a fringe practice to being an increasingly mainstream one by the 1970s and into the 1980s. And they've only become more entrenched in popular culture over time. As *The New York Times Magazine* wrote in 2008, "Though you may not know it, you live in Louise Hay's world."[25]

To a certain extent, we are still living in Louise Hay's world. Thanks to the ubiquity of Hay House, her thumbprint is everywhere, whether we think of ourselves as New Age or not: baby boomers who have never consulted a tarot card might have read Suze Orman's bestselling book *The Ultimate Retirement Guide for 50+*, published by Hay House in 2020. In any given year, Hay House still has multiple bestsellers on the *New York Times* list, on topics ranging from success at work to healthy eating. What's more, so many beliefs and practices that were once deemed New Age (many of them originating in Eastern spirituality) have become so integrated into mass culture now that they're not even seen as "alternative" any longer. Hay was an early believer in yoga and meditation—practices once considered fringe that have become hugely popular in the past few decades, in part because of the widespread nature of the New Age.

Belief in New Age philosophy even extends to the highest office in the land. Norman Vincent Peale—the author of *The Power of Positive Thinking*, which so inspired Louise Hay at the beginning of her spiritual journey—was Donald Trump's childhood pastor. Peale's teachings were crucial in the foundation of Trump's earliest beliefs. His family drove from Queens to Manhattan on Sundays just to hear Peale preach, and Trump could still remember those sermons decades later, saying "You could listen to him all day long. And when you left the church, you were disappointed it was over."[26] Peale's philosophy of relentless positivity offers a strangely poignant window into understanding Trump's character. Taken to its most extreme, the sense of self put forward by the New Age can begin to explain Trump's unflinching self-confidence and his unwavering belief in his own ability, even at moments when he's presented with overwhelming evidence to the contrary. When one's sense of self becomes purely a question of belief, no level of outside input or negative feedback can make any difference—it's where self-worth becomes self-worship. Even for people who never read a Louise Hay book—those who have not heard of Wayne Dyer or Norman Vincent Peale—their books shaped many of the people whose policies shape us.

You Can Heal Your Life combined all these different themes that are entrenched in American mythology—self-improvement, individualism, and positivity—and repackaged them into this new understanding of the self that was ideally suited to its time. It drew together ecumenical spirituality and old-fashioned success tropes to present an ideal American that was all-powerful, all-positive—and even a little magical—creating the perfect late twentieth-century update of the self-made man. The book responded to the new challenges of contemporary American life with this much older metaphysical ethos, creating a bootstrap spirituality for 1980s America.

❀

Much like Louise Hay and her Hayrides, Stephen Covey's initial success was rooted in his power as a public speaker. Where Hay's stage was a West Hollywood auditorium, Dr. Covey preached from conference centers across the United States and at his Covey Leadership Center in Provo, Utah, opened in 1984. Covey made a name for himself by training other leaders in the business world, but much of his skill as a public speaker came from another source entirely: his experience as a Mormon missionary. Covey was a devout Mormon, and one of his earliest public speaking experiences came while he was living as a missionary in England. Later, at Harvard Business School, when other students spent their free time at the local bars, Covey preached about Jesus from a wooden box in Boston Common.[27] By the time he was training CEOs in the 1980s, his message had no overt traces of Mormonism. The book was, however, clearly grounded in its author's understanding of Christian morality, drawing on values such as temperance and humility,[28] among others. Covey's use of business jargon could serve as a vehicle for spiritual ideas, and many who met him described an almost mystical touch to the way he moved through the world. Tom Peters, a fellow management guru and author of the bestselling book *In Search of Excellence*, said Covey had a spiritual magnetism. "I really felt like I was in the presence of a holy man. There was a certain gentleness, and there was a certain aura,"[29] Peters told me.

In that way, much like Hay, even the most mainstream authors had an interest in the divine—as the metaphysical and the transcendental found their way into 1980s pop culture in some surprising places. Even in this consumerist, rational time—or perhaps especially in that time—people were turning to much older ways of thinking, reshaping them to match this new context. Covey's work, while thoroughly late twentieth-century in its approach to business and productivity, was rooted in something much deeper and more ancient—not just the Bible but also some of the most important books in this canon.

Covey had spent years researching what he called "success literature," poring over hundreds of manuals, self-help books, and get-rich-quick books in order to write a Ph.D. dissertation on advice books across approximately the first two hundred years of American history. That research would form the basis of *The 7 Habits of Highly Effective People*. In writing his own book, one of Covey's touchstones that he returned to again and again was *The Autobiography of Benjamin Franklin*. Covey longed for a return to what he called the "character ethic"—something he saw as embodied in Franklin—with values such as "integrity, humility, fidelity, temperance, courage, justice, patience, industry, simplicity, modesty, and the Golden Rule."[30] Covey's seven habits feel explicitly drawn from Franklin's thirteen virtues, with both offering a framework to create lasting moral change. The first three habits were about becoming more independent: being proactive, making a plan for the goal you want and how to get there. The second three were about becoming more "interdependent," or learning how to cooperate with others at work or in your community. The seventh habit, "sharpen the saw," teaches readers that—much like Franklin's "project for moral perfection"—the process is ongoing and requires constant renewal through fitness, rest, and spiritual uplift. Like many of the authors whose work is profiled in this collection, Covey explicitly told readers that his text was much more than a book: it was a philosophy to be read and reread, practiced constantly, and taught to others. "I would recommend that you not 'see' this material as a book, in the sense that it is something to read once and put on a shelf," he wrote. He urged readers to instead understand it as a "continual process of change and growth."[31]

Covey's mixture of old and new, morality and money-making, resonated on a huge scale: *The 7 Habits of Highly Effective People* became one of the bestselling management books of all time, selling more than 40 million copies and earning a spot on the *New York Times* bestseller list for 220 weeks. Much like Hay, Covey is important not only for his personal contributions to this type of canon, but also for the way he inspired many hugely successful people to follow in his footsteps, from Martha Beck to Tony Robbins. Covey's legacy is evident in the business world writ large, too, with much of its lingua franca rooted in the jargon popularized by his book, from "win-win" to "proactive," "synergize," and "paradigm shift."[32] Even in 2020, the book continued to sell a staggering five thousand copies per week in North America alone, according to leadership at FranklinCovey.[33] Hundreds of thousands of people continue to write glowing reviews of the book online, with many calling it "life-changing."

The 7 Habits of Highly Effective People ostensibly taught readers how to be leaders, arguing for a kind of American individualism that was both ethical and efficient. This is an integral part of the "good American" story: that everybody can be a leader, that every man has heroism within him. Covey defined success for millions of people, reinforcing and updating ideas such as self-improvement, the power of your mindset, and the responsibility of the individual in shaping his own destiny. *The 7 Habits of Highly Effective People* created the perfect American marriage of capitalism and a kind of ecumenical spirituality—mixing Benjamin Franklin–era ideas with 1980s prosperity doctrine to create a thoroughly contemporary self-made man. Beyond the surface-level corporate material, Covey's philosophy was more expansive than a traditional understanding of success: it urged readers not to follow a list of steps blindly but to reexamine their very ways of thinking, to question not just what they did in the world but how they conceived of themselves and others within that world. In that way, it also represents a widening of the lens of this type of canonical advice book.

The book first landed on the *New York Times* bestseller list in the fall of 1990, but it was very much a product of the 1980s. It responded to some of the same fundamental anxieties and cultural shifts that had put Louise Hay on that same list just two years prior, such as job instability, the erosion of social programs, and a sense of general insecurity around jobs and families. "It just hit an inflection point where I think people were yearning for: How do I save my marriage? How do I save my kid? How do I save my business? What do I need to do differently?"[34] Scott Miller, an executive vice president at Franklin-Covey who worked with Covey for nearly twenty years, told me. At the same time, 1980s conservativism and the desire to access what one historian referred to as "an accelerating celebration of wealth"[35] created an expanding number of people who felt that they, too, could tap into some of the free-flowing prosperity of the era. While Covey's book was not explicitly about getting rich, it seemed to cater to a certain kind of young professional, and now more than 75 percent of Fortune 500 companies pay for Covey leadership training each year. That number alone is part of how "effective" Covey was: much like how the McGuffey Readers taught dozens of presidents and powerful businessmen alongside their millions of average readers, *The 7 Habits of Highly Effective People* deeply influenced many of the people who shape the American economy. Paradoxically, Covey's book also represented an inherent critique of leadership of the business world of the day. The 1980s had seen insider trading scandals, the collapse of multiple criminal banks, and a savings and loan fiasco that put the very basis of the U.S. financial system at risk.[36] In arguing for the necessity of moral leadership, Covey seemed to recognize that there was a present lack of it in the business world.

The foundation of creating moral leadership was built on personal responsibility, according to Covey. The heart of his bestselling book—deeply rooted in American mythology—was that you control your life. Where Hay encouraged people to heal their lives, Covey said that people could choose their response to situations, regardless of how dire. Covey did not tread into the New Age vision of an all-powerful self who could attract good or bad things his way; rather, he argued that humans' power lay in their ability to choose their response to any given situation. He even took the example of a friend who was dying of cancer and who chose to spend her last few weeks writing the history of her life and recording messages for her children. Terminal disease might be one of those life events over which we have no control, but Covey found himself awed by her courage. In his writing and lectures, he also makes frequent reference to Viktor Frankl, the Holocaust survivor who believed that we can choose our attitude to the things that happen to us—no matter how violent—and therefore choose our lives. That we can decide to create meaning, even in seemingly hopeless circumstances, is an attempt to give the power back to each individual—an idea that Covey argued was liberating. At the same time, this extreme version of personal responsibility—the command to be proactive even when we're dying—is a heavy burden.

A sizable chunk of Covey's book deals with suffering: not just death and disease but also more mundane frustration and a lack of meaning. The discomfort that Covey addressed in his book was the idea that life lacks not just certainty but coherence: as he points out, we can be ostensibly successful and still feel empty. What his book offered—much like self-help in general—was structure instead of certain happiness, a way of imposing cohesion on a chaotic world. Positivity is a fundamental part of the American mindset, and therein lies something that Covey realized: relentless optimism breeds its discontents. Unlike the authors of earlier success literature, Covey seemed to recognize that the pursuit of happiness long put forward by any number of advice books—and even the Constitution—was not always within reach. Whether because of disease, poverty, or any variety of suffering, "happiness" is not a perennial option. Purpose, however, might be.

Covey thereby brought Franklin's belief that reasonable creatures can "find or make a Reason for everything one has a mind to do"[37] to new heights. His philosophy pushed Franklin's version of self-reliance one step further: arguing for an individual who not only made the most of whatever came his way but used proactivity to create his own opportunities. This vision of proactivity and work ethic was a way of restoring people's personal power, reaffirming the core American belief that each person is free to choose his or her own life. Especially in an era of mass layoffs, when job instability became the "price of becoming more competitive,"[38] many Americans felt afflicted by a persistent lack of agency. This freedom of the mind was seemingly the last and only option for empowerment—and it resonated tremendously. Perhaps that's why the book has continued to maintain its popularity: as that kind of precarity in the job market persists—and has arguably accelerated in recent years—many workers may increasingly feel that they have no choice but to make their own opportunities.

Covey's book encouraged readers to go on a path to self-discovery that was based not on self-affirmation but on questioning their core beliefs, their "paradigms." Early on, for instance, he gives the example of a quiet New York City subway car one Sunday morning. Covey and the others around him are calmly reading or resting—until a father with his children boards the subway car. The children are loud and obnoxious, but the father sits there with his eyes closed until Covey's own irritation mounts to the point where he asks the man politely if he might control his children. The man responds softly, almost in a daze: "I guess I should do something about it. We just came from the hospital where their mother died about an hour ago. I don't know what to think, and I guess they don't know how to handle it either."[39] Covey described this interaction as a "paradigm shift": a moment that leads to a complete flip in understanding. This is what's radical about self-help books in general and about Covey's in particular: self-help is sometimes dismissed as the opiate of the masses, containing platitudes and ready-

made meaning, but the most successful books in this genre encourage people to question their own beliefs and to look at
things in a new way. Even if self-help books themselves tend to
offer some kind of prescription or a one-size-fits-all doctrine,
they encourage people to go on their own "journey." The book
may be offering suggestions, but there is a real mandate for readers to look at how they perceive the world, what they value, what
their priorities are, and what they want out of life. Covey even
encouraged more New Age practices such as visualization and
self-talk as part of this self-discovery.[40] By combining all these
various sources of wisdom—from scriptures to visualization—
Covey expanded the tools for self-discovery, widening both the
path to American success and its very definition.

In that way—underneath all its jargon—*The 7 Habits of
Highly Effective People* has a hint of *The Old Farmer's Almanac* in
its invitation to observe the world around us more closely.
Where *The Almanac* encouraged readers to count acorns, Covey
spoke of paradigms, but both philosophies called for a similar
kind of attention to detail. They share this notion that the answer might lie in the little things. Part of what self-help urges—
and what the good American is supposed to do, according to
these books—is to look at the clues of life as if he were a doctor
or detective. It is an attempt to turn the raw material of the everyday into a cohesive vision of the world and ourselves within
it. There is a grandiosity in this kind of thinking: that we can all
uncover something new, see what others do not, and be the heroes in our own lives (a mode of thinking that can also potentially open the door to con men and quacks). At the same time

there's a paradoxical humbleness to it, too, a calling to go back to basics, to take a closer look at the building blocks of habit and instinct.

Covey's vision of proactivity and paradigm shifts was bipartisan. While it seemed to resonate especially with corporate readers and MBA candidates, its readership was far broader than just that bloc. President Bill Clinton invited Covey to Camp David. The impetus to constantly improve transcends political parties. "You have to maintain your skills and update them. You're always engaged in self-training and in lifelong learning. . . . This became the mantra not just for conservatives but for a lot of people who were considered liberals as well,"[41] said Dr. Doug Rossinow, historian and author of the book *The Reagan Era: A History of the 1980s*. The uncertainty of the era and of the job market in particular engendered a culture of self-improvement that existed for everyone, where "retraining" and "refreshing skills" became prerequisites for just staying in the game of work or even love. "It would make perfect sense for self-help gurus, who were offering advice about continuing to update your skills and employability, to find a ready audience. People were not really hearing about any alternative to that,"[42] Rossinow said. Whether on the Left or the Right, politicians of the day continued to insist that people's individual power would determine their success or failure more than any federal policy, or national "paradigm shift," as it were.

Like many advice books before it, *The 7 Habits of Highly Effective People* mostly ignores systems of power that exist outside our immediate control, whether they be economic downturn or systemic prejudice. What was left unsaid in the book was that mastering all of Covey's skills might not prevent an employee from being laid off. A fundamental belief in American culture is personal freedom, but total agency as an individual does not exist in American society—and even less so within Covey's corporate audience. By taking personal responsibility, individual workers can certainly make themselves more attractive as employees, and they may even be able to advance to higher positions. But that straight line from proactivity to job promotion starts to fall apart when you tread into the territory of race, gender, and social class. For instance, a Black woman might follow all of Covey's advice by focusing on her character building and becoming a highly proactive employee. But if she has a boss affected by internal—even unconscious—biases, she may never advance to the levels of her white male colleagues, no matter how "effective" she is. She may even feel personally responsible for that failure outside of her control. Self-improvement is not made to address existing systems of racism and misogyny. Much like Carnegie's *How to Win Friends and Influence People* and Post's *Etiquette*, what Covey's book offered was not a radical overhaul of the system but a way of improving your relationship to that system. The book might not be able to put every reader into the boardroom of a Fortune 500 company, but it might allow a working-class person to become middle-class or help an employee of a company get promoted to middle management. Self-help is a game of marginal gains.

Covey's understanding of the relationship between the individual and his company, family, and community was what he called "interdependence." In a way that diverges from so many books about success, Covey wrote that independence should not be a reader's highest aspiration. Rather, people could achieve far more by working together. "Life is, by nature, highly interdependent. To try to achieve maximum effectiveness through independence is like trying to play tennis with a golf club—the tool is not suited to the reality,"[43] he wrote. By all accounts, Covey practiced this kind of teamwork in all areas of his life: along with his wife and his nine kids, he even created a mission statement for the family that hung on their living room wall. In interdependence, there was a recognition of individual limitations, even fallibility, in a way that rarely happens in this type of literature. Covey's book got rid of some of the loneliness of these old success archetypes by adding in this new layer of community.

Interdependence has actually been fundamental to American success, even if it's rarely part of our mythology. So many of the Americans we revere as individuals were admired because of their leadership skills, something that relied on their ability to ensure cooperation among a group, a community, or an army. Whether it was Benjamin Franklin organizing the philosophical society of the Junto Club or George Washington leading a battalion, their victories came out of the strength of the group they led. As one sociologist pointed out to me, even the archetypical American heroes we inherit have been mistakenly depicted as independent when they were in fact members of broader communities: The "lone cowboy" almost always traveled in a group. The frontiersman seeking his fortune out west was not a lone pioneer—or even a single family—slashing through the forest. He was usually accompanied by an entire caravan of friends and neighbors.[44] Self-help—much like the foundations of American identity—can be lonely and individualistic, and there is something admirable about crafting a philosophy that relies on something or someone outside of the self. Yes, cynics will say that it's a way of asserting social control over people—and to a certain extent Covey's philosophy likely benefits the bosses more than the employees—but when it's taken at its most sincere, interdependence reflects a fundamental truth about American society that has long been diminished: rugged individualism alone is woefully insufficient. Covey's book diverges from many of the books across *Americanon*, arguing that the ultimate goal should be cooperation and not just self-reliance.

⚛

Covey's seventh habit—"sharpen the saw"—was the one that made the rest of it possible. Sharpening the saw was the idea that in order to be "effective," to use Covey's terminology, everyone needs to cultivate his best self with exercise, sleep, nutrition, and spirituality. Like Franklin's system for moral perfection, cultivation of Covey's ideal individual required constant upkeep. Covey took his own advice very seriously, and he started most days the same way: First, he read from the Bible while working out for at least thirty minutes on a stationary bike.[45] From there, it was fifteen minutes of vigorous laps in a swimming pool and then fifteen minutes of yoga in the shallow end of the pool. After his exercise, he retreated to his library to "pray with a listening spirit"[46] and visualize his entire day. "I see myself living by correct principles and accomplishing worthy purposes,"[47] he said of his morning routine in an interview. "Much of this listening and visualizing work is very challenging, so I win the private victory when I have made my mind up and commit to live by correct principles and to serve worthy purposes,"[48] he added. Covey, the man who literally wrote the book on effectiveness, did not believe in shortcuts, but he certainly appreciated efficiency. One observer once saw Covey, a veritable multitasker, lying on the locker room floor of a gym, being sprayed by at least two different showerheads as he attempted to shave and brush his teeth at the same time.[49]

Sharpening the saw was an acknowledgment that readers had a life outside their desire to be successful in business. In that way, Covey complicated the American relationship with productivity, putting into question certain aspects of the work ethic and bringing a more holistic approach than so many other self-help books had done. For instance, Covey put forward the idea that true efficiency is not about getting more things done in less time; it's about prioritizing things that are important. *The 7 Habits of Highly Effective People* popularized the idea of quadrant planning,[50] where each person divides tasks into things that are urgent or not urgent and important or not important. That way, he or she can focus on that which is urgent and important (such as a deadline for a big project) rather than getting lost in what is urgent but not important (sending emails), or not important and not urgent (social media). Sharpening the saw fell into the category of activities that were not urgent but still important. Unlike many earlier books that relied on the American work ethic, *The 7 Habits of Highly Effective People* was not an edict to work ever-longer hours. It encouraged readers to examine their priorities, to look at the ways in which working more did not necessarily mean working better. Contrary to someone such as Tim Ferriss, for instance, and other later gurus who emphasized "life hacking," Covey insisted that there were no shortcuts. Prioritizing simply meant some things would not be done.

Covey essentially transformed Franklin's obsession with "usefulness" to talk about "effectiveness." And our contemporary culture has in turn morphed that into "optimization." In a way that Covey could not have predicted, sharpening the saw may have laid the foundation for our culture's current, almost pathological obsession with health and wellness. In our world of meditation apps and meal-delivery kits, leisure activities have become an integral part of making us more attractive individuals—and doing so in record time. Efficiency has long been our national ethos when it comes to the pursuit of wealth, but we've seemingly tried to adapt that mentality to everything else in our lives, including activities that are meant to be relaxing or fun. As Alexis de Tocqueville observed of Americans when the country was little more than fifty years old, "It is strange to see with what feverish ardour the Americans pursue their own welfare; and to watch the vague dread that constantly torments them lest they should not have chosen the shortest path which may lead to it."[51] Americans today seem tormented by that same vague dread not just about making money but about shaping the commodity that has become ourselves. Americans shuttle between their office and CrossFit gym, stopping only to refuel with a green juice, fearing that they are not getting healthy enough fast enough. It's what *New Yorker* staff writer Jia Tolentino described as the mandate to "always be optimizing."[52] Routines that were meant to bring peace now bring a fraught angst, but we keep doing them partially because they have become integral to the story we are telling about ourselves—that we're the kind of people who do yoga every day or cook gourmet meals each night.

Much like our own mythmaking about the American story, the cycle of self-improvement—renewed and repeated throughout our history—is constant. This is at the heart of both Covey's brand of self-improvement and the many similar business and productivity books that would come after him: the process never ends. It's an idea that is omnipresent in American life—because if you are responsible for your destiny, if only you stand between your current state and a better, more prosperous self, then potentially you could always have more, always be better. It engenders a culture of self-improvement that exists for everyone in the United States, regardless of whether they read this type of literature or not. Even if we don't shop in the self-help aisle, we live in a society that values the acceleration of personal achievement and productivity over nearly anything else. We might not be able to draw a straight line from Franklin's plan for moral perfection to Covey's proactivity to our current obsessions with optimization, but a thread certainly ties them together, as this canon of how-to books and advice continually adds layers to earlier books' frameworks, each book's ideology building the blocks to form the foundation of the next wave of advice literature.

In that way, nothing is ever completely new, but neither do those powerful early stories about American identity entirely disappear. Covey's book came out of several generations of advice books, and those books were built on the advice that came before them. For all of the United States' desire to create a new experiment, it's impossible to build something that has no point of reference. These books scaffold one another, and their values might be reshaped or temporarily lose potency, but the storytelling never goes away. Much like religious practice or Covey's own fitness regimen, an eternity is built into the activity itself.

Epilogue

Whether in 1821 or 2021, Americans tend to respond to uncertainty in much the same way they always have: with a desire for clarity, for absolute truths. The need for definition has not gone away, even if the market for print dictionaries wanes. The difference now is that 30 or 60 or 100 million people might no longer buy the same book to ease their anxiety. Instead, each how-to book today tends to address a far more specific audience than ever before, with books being published on navigating sexism in the corporate world or an evangelical homeschooler's guide to college prep. The authority of reference books (made of paper, held in your hands) has shifted, too. People might turn to Google, to Wikipedia, or even to Quora with the burning how-to questions that they once brought to a domestic manual or a sex book. It is why huge brands like *The Old Farmer's Almanac* and Merriam-Webster have focused increased energy on their online presences, with everything from Twitter accounts to YouTube channels.

Even if today's bestselling how-to books are not consciously thinking about shaping a single definition of American identity in the way that someone like Noah Webster was, they still cannot help but encode messages about Americanness. Language about autonomy or the self-made man is updated to "leaning in" or being a "girlboss," but the core beliefs remain mostly unchanged. Dale Carnegie might not appreciate the comparison, but books such as Rachel Hollis's *Girl, Wash Your Face* bear a striking resemblance in their ability to combine magical thinking, Protestantism, and a can-do attitude. Even books that frame themselves as anti–self-help—*Unfu*k Yourself* or *You Are a Badass*—still build on the same foundation as so many of these books: one of individualism, work ethic, positive thinking, meritocracy, and exceptionalism.

People tend to understand the American story as something to be slowly uncovered, piece by piece, like a natural object. The actual origins of our culture are far more disparate, coming not only from presidents and revolutionaries but also from fanatical schoolteachers and scorned socialites. And the narrative threads they created were there to be picked up by others, braided into new books or fresh updates on old philosophies. There's something a little democratic about the codification of our values through these commonplace books over the course of generations. At the same time, these authors created their books based on a mix of their own personal anxieties and desires, crafting our national narrative with their chosen values. Their books tended to ignore all those elements of our origin story that have been collectively cast aside or violently excised: American mythology tends only to incorporate a certain kind of immigrant story, a very limited number of books from Black communities and writers of color, much less the stories and folklore of Indigenous peoples. Our identity is not organically grown; it is constructed, created piece by piece like jagged shards of pottery being shaped into a mosaic—only to be smashed again and put back together in a slightly new way.

In revisiting these familiar books in this new way, we are forced to look at the unreliable nature of memory. Ralph Ellison described memory and identity as "ever at odds," and in one sense that's true: American identity has long constructed itself through an amnesia about its most definitive and ugliest moments. The stories we tell so frequently about meritocracy, self-reliance, and equality must ignore centuries of slavery, genocide against Indigenous peoples, and the free labor of women. The darkest chapters of our history show up only as subtext in the books featured in these chapters precisely because their violence is incompatible with the story that the United States is telling about itself. The books across *Americanon* often bypassed national mourning or reckoning and instead created idealized visions of the America they inhabited. Whether it was Noah Webster projecting a linguistically superior nation of independence and Christianity, or Dale Carnegie imagining that the cure to even the Great Depression was positivity, these books are not straightforward accounts of the United States but rather constant, mythical retellings, told and retold to the point of feeling like truth. Those myths in turn exhibit a very real pull over our daily reality.

Much like Scheherazade, telling a new story each night so that she might live to see another day, we tell stories to survive.

Mythmaking is the amulet to ward off a national death. The narrative is revised to incorporate new fears and fresh trauma, but the story never goes away. Culture, myth, and identity are fashioned over time—cobbled together in moments of doubt as a way of reassuring ourselves not just of who we were but of who we are. What might it look like to do something new? To give people more questions, less certainty, and a sense of just how vast and ambiguous the term "American" can be—because memory and identity do not necessarily have to be at odds. We have the choice to put to rest a sanitized version of the United States as a country on a hill. I wrote this book because I wanted to grapple with our canon's quirks, its extremes, and even its darkness. It is freeing rather than frightening to see our beliefs not as absolute truths but as stories that we've picked up along the way—because that means we can put some of them down when they no longer serve us, or at least attempt to stop telling the ones that harm us.

The creation of American identity is ongoing, a process that comes from a continual questioning of what this country might represent. Reexamining the tumultuous moments that produced the bestsellers across *Americanon* can feel eerily prescient for our own period in history, one that is increasingly defined by conflict, upheaval, and sheer anxiety. The same cycle plays out: much like Catharine Beecher or William Holmes McGuffey, some swath of the population decries rapid change or fears a loss of culture—without recognizing the fact that culture is being created all the time. Mythology is that way, too: constructed based on fear, hope, and necessity—a kind of trench ingenuity. "We hunger to understand, so we invent myths about how we imagine the world is constructed—and they're, of course, based upon what we know, which is ourselves and other animals," the astronomer Carl Sagan once said. "But we're not fully satisfied with those stories, so we keep broadening the horizon of our myths; and then we discover that there's a totally different way in which the world is constructed, and things originate."[1] This broadening of our mythology's horizons might be the only way to tell a new, truer story, one that does not respond to uncertainty with a rush to create meaning but instead embraces the ambiguity of an ever-changing nation.

Acknowledgments

This book has been such a collective effort that I'm tempted to make this section as long as the chapters themselves. I want to thank my agent, Anna-Sproul Latimer, without whom I would never have thought that writing a book was possible. Her no-nonsense calls, texts, and emails have kept me going. An enormous thank-you to Cassidy Sachs, who is my perfect editor—her brilliance astounds me, and she always has just the right thing to say or the perfect note to put things in perspective. Her astute eye has made this book immeasurably better. Thank you to the entire publicity and marketing team at Dutton, especially Natalie Church, Stephanie Cooper, and Becky Odell. My fact-checkers—Parker Richards and Hannah Steinkopf-Frank—are both incredible. Their thoroughness and attention to detail have put even my very neurotic mind to rest.

The many archives, both private and public, that graciously allowed me access to their trove of books and manuscripts have made this book possible. Digging through old manuscripts and letters is always my favorite part of the writing process, so a big thank-you to the Schlesinger Library at Radcliffe, the Beinecke Rare Book & Manuscript Library at Yale, the American Library in Paris, the American Antiquarian Society, the New York Public Library, the Emily Post Institute, the General Mills archive, and the Dale Carnegie & Associates archive. A special thanks to the many present-day legacy keepers of these books who gave me such a warm welcome into their offices and histories, including Tim Clark, Judson Hale, and Janice Stillman at *The Old Farmer's Almanac*, Peter Sokolowski of Merriam-Webster, Lizzie Post and Daniel Post Senning, Dale Carnegie & Associates, the team at FranklinCovey, and the leadership of Hay House. The Betty Crocker chapter would not have been possible without the open access and tireless efforts of General Mills, especially Natasha Bruns. Being able to read through dozens of personal letters and artifacts related to Betty Crocker was a delight, and Natasha's ability to locate exactly what I was looking for in record time was nothing short of impressive. I can't thank her enough for responding to dozens of emails in the past few years as I refined my research. Both she and the Betty Crocker team were invaluable in assisting me in fact-checking this chapter.

So many historians, sociologists, writers, and experts in literature (by my most recent count, nearing one hundred) have graciously shared their time and expertise with me in the writing of this book. I am grateful to every one of them, all of whom were incredibly gracious and patient in making complex historical figures and periods digestible to a non-historian such as myself. I want to give special thanks to Michael Hattem,

Micki McGee, Trysh Travis, Johann Neem, Allison Speicher, Shelby Balik, Leni Sorensen, Andrea Voyer, and Doug Rossinow. Thank you to Maria Trumpler, who first introduced me to Catharine Beecher's work when I was an undergraduate and who continues to teach and speak about Beecher's legacy in a way that never flattens Beecher's nuance. This book owes a debt of gratitude to the biographers of the authors across *Americanon*, especially Joshua Kendall, Laura Claridge, Walter Isaacson, Kathryn Kish Sklar, Dolores P. Sullivan, and Steven Watts. Thank you to the many people who shared their personal stories with me about their experiences with these books and authors: Marion Schmidt, Kateri Lukkes, Karley Sciortino, Aaron Jagt, Mark S. King, and Colin Clews—I consider it an honor.

Thank you to my mother, who has been the most faithful reader of my writing for a couple decades now. She has very patiently endured many fraught phone calls in the past three years I spent writing this book, and her suggestions on early drafts were some of the most surprisingly frank and constructive I've ever encountered. It was often her voice in my head as I wrote this book, her reminder to see beyond people's flaws and to their humanity. I thank her for my love of literature, and I credit her for imbuing me with a reverence for all books, even the humblest. My father is a wonderful cheerleader who never ceases to beat the drum for my success. He is excellent in a crisis, and I'll never forget him coming to the rescue with great calm and wonderful tacos when I lost many of my early notes in a horrific glass-of-water-meets-laptop crisis early in the writing process of this book. Thank you to Abby, my oldest friend and the best sister there is. You were the first person to hear the news about this book, and I'll never forget celebrating with you. I am grateful to James, the person I'm closest to who can most sympathize with the less-than-fun-and-bohemian aspects of working in the arts; I cherish our conversations about what the hell it is we're doing out here.

Given the nature of this book, I cannot resist thanking all of my familial founding fathers and mothers, the Irish maids and the Italian barbers, who somehow clustered together in New England. To keep this slightly shorter, I'll stick with the most recent. Thanks especially to Elena McHugh, who has been my role model for many years. Since the time I was a child, she made me feel that anything was possible, and she set the example of how to do that. Thank you to David McHugh, who never stopped checking in on me and cracking jokes through one of the most difficult years in our family. Papa may not be the loudest member in our family, but he has a knack for storytelling, too. My maternal grandfather, to whom this book is dedicated, was the George Bailey of his corner of Massachusetts. And thank you to his wife, Katherine, who has kept his memory alive for our family.

I am forever grateful to my wonderfully talented friend Mariah Tyler. From our first days as colleagues at a magazine, she has been a constant source of encouragement. And I can never thank her enough for taking the best author portrait I could have imagined. Her ability to put others at ease and to capture the essence of strangers and friends alike is part of what makes her such an exceptional photographer. I am in her debt. I'd also like to thank all the colleagues, friends, and family who gave me early feedback on drafts of the book, including Zoey,

Hannah, Quentin, my mother, and the members of Study Hall in Paris. A particular thanks to Quentin, who has put up with my dishes molding in the sink and my overall mole-person tendencies while I work. His loving reminders to take a walk, eat something, or just *"arrête un peu"* have kept me from falling into total despair while finishing a first book during a pandemic. Special thanks to dear friends near and far: Eleni Zafiroulis, Julian Debenedetti, Clark Mindock, Pearce Groover, and Christy Savery.

I have been lucky enough to have enjoyed the support and encouragement of several wonderful mentors over the years, especially Jake Halpern and Robert MacPherson. Thank you also to some of the first people who encouraged my writing and made me think being a writer was possible, in particular Briallen Hopper, Carlotta Zilliax, Jessica Bond, and Michaela Steimle.

Thank you also to Philip Glass, who doesn't know me personally but whose music has been playing constantly as I write this book. I thank him, too, for his openness about being an artist with a day job. In that spirit, I want to pour one out for the patrons and staff of Sophie's bar, who supported me in more ways than one while I wrote the proposal that would become this book. The Sunday regulars at Sophie's have been some of my faithful readers for many years, and I owe them a debt of gratitude that a few kickbacks will never repay.

Notes

1. Ralph Ellison, "The Golden Age of Jazz: Time Past," *Esquire*, January 1959.

INTRODUCTION

1. Jill Lepore, "Noah's Mark," *The New Yorker*, October 30, 2006.
2. *Aurora General Advertiser* (Philadelphia), June 9, 1800, cited in Tim Cassedy, "'A Dictionary Which We Do Not Want': Defining America Against Noah Webster, 1783–1810," *The William and Mary Quarterly* 71, no. 2 (2014): 238.
3. "Walker's Criticism," *Polyanthos* (Boston), August 1, 1806, cited in Cassedy, "'A Dictionary Which We Do Not Want,'" 247.
4. "Art. 14," *Monthly Anthology*, May 1808, cited in Cassedy, "'A Dictionary Which We Do Not Want,'" 229.
5. *Marquette Law School Supreme Court Survey* (distributed by Marquette University, 2019), https://law.marquette.edu/poll/wp-content/uploads/2019/10/MULawSC2019Toplines.pdf.
6. *The New York Times* bestseller list; *Publishers Weekly* bestseller list; *Books That Shaped America*, exhibition, Library of Congress, Washington, D.C., June 25–September 29, 2012.
7. *Merriam-Webster.com Dictionary*, s.v. "nostalgia," accessed March 1, 2020, https://www.merriam-webster.com/dictionary/nostalgia.

CHAPTER ONE

1. U.S. Census Bureau, population data (2018), https://www.nhes.nh.gov
    /elmi/products/cp/profiles-htm/dublin.htm.
2. Tim Clark, "100 Ways to Avoid Dying," *The Old Farmer's Almanac*,
    January 1990.
3. Tim Clark, interview by the author, Dublin, NH, September 16, 2019,
    digital recording.
4. Clark interview.
5. Numbers from *The Old Farmer's Almanac*, editor Tim Clark, provided
    June 16, 2020.
6. Clark interview.
7. Maria Leach, S*tandard Dictionary of Folklore, Mythology, and Legend* (New
    York: Funk & Wagnalls, 1972), cited in Clark interview.
8. Clark interview.
9. Judson D. Hale, *The Best of the Old Farmer's Almanac: The First 200 Years*
    (New York: Random House, 1991), 6–9.
10. Jack Larkin, "'Printing Is Something Every Village Has in It': Rural
    Printing and Publishing," in *A History of the Book in America*, vol. 2, *An
    Extensive Republic: Print, Culture, and Society in the New Nation,
    1790–1840*, ed. Robert A. Gross and Mary Kelley (Chapel Hill:
    University of North Carolina Press, 2010), 158.
11. George Kittredge, *The Old Farmer and His Almanack* (Cambridge, MA:
    Harvard University Press, 1904).
12. Kittredge, *Old Farmer*, 4.
13. U.S. Census Bureau, population data (2010), https://www.westboylston
    -ma.gov/about-our-town/pages/demographics.
14. Abigail Tucker, "The Great New England Vampire Panic," *Smithsonian*,
    October 2012.
15. "Black Cats, Lucky Bones and Superstitious New Englanders," New
    England Historical Society, October 25, 2019, https://www
    .newenglandhistoricalsociety.com/black-cats-lucky-bones-superstitious
    -new-englanders/.
16. Robert B. Thomas, *The (Old) Farmer's Almanac 1833* (Boston: Carter,
    Hendree and Co., 1832), cited in Editors of *The Old Farmer's Almanac*,
    "The Life and Times of Robert B. Thomas," *Old Farmer's Almanac*, April
    21, 2020, https://www.almanac.com/extra/life-and-times-robert-b
    -thomas.
17. Adrienne LaFrance, "How *The Old Farmer's Almanac* Previewed the
    Information Age," *The Atlantic*, November 13, 2015, https://www
    .theatlantic.com/technology/archive/2015/11/how-the-old-farmers
    -almanac-previewed-the-information-age/415836/.

18. Catherine Boeckmann, "How the *Old Farmer's Almanac* Predicts the Weather," *The Old Farmer's Almanac*, August 10, 2020, https://www.almanac.com/content/how-old-farmers-almanac-predicts-weather.

19. Kitteridge, *Old Farmer*, 8.

20. Kitteridge, *Old Farmer*, 14.

21. Andrew Wehrman, "Smallpox Inoculation in 18th Century New England" (lecture, Massachusetts Historical Society, Boston, MA, October 25, 2014).

22. Wehrman, "Smallpox Inoculation."

23. Kitteridge, *Old Farmer*, 15.

24. Robert B. Thomas, *The (Old) Farmer's Almanac 1833* (Boston: Carter, Hendree and Co., 1832), cited in Kitteridge, *Old Farmer*, 15.

25. Hale, *Best of the Old Farmer's Almanac*, 6–9.

26. Hale, *Best of the Old Farmer's Almanac*, 6–9.

27. Hale, *Best of the Old Farmer's Almanac*, 16.

28. Robert B. Thomas, *The (Old) Farmer's Almanac 1794* (Boston: Belknap and Hall, 1793, published annually since 1792).

29. Thomas, *(Old) Farmer's Almanac 1794*.

30. Thomas, *(Old) Farmer's Almanac 1794*.

31. John E. Walsh and David Allen, "Testing the Farmer's Almanac," *Weatherwise* 34, no. 5 (1981): 212–15.

32. Clark interview.

33. Clark interview.

34. Clark interview.

35. Clark interview.

36. LaFrance, "How *The Old Farmer's Almanac*."

37. Clark interview.

38. LaFrance, "How *The Old Farmer's Almanac*."

39. Robert B. Thomas, *The Old Farmer's Almanac 1793* (Boston: Manning & Loring, 1792).

40. Robert B. Thomas, *The Old Farmer's Almanac 1800* (Boston: Manning & Loring, 1799, published annually since 1792).

41. Thomas, *Old Farmer's Almanac 1800*.

42. Thomas, *Old Farmer's Almanac 1800*.

43. J. Hector St. John de Crèvecoeur, *Letters from an American Farmer: Describing Certain Provincial Situations, Manners, and Customs, Not Generally Known* (Dublin, Ireland: John Exshaw, 1782).

44. Thomas Jefferson, *Notes on the State of Virginia* (Boston: Lilly and Wait, 1832), pdf, https://www.loc.gov/item/03004902/.

45. Jefferson, *Notes*.

46. "About Our Town: History," Town of West Boylston, MA, n.d., https://www.westboylston-ma.gov/about-our-town/pages/history.

47. Roxanne Dunbar-Ortiz, *An Indigenous Peoples' History of the United States* (Boston: Beacon Press, 2014), 1.

48. Robb Sagendorph, *America and Her Almanacs* (Dublin, NH: Yankee Publishing Company, 1970), 31.

49. David J. Silverman, *This Land Is Their Land: The Wampanoag Indians, Plymouth Colony, and the Troubled History of Thanksgiving* (New York: Bloomsbury, 2019), 137.

50. Jill Lepore, *These Truths* (New York: W. W. Norton, 2018), 56.

51. Lepore, *These Truths*.

52. Laura Miles, "From Tablet to Tablet: A History of the Book," University of Michigan, n.d., https://sites.google.com/a/umich.edu/from-tablet-to -tablet/home.

53. Miles, "From Tablet to Tablet."

54. Miles, "From Tablet to Tablet."

55. Allan R. Raymond, "To Reach Men's Minds: Almanacs and the American Revolution, 1760–1777," *The New England Quarterly* 51, no. 3 (1978): 370–95.

56. Raymond, "To Reach Men's Minds."

57. Raymond, "To Reach Men's Minds."

58. Robert B. Thomas, *The Old Farmer's Almanac 1864* (Boston: Brewer & Tileston, 1863, published annually since 1792).

59. Robert B. Thomas, *The Old Farmer's Almanac 1846* (Boston: Jenks & Palmer, 1845, published annually since 1792).

60. Robert B. Thomas, *The Old Farmer's Almanac* (Boston: various publishers, 1792—).

61. Robert B. Thomas, *The Old Farmer's Almanac 1847* (Boston: Jenks & Palmer, 1846, published annually since 1792).

62. Judson Hale, "Predicting Snow for the Summer of 1816," *The Old Farmer's Almanac*, August 4, 2016, https://www.almanac.com/content/predicting -snow-summer-1816.

63. Paul W. Gates, "Problems of Agricultural History, 1790–1840," *Agricultural History* 46, no. 1 (1972): 33–58, www.jstor.org/stable /3741556.

64. Hale, *Best of the Old Farmer's Almanac*, 7.

65. Robert B. Thomas, quoted in *The Old Farmer's Almanac* (Dublin, NH: Yankee Publishing, 2012).

66. Samuel Green, "The Founder of the Old Farmer's Almanac," in *The Best of the Old Farmer's Almanac*, ed. Will Forpe (Middle Village, NY: Jonathan David Publishers, 1977), 4.

67. Hale, *Best of the Old Farmer's Almanac*, 26.

68. Hale, *Best of the Old Farmer's Almanac*, 26.

69. Editors of *The Old Farmer's Almanac*, "History of *The Old Farmer's Almanac*," *Old Farmer's Almanac* online, August 4, 2016, https://www .almanac.com/content/history-old-farmers-almanac.

70. Hale, *Best of the Old Farmer's Almanac*, 41.

71. "History of *The Old Farmer's Almanac*."

72. "History of *The Old Farmer's Almanac*."

73. L. H. Robbins, "Counselor & Friend," *The New York Times*, March 9, 1947, sec. SM, 18, https://www.nytimes.com/1947/03/09/archives /counselor-friend-the-farmers-almanac-has-offered-wisdom-wit-and.html.

74. Editors of *The Old Farmer's Almanac*, "Supplying Information to the Enemy," *The Old Farmer's Almanac*, March 8, 2019, https://www.almanac .com/content/supplying-information-enemy.

75. Editors of *The Old Farmer's Almanac*, "Supplying Information."

76. "History of *The Old Farmer's Almanac*."

77. Judson D. Hale, phone interview by the author, Paris, October 16, 2019, digital recording.

78. "Robb Sagendorph, 69, Publisher of Farmer's Almanac Is Dead," *The New York Times*, July 6, 1970, https://www.nytimes.com/1970/07/06/archives /robb-sagendorph-69-publisher-of-farmers-almanac-is-dead-served-a .html.

79. "Robb Sagendorph."

80. "Robb Sagendorph"; Robbins, "Counselor & Friend."

81. Robbins, "Counselor & Friend."

82. Hale interview.

83. Robbins, "Counselor & Friend."

84. Robbins, "Counselor & Friend."

85. Robbins, "Counselor & Friend."

86. Robbins, "Counselor & Friend."

87. Hale interview.

88. Hale interview.

89. Hale interview.

90. "Introducing . . . YANKEE," New England Today, *Yankee*, November 9, 2018, https://newengland.com/yankee-magazine/living/new-england -history/introducing-yankee/.

91. Robbins, "Counselor & Friend."

92. Robbins, "Counselor & Friend."

93. Hale interview.

94. Janice Stillman, phone interview by the author, Paris, October 9, 2020, digital recording.

95. Leni Sorensen, phone interview by the author, Paris, October 25, 2019, digital recording.

96. Stephanie Leydon, "How a Long-Ago Map Created Racial Boundaries That Still Define Boston," GBH News, November 13, 2019.
97. Richard Hofstadter, "The Myth of the Happy Yeoman," *American Heritage*, April 1956.
98. Statistic from the American Farm Bureau Federation, "Fast Facts About Agriculture & Food," Voice of Agriculture—American Farm Bureau Federation, 2019, https://www.fb.org/newsroom/fast-facts.
99. Clark interview.

CHAPTER TWO

1. Joshua Kendall, *The Forgotten Founding Father: Noah Webster's Obsession and the Creation of an American Culture* (New York: G.P. Putnam's Sons, 2010), 77.
2. Kendall, *Forgotten Founding Father*, 78.
3. Harry R. Warfel, *Noah Webster: Schoolmaster to America* (New York: Macmillan Company, 1936), 53.
4. Noah Webster, *A Collection of Papers on Political, Literary, and Moral Subjects* (New York: Webster & Clark, 1843), 309.
5. Warfel, *Noah Webster*, 53.
6. Jesse Sheidlower, "Noah Webster, Founding Father," *The New York Times*, May 27, 2011.
7. Noah Webster, *The American Spelling Book, Containing an Easy Standard of Pronunciation: Being the First Part of a Grammatical Institute of the English Language* (Boston: Thomas and Andrews, 1783), 87.
8. Webster, *American Spelling Book*, 148.
9. Kendall, *Forgotten Founding Father*, 84.
10. Noah Webster, *A Grammatical Institute of the English Language, Part I* (Hartford, CT: Hudson & Goodwin, 1783), 162.
11. Webster, *Grammatical Institute*, 6.
12. Webster, *Grammatical Institute*, preface.
13. Noah Webster, "Essays Against Abbé Raynal," cited in Warfel, *Noah Webster: Schoolmaster to America* (New York: Macmillan, 1936), 47–49.
14. Kendall, *Forgotten Founding Father*, 79.
15. Webster, "On the Education of Youth in America," *American Magazine* (New York), December 1787.
16. Webster, "On the Education."
17. *Merriam-Webster.com Dictionary*, s.v. "nationalism," accessed January 17, 2020, https://www.merriam-webster.com/dictionary/nationalism.

18. Webster, "On the Education."
19. Webster, *Grammatical Institute*, introduction.
20. Rosemarie Ostler, "Trial by Stagecoach," *American History* 52, no. 5 (December 2017): 44–51.
21. Ostler, "Trial by Stagecoach."
22. Ostler, "Trial by Stagecoach."
23. Ostler, "Trial by Stagecoach."
24. Noah Webster, *Dissertations on the English Language* (Boston: Isaiah Thomas, 1789), 36.
25. Ostler, "Trial by Stagecoach."
26. Horace E. Scudder, *American Men of Letters: Noah Webster* (Cambridge, MA: Riverside Press, 1881), 71.
27. Scudder, *American Men of Letters*.
28. William Kretzschmar, phone interview by the author, Brooklyn, NY, March 6, 2020, digital recording.
29. Kretzschmar interview.
30. Peter Martin, *The Dictionary Wars: The American Fight over the English Language* (Princeton, NJ: Princeton University Press, 2019), 23.
31. Harlow G. Unger, *Noah Webster: The Life and Times of an American Patriot* (New York: John Wiley & Sons, 1998), 34.
32. Freeman Meyer, "Noah Webster's Story," Noah Webster House, 1987, https://noahwebsterhouse.org/noah-websters-story/.
33. Jill Lepore, "Noah's Mark," *The New Yorker*, October 30, 2006.
34. Joshua Kendall, phone interview by the author, Brooklyn, NY, February 28, 2018, digital recording.
35. Noah Webster, *Plan of Policy for Improving the Advantages and Perpetuating the Union of the American States* (Hartford, CT: Hudson & Goodwin, 1785).
36. Kendall, *Forgotten Founding Father*, 3.
37. Webster, *Dissertations*, 19.
38. Sarah Etter, "Probing Question: How Did Regional Accents Originate?," *Penn State News*, August 2005.
39. Etter, "Probing Question."
40. Megan Melancon, "Do You Speak American? Cajun English," Public Broadcasting Service, 2005, https://www.pbs.org/speak/seatosea/americanvarieties/cajun/.
41. "Talking the Tawk," *The New Yorker*, November 2005.
42. "Talking the Tawk."
43. "Noah Webster Cures the Blues with a Spelling Book," New England Historical Society, October 16, 2015, https://www.newenglandhistoricalsociety.com/noah-webster-cures-the-blues-with-a-spelling-book/.
44. Rosemarie Ostler, *Founding Grammars: How Early America's War over Words Shaped Today's Language* (New York: St. Martin's Press, 2015).

45. Frederick Douglass, *Narrative of the Life of Frederick Douglass, an American Slave* (Boston: Anti-Slavery Office, 1845), 43.

46. Douglass, *Narrative*, 43–44.

47. Hugh Rawson, "Slang," *American Heritage*, October 2003.

48. Rawson, "Slang."

49. Kendall interview.

50. Kendall interview.

51. Kendall, *Forgotten Founding Father*, 59.

52. Noah Webster, *Diary*, published in *The Autobiographies of Noah Webster*, ed. Richard M. Rollins (Columbia: University of South Carolina Press, 1989), 347.

53. Webster, *Diary*, 349.

54. "Noah Webster, Father of the American Dictionary, Was Unemployable," *The Atlantic*, October 16, 2012.

55. "Noah Webster, Father of the American Dictionary."

56. Warfel, *Noah Webster*, 240–41.

57. Kendall, *Forgotten Founding Father*, 173.

58. "An Essay on Slavery," *The American Minerva*, December 9, 1793.

59. Noah Webster, *Effects of Slavery on Morals and Industry* (Hartford, CT: Hudson and Goodwin, 1793), 48.

60. Noah Webster, *An American Dictionary of the English Language*, 1st ed. (New York: S. Converse, 1828), s.v. "slavery."

61. Noah Webster to Eliza Webster, March 1837, cited in Kendall, *Forgotten Founding Father*, 202.

62. Lepore, "Noah's Mark."

63. Warfel, *Noah Webster*, 315.

64. Lepore, "Noah's Mark."

65. Martin, *Dictionary Wars*, 35.

66. Lepore, "Noah's Mark."

67. Warfel, *Noah Webster*, 346.

68. Warfel, *Noah Webster*, 127.

69. Kendall, *Forgotten Founding Father*, 310.

70. Leslie Landrigan, "16 Fun Facts about Noah Webster, the Dictionary Writer Who Was Slightly Nuts," New England Historical Society, November 8, 2019, https://www.newenglandhistoricalsociety.com /16-fun-facts-noah-webster-dictionary-writer-slightly-nuts/.

71. Webster, *American Dictionary of the English Language*, s.v. "center."

72. Webster, *American Dictionary of the English Language*, preface.

73. Webster, *American Dictionary of the English Language*, s.v. "senate."

74. Webster, *American Dictionary of the English Language*, s.v. "plantation."

75. Webster, *American Dictionary of the English Language*, preface.

76. Webster, *American Dictionary of the English Language*.

77. Erin Duffin, "Most Spoken Languages in the World," Statista, April 3, 2020, https://www.statista.com/statistics/266808/the-most-spoken -languages-worldwide/.

78. Webster, *American Dictionary of the English Language*, s.v. "racoon."

79. Webster, *American Dictionary of the English Language*, s.v. "Americanize."

80. Noah Webster, *A Compendious Dictionary of the English Language*, 1st ed. (Hartford, CT: Hudson and Goodwin, 1806), s.v. "immigrate."

81. Webster, *Compendious Dictionary*.

82. Webster, *American Dictionary of the English Language*, s.v. "immigrate."

83. Neil Larry Shumsky, "Noah Webster and the Invention of Immigration," *The New England Quarterly* 81, no. 1 (2008): 126–35, www.jstor.org /stable/20474606.

84. Webster, *American Dictionary of the English Language*, preface.

85. Webster, *American Dictionary of the English Language*, s.v. "love."

86. Webster, *American Dictionary of the English Language*, s.v. "nature."

87. Webster, *American Dictionary of the English Language*, s.v. "devotion."

88. "How to Use Noah Webster's Reading Handbook," DIY Homeschooler, June 4, 2020, https://diyhomeschooler.com/how-to-use-noah-websters -reading-handbook/.

89. Peter Sokolowski, phone interview by the author, Paris, November 6, 2019, digital recording.

90. Martin, *Dictionary Wars*, 203–209.

91. Martin, *Dictionary Wars*, 281.

92. Sokolowski interview.

93. Sokolowski interview.

94. Martin, *Dictionary Wars*, 190.

95. Merriam-Webster Editors, "About Us," Merriam-Webster, n.d., https:// www.merriam-webster.com/about-us/noah-webster-legacy.

96. Webster, *American Dictionary of the English Language*, s.v. "tung."

97. Martin, *Dictionary Wars*, chap. 17, 273–87.

98. William Greenleaf Webster, letter, n.d., courtesy of Merriam-Webster.

99. Sales figures from Peter Sokolowski of Merriam-Webster, received November 27, 2020.

100. Herbert C. Morton, *The Story of Webster's Third: Philip Gove's Controversial Dictionary* (Cambridge, UK: Cambridge University Press, 1994), 92.

101. *Merriam-Webster's Dictionary 2nd ed.* (Springfield, MA: G&C Merriam Company, 1934), cited in David Skinner, *The Story of Ain't: America, Its Language, and the Most Controversial Dictionary Ever Published* (New York: HarperCollins, 2012), 2.

102. Morton, *Story of Webster's Third*, 168.

103. Morton, *Story of Webster's Third*, 90–91.

104. Skinner, *Story of Ain't*, 12.

105. Quoted in Skinner, *Story of Ain't*, 282.
106. "Explore the DARE Survey," *Dictionary of American Regional English* (Cambridge, MA: Harvard University Press, 2013), https://www.daredictionary.com/.
107. *Dictionary of American Regional English*, s.v. "honeyfuggle."
108. *Dictionary of American Regional English*, s.v. "jugarum."
109. Gretchen McCulloch, *Because Internet*: *Understanding the New Rules of Language* (New York: Riverhead Books, 2019).
110. Figures from editor at large Peter Sokolowski of Merriam-Webster, provided November 6, 2019.
111. McCulloch, *Because Internet*, 266.
112. Lynda Mugglestone, *Dictionaries*: *A Very Short Introduction* (Oxford, UK: Oxford University Press, 2011), 30.
113. Sokolowski interview.
114. Sokolowski interview.
115. Sokolowski interview.
116. Sokolowski interview.
117. Merriam-Webster Editors, "Looking for Love," *Merriam-Webster*, accessed October 2020, https://www.merriam-webster.com/words-at-play/why-do-we-look-up-love.
118. Sokolowski interview.

CHAPTER THREE

1. Gordon S. Wood, *The Americanization of Benjamin Franklin* (New York: Penguin Books, 2005), 17.
2. Michael Zuckerman, "Franklin's Masks," in *Benjamin Franklin's Intellectual World*, ed. Paul E. Kerry and Matthew S. Holland (Lanham, MD: Rowman & Littlefield, 2012), 7.
3. Susan Garfinkel, "Benjamin Franklin's *Autobiography*," Finding Franklin: A Resource Guide, Virtual Programs and Services, Library of Congress, 2016, https://www.loc.gov/rr/program/bib/franklin/autobiography.html.
4. Benjamin Franklin, *Benjamin Franklin's Autobiography*, ed. Joyce E. Chaplin (New York: W. W. Norton, 2012), 70.
5. Wood, *Americanization of Benjamin Franklin*, 239.
6. Carla Mulford and Nian-Sheng Huang, "Benjamin Franklin and the American Dream," in *The Cambridge Companion to Benjamin Franklin*, ed. Carla Mulford (Cambridge, UK: Cambridge University Press, 2009), 150.
7. Data provided by Joe Karaganis, director of Open Syllabus, June 9, 2020, https://opensyllabus.org/.

8. Marguerite Ward, "5 Ways a Biography of Ben Franklin Shaped Elon Musk's World View," CNBC, April 19, 2017, https://www.cnbc.com /2017/04/19/5-things-we-can-learn-from-one-of-elon-musks-favorite -books.html.

9. Benjamin Franklin, *Benjamin Franklin's Autobiography: An Authoritative Text, Backgrounds, Criticism,* ed. J. A. Leo Lemay and P. M. Zall (New York: W. W. Norton, 1986), xiii.

10. Carla Mulford, "Figuring Benjamin Franklin in American Cultural Memory," *The New England Quarterly* 72, no. 3 (1999): 415–43.

11. Walter Isaacson, *Benjamin Franklin: An American Life* (New York: Simon & Schuster, 2003), 479.

12. Mulford, "Figuring Benjamin Franklin," 426.

13. Mulford, "Figuring Benjamin Franklin," 443.

14. Benjamin Franklin, *Benjamin Franklin's Autobiography*, ed. Joyce E. Chaplin (New York: W. W. Norton, 2012), 11. The autobiography was originally published in 1793.

15. Franklin, *Autobiography*, 14.

16. Franklin, *Autobiography*.

17. All details are from Franklin, *Autobiography of Benjamin Franklin*, 15.

18. Franklin, *Autobiography*.

19. John Griffith, "Franklin's Sanity and the Man Behind the Masks," in *The Oldest Revolutionary: Essays on Benjamin Franklin*, ed. J. A. Leo Lemay (Philadelphia: University of Pennsylvania Press, 1976), 126.

20. Franklin, *Autobiography*, 37.

21. Carl Van Doren, *Benjamin Franklin* (New York: Viking, 1938), 91.

22. Van Doren, *Benjamin Franklin*.

23. Franklin, *Autobiography*, 64.

24. Benjamin Franklin, *Poor Richard's Almanack* (New York: Skyhorse, 2007), 55.

25. Franklin, *Autobiography*, 50.

26. Franklin, *Autobiography*, 50.

27. Franklin, *Autobiography*, 79.

28. Franklin, *Autobiography*, 79.

29. U.S. Census Bureau, population data (1790), https://www.census.gov /programs-surveys/decennial-census/decade/decennial-publications.1790 .html.

30. Franklin, *Autobiography*, 9.

31. Isaacson, *Benjamin Franklin*, 254.

32. Benjamin Franklin to Mary Stevenson, November 28, 1768, Papers of Benjamin Franklin, 1706–1790, Yale University Library.

33. Isaacson, *Benjamin Franklin*, 253.

34. Isaacson, *Benjamin Franklin*, 256.

35. Isaacson, *Benjamin Franklin*, 2.
36. Erving Goffman, *The Presentation of the Self in Everyday Life* (New York: Doubleday, 1956), cited in Griffith, "Franklin's Sanity."
37. Goffman, *Presentation of the Self*.
38. Michael Hattem, phone interview by the author, Paris, August 29, 2019, digital recording.
39. Hattem interview.
40. Griffith, "Franklin's Sanity"; Zuckerman, "Franklin's Masks"; Judith P. Saunders, "The Autobiography of Benjamin Franklin: The Story of a Successful Social Animal," in *American Classics: Evolutionary Perspectives* (Boston: Academic Studies Press, 2018), 1–22.
41. Franklin, *Autobiography of Benjamin Franklin*, 9.
42. Micki McGee, phone interview by the author, Paris, January 16, 2020, digital recording.
43. Gary B. Nash, "Franklin and Slavery," *Proceedings of the American Philosophical Society* 150, no. 4 (2006): 618–35.
44. William Cushing, "Legal Notes about the Quock Walker Case," Massachusetts Historical Society (Boston), 1783, http://www.masshist .org/database/viewer.php?old=1&item_id=670.
45. Cushing, "Legal Notes."
46. Noah Webster, *Effects of Slavery on Morals and Industry* (Hartford: Hudson and Goodwin, 1793), cited in K. Alan Snyder, *Defining Noah Webster: A Spiritual Biography* (Maitland, FL: Xulon Press, 2002), 106.
47. Wood, *Americanization of Benjamin Franklin*, 228.
48. Benjamin Franklin to *The Federal Gazette*, March 23, 1790, Papers of Benjamin Franklin, 1706–1790, Yale University Library.
49. Benjamin Franklin to Sarah Franklin Bache, June 3, 1779, Papers of Benjamin Franklin, 1706–1790, Yale University Library.
50. Isaacson, *Benjamin Franklin*, 325.
51. Franklin to Franklin Bache.
52. Franklin to Franklin Bache.
53. Isaacson, *Benjamin Franklin*, 327.
54. Isaacson, *Benjamin Franklin*, 390.
55. Benjamin Franklin to Elizabeth Partridge, October 11, 1779, Papers of Benjamin Franklin, 1706–1790, Yale University Library.
56. Isaacson, *Benjamin Franklin*, 330.
57. Franklin, *Autobiography*, 79.
58. Franklin, *Autobiography*, 69.
59. Franklin, *Autobiography*, 82.
60. Franklin, *Autobiography*, 18.
61. Franklin, *Autobiography*, 75.
62. Simon Worrall, "Ben Franklin Slept Here," *Smithsonian*, March 2006.

63. Benjamin Franklin, *Fart Proudly: Writings of Benjamin Franklin You Never Read in School*, ed. Carl Japikse (New York: Penguin Random House, 2003).

64. "Few with Family Incomes of $100K+ Embrace the Label 'Upper Class,'" Pew Research Center—U.S. Politics & Policy, March 4, 2015.

65. Benjamin Franklin, *Plain Truth: or, Serious Considerations on the Present State of the City of Philadelphia, and Province of Pennsylvania* (1747), cited in Founders Online, National Archives. Original source: *The Papers of Benjamin Franklin, vol. 3, January 1, 1745, Through June 30, 1750*, ed. Leonard W. Labaree (New Haven, CT: Yale University Press, 1961), 180–204.

66. Anat Shenker-Osorio, "Why Americans All Believe They Are 'Middle Class,'" *The Atlantic*, August 1, 2013.

67. Marzuki Jamil Baki Bin Haji Mohamed Johar, "Benjamin Franklin and His Critics: John Adams, Mark Twain, and David Herbert Lawrence," Master's thesis, Eastern Illinois University, 1997.

68. Herman Melville, *Israel Potter* (New York: G. P. Putnam, 1855), 65.

69. Mark Twain, "The Late Benjamin Franklin," *The Galaxy*, July 1870.

70. D. H. Lawrence, *Studies in Classic American Literature* (New York: Thomas Seltzer, 1923), 26.

71. Lawrence, *Studies*, 27.

72. Hattem interview.

CHAPTER FOUR

1. U.S. Census Bureau, population data (1790), https:// www.census.gov /programs-surveys/decennial-census/ decade/decennial-ublications.1790 .html.

2. U.S. Census Bureau, population data (1830), https://www.census.gov /population/www/censusdata/files/table-2.pdf.

3. "Dr. McGuffey, the Man Behind the Readers," *The New York Times*, April 29, 1923.

4. "Dr. McGuffey."

5. Daniel Drake (writer and physician) to Charles McGuffey (grandson of Alexander McGuffey), cited in Harvey Minnich, *William Holmes McGuffey and His Readers* (New York: American Book Company, 1936), 3.

6. Ohio Historical Society, "Historic American Indian Tribes of Ohio, 1654–1843," n.d., https://www.rrcs.org/Downloads/Ohios%20historic %20Indians%2038%20pages.pdf.

7. Minnich, *William Holmes McGuffey*, 3–4.

8. Dolores P. Sullivan, *William Holmes McGuffey: Schoolmaster to the Nation* (Rutherford, NJ: Fairleigh Dickinson University Press, 1994), 40.
9. Minnich, *William Holmes McGuffey*, 8.
10. Quentin Skrabec, *William McGuffey: Mentor to American Industry* (Sanford, NC: Algora Publishing, 2009), 35.
11. Sullivan, *William Holmes McGuffey*, 41.
12. Sullivan, *William Holmes McGuffey*.
13. Skrabec, *William McGuffey*, 45.
14. Henry H. Vail, *A History of the McGuffey Readers* (Cleveland, OH: Burrows Brothers, 1911), 23.
15. Sullivan, *William Holmes McGuffey*, 30.
16. Sullivan, *William Holmes McGuffey*, 44.
17. Skrabec, *William McGuffey*, 58.
18. Sullivan, *William Holmes McGuffey*, 48.
19. Sullivan, *William Holmes McGuffey*, 46.
20. Minnich, *William Holmes McGuffey*, 148.
21. Vail, *A History of the McGuffey Readers*, 28.
22. William Holmes McGuffey, *Sermons Given by William Holmes McGuffey 1826, 1828*, Walter Havighurst Special Collections: McGuffey Collection, Miami University.
23. Minnich, *William Holmes McGuffey*, 16.
24. Minnich, *William Holmes McGuffey*, 16–17.
25. Walter Havighurst, *The Miami Years* (New York: G. P. Putnam's Sons, 1958–1969), cited in Sullivan, *William Holmes McGuffey*, 60.
26. Sullivan, *William Holmes McGuffey*, 51.
27. Sullivan, *William Holmes McGuffey*, 60.
28. "McGuffey Reader Staging a Comeback Amid 'Back to Basics' Education Drive," *New York Times*, June 18, 1975, 31.
29. Sullivan, *William Holmes McGuffey*, 60–61.
30. Sullivan, *William Holmes McGuffey*, 63.
31. Minnich, *William Holmes McGuffey*, 30–32.
32. Minnich, *William Holmes McGuffey*, 24.
33. Stephen Gordon (McGuffey House and Museum), phone interview by the author, New York, October 5, 2018, digital recording.
34. Vail, *A History of the McGuffey Readers*, 33–34.
35. Lyman Beecher, *A Plea for the West* (Cincinnati, OH: Truman and Smith, 1835).
36. Beecher, *A Plea*.
37. Minnich, *William Holmes McGuffey*, 31.
38. Sullivan, *William Holmes McGuffey*, 56.
39. Minnich, *William Holmes McGuffey*, 19.
40. Minnich, *William Holmes McGuffey*, 20.

41. Robert W. Lynn, "Civil Catechetics in Mid-Victorian America: Some Notes About American Civil Religion, Past and Present," *Religious Education* (January–February 1972), cited in James W. Fraser, *Between Church and State: Religion and Public Education in Multicultural America* (Baltimore, MD: Johns Hopkins University Press, 1999), 36.

42. William Holmes McGuffey, *The Eclectic Fourth Reader* (Cincinnati, OH: Truman and Smith, 1837), 145.

43. Minnich, *William Holmes McGuffey*, 36.

44. William Holmes McGuffey, *McGuffey's Newly Revised Eclectic Fourth Reader: Containing Elegant Extracts in Prose and Poetry, with Rules for Reading, and Exercises in Articulation, Defining, Etc.*, rev. and improved (New York: Clark, Austin & Smith; Cincinnati, OH: W. B. Smith & Co., 1853), preface.

45. McGuffey, *McGuffey's Newly Revised Eclectic Fourth.*

46. McGuffey, *McGuffey's Newly Revised Eclectic Fourth.*

47. McGuffey, *McGuffey's Newly Revised Eclectic Fourth.*

48. McGuffey, *McGuffey's Newly Revised Eclectic Fourth.*

49. McGuffey, *McGuffey's Newly Revised Eclectic Fourth.*

50. McGuffey, *McGuffey's Fourth Eclectic Reader*, 211.

51. McGuffey, *McGuffey's Fourth Eclectic Reader*, 110.

52. McGuffey, *McGuffey's Fourth Eclectic Reader*, 110.

53. McGuffey, *McGuffey's Fourth Eclectic Reader*, 112.

54. Samuel J. Smith, "McGuffey Readers" (2008), Faculty Publications and Presentations, 101, http://digitalcommons.liberty.edu/educ_fac_pubs /101.

55. Alexander McGuffey, *McGuffey's Rhetorical Guide or Fifth Reader* (Cincinnati, OH: Truman & Smith, 1844), 22.

56. Louise L. Stevenson, *The Victorian Homefront: American Thought and Culture, 1860–1880* (Ithaca, NY: Cornell University Press, 2001), 96.

57. McGuffey, *McGuffey's Rhetorical Guide or Fifth Reader*, 22.

58. Skrabec, *William McGuffey*, 193.

59. McGuffey, *McGuffey's Fourth Eclectic Reader*, 154.

60. McGuffey, *McGuffey's Fourth Eclectic Reader*, preface.

61. James Fraser, phone interview by the author, New York, January 18, 2019, digital recording.

62. Fraser interview.

63. William B. Kennedy, cited in Thomas C. Hunt et al., eds., "Introduction," in *Encyclopedia of Educational Reform and Dissent*, vol. 1 (Thousand Oaks, CA: Sage, 2010), xxxviii.

64. Sandy Hingston, "Bullets and Bigots: Remembering Philadelphia's 1844 Anti-Catholic Riots," *Philadelphia*, December 17, 2015.

65. Hingston, "Bullets and Bigots."

66. Hingston, "Bullets and Bigots."

67. Benjamin Harris, *New England Primer* (Boston: Edward Draper, 1777). This was originally published in 1688.

68. Noah Webster to Alexander McGuffey, March 3, 1837, Walter Havighurst Special Collections: McGuffey Collection, Miami University.

69. Webster to McGuffey.

70. McGuffey, *McGuffey's Rhetorical Guide or Fifth Reader*, 249.

71. Brent Staples, "How Italians Became 'White,'" *The New York Times*, October 12, 2019.

72. Stanley W. Lindberg, quoted in Susan Walton, "(Re)Turning To W. H. McGuffey's Frontier Virtues," *Edweek*, February 2, 1983.

73. Skrabec, *William McGuffey*, 129.

74. McGuffey, *McGuffey's Rhetorical Guide or Fifth Reader*, 16.

75. McGuffey, *McGuffey's Rhetorical Guide or Fifth Reader*, 10.

76. W. H. McGuffey, *Laguna Indian Translation of McGuffey's New First Eclectic Reader* (Laguna Pueblo, NM: Laguna Mission Press, 1882).

77. Minnich, *William Holmes McGuffey*, vii.

78. Minnich, *William Holmes McGuffey*, 5.

79. Steven Watts, *The People's Tycoon: Henry Ford and the American Century* (New York: Random House, 2005), 11.

80. Bill McGraw, "A Special Report: Henry Ford and 'The International Jew,'" *The Dearborn Historian*, Autumn 2018.

81. Neil Baldwin, *Henry Ford and the Jews: The Mass Production of Hate* (New York: Public Affairs, 2002).

82. Richard Haitch, "Follow Up on the News; McGuffey Revival," *The New York Times*, April 3, 1983, https://www.nytimes.com/1983/04/03/nyregion/follow-up-on-the-news-mcguffey-revival.html.

83. Haitch, "Follow Up."

84. Johann Neem, "The Strange Afterlife of William McGuffey and His Readers," *The Hedgehog Review*, Summer 2018.

85. Sherry Hayes, "Homeschool McGuffey's Lesson Tutorial Level One," YouTube video, 18:08, January 25, 2020.

86. Aaron Jagt, phone interview by the author, Paris, April 11, 2020, digital recording.

87. Arthur Robinson, "More Than a Fighting Chance," Robinson Curriculum, July 6, 2015, https://www.robinsoncurriculum.com/more-than-a-fighting-chance/.

88. Jagt interview.

89. Jagt interview.

90. Jagt interview.

91. Jagt interview.

92. Chimamanda Ngozi Adichie, "The Danger of a Single Story," filmed July 2009 in Oxford, England, TED video, 18:34.

93. Johann Neem, phone interview by the author, Paris, April 7, 2020, digital recording.

CHAPTER FIVE

1. Barbara A. White, *The Beecher Sisters* (New Haven, CT: Yale University Press, 2003), 6.

2. Catharine Esther Beecher to Edward Beecher, June 4, 1822, cited in White, *Beecher Sisters*, 7.

3. Catharine Beecher to Edward Beecher.

4. Kathryn Kish Sklar, *Catharine Beecher: A Study in American Domesticity* (New York: W. W. Norton, 1976), 33.

5. White, *Beecher Sisters*, 22.

6. Harriet Beecher Stowe to Lyman Beecher and Henry Ward Beecher, September 1851, cited in White, *Beecher Sisters*, 59.

7. Alexis de Tocqueville, *Democracy in America* (New York: G. Dearborn, 1835–40).

8. Catharine Beecher, *An Essay on Slavery and Abolitionism, with Reference to the Duty of American Females* (Philadelphia: Henry Perkins, 1837).

9. White, *Beecher Sisters*, 119.

10. Catharine Beecher, *Educational Reminiscences and Suggestions* (New York: J. B. Ford & Co., 1874), cited in Sklar, *Catharine Beecher*, 21.

11. White, *Beecher Sisters*, 9.

12. White, *Beecher Sisters*, 9.

13. Allison Speicher, "Catharine Beecher Educates the West," *Grating the Nutmeg*, podcast, March 8, 2017, 43:51.

14. Beecher, *An Essay on Slavery*.

15. Alisse Theodore, "'A Right to Speak on the Subject': The U.S. Women's Antiremoval Petition Campaign, 1829–1831," *Rhetoric and Public Affairs* 5, no. 4 (2002): 601–23.

16. Sklar, *Catharine Beecher*, 139.

17. Sklar, *Catharine Beecher*, 139.

18. Sklar, *Catharine Beecher*, 115.

19. Sklar, *Catharine Beecher*, 117.

20. Catharine Beecher to *The Cincinnati Gazette*, February 21, 1837, cited in Sklar, *Catharine Beecher*, 131.

21. Sklar, *Catharine Beecher*, 139.
22. C. Beecher, "How to Redeem Woman's Profession from Dishonor," *Harper's Magazine*, November 1865.
23. Joan N. Burstyn, "Catharine Beecher and the Education of American Women," *The New England Quarterly* 47, no. 3 (1974): 389.
24. C. Beecher, *A Treatise on Domestic Economy* (New York: Harper & Brothers, 1841), 37.
25. Linda Kerber, "The Republican Mother: Women and the Enlightenment— An American Perspective," *American Quarterly* 28, no. 2 (1976): 187–205.
26. Beecher, *Treatise on Domestic Economy*, 62.
27. Beecher, *Treatise on Domestic Economy*.
28. Beecher, *Treatise on Domestic Economy*, 124.
29. Beecher, *Treatise on Domestic Economy*.
30. C. Beecher, *An Essay on the Education of Female Teachers* (New York: Van Nostrand & Dwight, 1835).
31. C. Beecher, *The Duty of American Women to Their Country* (New York: Harper & Brothers, 1845), 34.
32. Beecher, *Duty of American Women*, 64.
33. Allison Speicher (vice president of the Harriet Beecher Stowe Society), phone interview by the author, Paris, March 24, 2020, digital recording.
34. Lydia Maria Child, *The American Frugal Housewife* (Boston: Marsh & Capen; Carter & Hendee, 1829), 1.
35. Child, *American Frugal Housewife*, 4.
36. Child, *American Frugal Housewife*, 5.
37. Tracy A. Thomas, *Elizabeth Cady Stanton and the Feminist Foundations of Family Law* (New York: New York University Press, 2016).
38. Claudia Goldin and Lawrence F. Katz, *The Race Between Education and Technology* (Cambridge, MA: Harvard University Press, 2008), and David B. Tyack and Elisabeth Hansot, *Learning Together: A History of Coeducation in American Schools* (New Haven: Yale University Press, 1990), cited in Johann Neem, *Democracy's Schools: The Rise of Public Education in America* (Baltimore, MD: Johns Hopkins University Press, 2017), 3.
39. Burstyn, "Catharine Beecher," 393.
40. Nancy F. Cott, *The Bonds of Womanhood: "Woman's Sphere" in New England, 1780–1835* (New Haven, CT: Yale University Press, 1977), 10.
41. Sklar, *Catharine Beecher*, 152.
42. Glenna Matthews, *"Just a Housewife": The Rise and Fall of Domesticity in America* (New York: Oxford University Press, 1987), 21.
43. Matthews, *"Just a Housewife."*
44. "Americana," *Time*, February 3, 1930, cited in Olivia B. Waxman, "Thanksgiving Wasn't Always a National Holiday. This Woman Made It Happen," *Time*, November 23, 2016.

45. John Egerton, foreword to Toni Tipton-Martin, *The Jemima Code: Two Centuries of African American Cookbooks* (Austin: Texas University Press, 2015), x.

46. Kelley Fanto Deetz, *Bound to the Fire: How Virginia's Enslaved Cooks Helped Invent American Cuisine* (Lexington: University of Kentucky Press, 2017).

47. Barbara Haber, foreword to Tipton-Martin, *Jemima Code*, xiv.

48. "Henry Ward Beecher on the Crisis," *The New York Times*, April 15, 1861, https://www.nytimes.com/1861/04/15/archives/henry-ward-beecher-on -the-crisis-what-will-you-do-stand-still-or-go.html.

49. "Henry Ward Beecher on the Crisis."

50. Beecher, "How to Redeem Woman's Profession," 716.

51. Beecher, "How to Redeem Woman's Profession," 716.

52. Jenifer Frank, "Hartford's Nook Farm," Connecticut History: A CTHumanities Project, June 5, 2014, https://connecticuthistory.org /hartfords-nook-farm/.

53. Frank, "Hartford's Nook Farm."

54. Sklar, *Catharine Beecher*, 263–264.

55. C. Beecher and H. Beecher Stowe, *The American Woman's Home: or, Principles of Domestic Science* (New York: J. B. Ford, 1869), 13.

56. *Books That Shaped America*, exhibition, Library of Congress, Washington, D.C., June 25–September 29, 2012.

57. Beecher and Stowe, *American Woman's Home*, 171.

58. Speicher interview.

59. Beecher and Stowe, *American Woman's Home*, 333.

60. Beecher and Stowe, *American Woman's Home*, 19.

61. Beecher and Stowe, *American Woman's Home*, 19.

62. Beecher and Stowe, *American Woman's Home*, 20.

63. Beecher and Stowe, *American Woman's Home*, 19.

64. Beecher, "How to Redeem Woman's Profession," 712.

65. Beecher, "How to Redeem Woman's Profession," 716.

66. Beecher and Stowe, *American Woman's Home*, 23.

67. Sarah Leavitt, phone interview by the author, Paris, March 18, 2020, digital recording.

68. Leavitt interview.

69. Speicher interview.

CHAPTER SIX

1. Edwin Post, *Truly Emily Post* (New York: Funk & Wagnalls, 1961), 146.

2. Post, *Truly Emily Post*, 146.

3.   Laura Claridge, *Emily Post: Daughter of the Gilded Age, Mistress of American Manners* (New York: Random House, 2008), 5.

4.   Marie Weldon, "Society at Home and Abroad," *The New York Times*, July 23, 1905, SM8, cited in Claridge, *Emily Post*, 169.

5.   Elizabeth Kolbert, "Place Settings," *The New Yorker*, October 20, 2008.

6.   Weldon, "Society at Home and Abroad."

7.   Post, *Truly Emily Post*, 150.

8.   Emily Post, "Mrs. Post's Own Story About Herself," *Bell Syndicate*, n.d. (courtesy of the Emily Post Institute).

9.   Helena Huntington Smith, "Lady Chesterfield," *The New Yorker*, August 16, 1930.

10. Smith, "Lady Chesterfield."

11. Post, *Truly Emily Post*, 105.

12. Post, *Truly Emily Post*, 106; Claridge, *Emily Post*, 147.

13. Emily Post, *The Flight of a Moth* (New York: Dodd, Mead, 1904), 5.

14. Post, *Flight of a Moth*, 2.

15. Post, *Flight of a Moth*, 3.

16. Emily Post, *By Motor to the Golden Gate* (New York: Appleton, 1916).

17. Post, *Truly Emily Post*, 208.

18. Emily Post, *Etiquette in Society, in Business, in Politics and at Home* (New York: Funk & Wagnalls, 1922).

19. Claridge, *Emily Post*, 253.

20. Smith, "Lady Chesterfield."

21. Post, *Truly Emily Post*, 238.

22. Douglas Martin, "Elizabeth Post of the Etiquette Family Dies at 89," *The New York Times*, April 27, 2010.

23. Kolbert, "Place Settings."

24. Post, *Truly Emily Post*, 20.

25. Post, *Truly Emily Post*, 4.

26. "Celebrate Mark Twain's Seventieth Birthday," *The New York Times*, December 6, 1905, 1.

27. Claridge, *Emily Post*, 168.

28. Claridge, *Emily Post*, 20.

29. Lizzie Post, interview by the author, Burlington, VT, September 17, 2019, digital recording; Post, *Truly Emily Post*, 26.

30. Post, *Truly Emily Post*, 16.

31. Post, *Truly Emily Post*, 39.

32. Claridge, *Emily Post*, 21.

33. Claridge, *Emily Post*, 12.

34. Claridge, *Emily Post*, 11.

35. Post, *Truly Emily Post*, 34.

36. Post, *Truly Emily Post*, 34.

37. Post, *Truly Emily Post*, 34.
38. Claridge, *Emily Post*, 80.
39. Post, *Truly Emily Post*, 38.
40. Post, *Truly Emily Post*, 40.
41. Daniel Post Senning, interview by the author, Burlington, VT, September 17, 2019, digital recording.
42. Press clippings from Emily Post, personal scrapbook, courtesy of the Emily Post Institute.
43. Claridge, *Emily Post*, 244.
44. All details are from Claridge, *Emily Post*, 245.
45. Claridge, *Emily Post*, 245.
46. Claridge, *Emily Post*, 245.
47. Senning interview; Post interview.
48. Claridge, *Emily Post*, 246.
49. Post, *Truly Emily Post*, 210.
50. Post, *Truly Emily Post*, 181.
51. Claridge, *Emily Post*, 249.
52. Claridge, *Emily Post*, 250.
53. Claridge, *Emily Post*, 211.
54. Claridge, *Emily Post*, 214.
55. Figures courtesy of Emily Post Institute.
56. Smith, "Lady Chesterfield."
57. Post, *Etiquette*.
58. Senning interview.
59. Senning interview.
60. Post, scrapbook, multiple years (courtesy of the Emily Post Institute).
61. Post, *Etiquette*, 58.
62. Post, *Etiquette*, 58.
63. Eric Bennett, "1922: The Year That Transformed English Literature," *The New York Times*, August 9, 2017.
64. Claridge, *Emily Post*, 254.
65. Advertisement for *Etiquette*, *The Literary Digest*, October 14, 1922 (courtesy of the Emily Post Institute.)
66. Senning interview.
67. Post, *Etiquette*, 65.
68. Post, *Etiquette*, 68.
69. Post, *Etiquette*, 70.
70. Post, *Etiquette*, 98–131.
71. Post, *Etiquette*.
72. Post, *Etiquette*, 65.
73. Theodore Roosevelt, "Americanism (Knights of Columbus)" (speech, Carnegie Hall, New York, October 13, 1915).

74. Claridge, *Emily Post*, 242.
75. Claridge, *Emily Post*, 270.
76. Post, *Etiquette*, 288–380.
77. Randy Olson, "144 Years of Marriage and Divorce in 1 Chart," February 25, 2020, http://www.randalolson.com/2015/06/15/144-years-of-marriage-and-divorce-in-1-chart/.
78. Post, *Etiquette*, 509.
79. Andrea Voyer, phone interview by the author, Boston, November 26, 2019, digital recording.
80. Voyer interview.
81. William Curtis, "Some Recent Books," *Town & Country*, September 1, 1922 (courtesy of the Emily Post Institute).
82. Curtis, "Some Recent Books."
83. Katherine Anne Porter, "Etiquette in Action," *New York Tribune*, December 26, 1925 (courtesy of the Emily Post Institute).
84. Porter, "Etiquette."
85. Claridge, *Emily Post*, 283.
86. Post, *Truly Emily Post*, 231.
87. Post, *Etiquette*, 387.
88. Claridge, *Emily Post*, 284.
89. Post, scrapbooks, various years (courtesy of the Emily Post Institute).
90. Post, scrapbooks.
91. Julia Child, Simone Beck, and Louisette Bertholle, *Mastering the Art of French Cooking* (New York: Alfred A. Knopf, 1961).
92. C. Dallett Hemphill, "Middle Class Rising in Revolutionary America: The Evidence from Manners," *Journal of Social History* 30, no. 2 (1996): 317–44.
93. Alexis de Tocqueville, *Democracy in America* (New York: G. Dearborn, 1835–40), 58.
94. Arthur Schlesinger, *Learning How to Behave: A Historical Study of American Etiquette Books* (New York: Macmillan, 1946), 18.
95. *Chicago Tribune* article (1897), cited in Ron Grossman, "How Andrew Jackson's Inauguration Day Went off the Rails," *Chicago Tribune*, January 13, 2017.
96. Schlesinger, *Learning How to Behave*, 17.
97. Ralph Waldo Emerson, *Essays: Second Series* (Boston: James Munroe, 1844), 129.
98. Samuel R. Wells, *How to Behave: A Pocket Manual of Republican Etiquette* (New York: Fowler & Wells, 1856), vii.
99. Post, *Etiquette*, 59.
100. Post, *Etiquette*, 61.

101. Post, *Etiquette*, 58–61.

102. Post, *Etiquette*, 64.

103. "The Most Powerful Women in America," *Pageant*, April 1950, cited in Claridge, *Emily Post*, 261.

104. "Remarkable American Women, 1776–1976," *Life*, special report, 1976 (courtesy of the Emily Post Institute).

105. Deborah G. Felder, *A Century of Women: The Most Influential Events in Twentieth-Century Women's History* (New York: Kensington Books, 1999).

106. Dorothy Parker, "Mrs. Post Enlarges on Etiquette," *The New Yorker*, December 24, 1927.

107. Post, *Etiquette*, 2nd ed. (New York: Funk & Wagnalls, 1928), cited in Parker, "Mrs. Post Enlarges."

108. Jeanne Perkins, "Close Up: Emily Post," *Life*, May 6, 1946 (courtesy of the Emily Post Institute).

109. Perkins, "Close Up."

110. Post, *Etiquette* (New York: Funk & Wagnalls 1942), cited in Claridge, *Emily Post*, 395.

111. Post, *Etiquette* (New York: Funk & Wagnalls 1942), cited in Claridge, *Emily Post*, 395.

112. Lizzie Post, *Higher Etiquette: A Guide to the World of Cannabis from Dispensaries to Dinner Parties* (New York: Ten Speed Press, 2019).

113. Post, *American Weekly* article, seen at the Emily Post Institute.

114. Post interview.

115. Emily Post, personal photo album, 1895 (courtesy of the Emily Post Institute).

116. Post interview.

117. Post interview.

118. Post interview.

CHAPTER SEVEN

1. Dale Carnegie to Donna Carnegie (The Story of My Life), January 30, 1952, letter (courtesy of Dale Carnegie & Associates).

2. Dale Carnegie, *How to Stop Worrying and Start Living* (New York: Simon & Schuster, 1948), 150–51, cited in Steven Watts, *Self-Help Messiah: Dale Carnegie and Success in Modern America* (New York: Other Press, 2013), 15.

3. Dale Carnegie to Donna Carnegie.

4. Dale Carnegie to Donna Carnegie.

5. Dale Carnegie to Donna Carnegie.

6. Dale Carnegie to Donna Carnegie.
7. Dale Carnegie to Donna Carnegie.
8. Dale Carnegie to Donna Carnegie.
9. Dale Carnegie to Donna Carnegie.
10. Dale Carnegie to Donna Carnegie.
11. Dale Carnegie to Donna Carnegie.
12. Margaret Case Harriman, "He Sells Hope," *Saturday Evening Post*, August 14, 1937.
13. Dale Carnegie to Donna Carnegie.
14. Dale Carnegie to Donna Carnegie.
15. Dale Carnegie to Donna Carnegie.
16. Dale Carnegie to Donna Carnegie.
17. Harriman, "He Sells Hope."
18. Dale Carnegie, "Eleven Ways for Developing Your Personality," public speaking notes, ca. 1940s (courtesy of Dale Carnegie & Associates).
19. Watts, *Self-Help Messiah*, 80–81.
20. Watts, *Self-Help Messiah*, 71.
21. Dale Carnegie to Donna Carnegie.
22. Watts, *Self-Help Messiah*, 105.
23. Dale Carnegie to Donna Carnegie.
24. Dale Carnegie to Donna Carnegie.
25. Dale Carnegie to Donna Carnegie.
26. Watts, *Self-Help Messiah*, 111.
27. Watts, *Self-Help Messiah*, 258.
28. Watts, *Self-Help Messiah*.
29. Watts, *Self-Help Messiah*, 259.
30. Dale Carnegie, *How to Win Friends and Influence People* (New York: Simon & Schuster, 1936), xvi.
31. "Bankers v. Panic," *Time*, November 4, 1929, cited in Olivia B. Waxman, "What Caused the Stock Market Crash of 1929—and What We Still Get Wrong About It," *Time*, October 24, 2019.
32. Watts, *Self-Help Messiah*, 226.
33. Robert C. Goldston, *The Great Depression: The United States in the Thirties* (Indianapolis, IN: Bobbs-Merrill, 1968), 163.
34. Carnegie, *How to Win Friends and Influence People*, 67.
35. Watts, *Self-Help Messiah*, 260.
36. Carnegie, *How to Win Friends and Influence People*, xxii.
37. Harriman, "He Sells Hope."
38. Barbara Ehrenreich, *Bright-Sided: How the Relentless Promotion of Positive Thinking Has Undermined America* (New York: Henry Holt and Company, 2009), 4.

39. Nancy Shulins, "'How to Win Friends and Influence People': Best Seller Turns 50, but Its Advice Is Timeless," Associated Press, August 24, 1986.

40. Dale Carnegie, "17 Things This Training Will Help You Do," promotional material, n.d. (courtesy of Dale Carnegie & Associates).

41. Carlos Ferran and Stephanie Watts, "Videoconferencing in the Field: A Heuristic Processing Model," *Management Science* 54, no. 9 (September 2008), iv–1683, cited in Sue Shellenbarger, "Why Likability Matters More at Work," *The Wall Street Journal*, March 24, 2014.

42. Barbara Gerbert, "Perceived Likeability and Competence of Simulated Patients: Influence on Physicians' Management Plans," *Social Science and Medicine* 18, no. 12 (1984): 1053–59.

43. Watts, *Self-Help Messiah*, 120.

44. Carnegie, *How to Win Friends and Influence People*, xxii.

45. Gail Thain Parker, "How to Win Friends and Influence People: Dale Carnegie and the Problem of Sincerity," *American Quarterly* 29, no. 5 (1977): 506–518.

46. Parker, "How to Win Friends," 51.

47. Harriman, "He Sells Hope."

48. Dorothy Carnegie (Dale's wife) and Rosemary Crom (Dale's stepdaughter), personal communication with Brenda Johnson (chief archivist of Dale Carnegie Archive).

49. Watts, *Self-Help Messiah*, 261.

50. Figure courtesy of Dale Carnegie & Associates, provided by Brenda Johnson (archivist at DCA), December 2, 2019.

51. Watts, *Self-Help Messiah*, 314.

52. "Soft Answers," *The New York Times*, February 14, 1937.

53. Concepción de León, "The 10 Most Checked-Out Books in N.Y. Public Library History," *The New York Times*, January 13, 2020.

54. *Collier's*, January 15, 1949, and *Cosmopolitan*, January 1959, 146, cited in Parker, "How to Win Friends."

55. Dale Carnegie to Donna Carnegie.

56. Joe Hart, phone interview by the author, Paris, May 5, 2020, digital recording.

57. Allen E. Grabo and Mark Van Vugt, "Charismatic Leadership and the Evolution of Cooperation," *Evolution and Human Behavior* 37, no. 5 (March 2016).

58. Maia J. Young, Michael W. Morris, and Vicki Scherwin, "Managerial Mystique: Magical Thinking in Judgments of Managers' Vision, Charisma, and Magnetism," *Journal of Management* 39, no. 4 (March 2011).

59. Joshua Derman, "Max Weber and Charisma: A Transatlantic Affair," *New German Critique*, no. 113 (2011): 51–88.

60. *Merriam-Webster.com Dictionary*, s.v. "charisma," accessed April 26, 2020, https://www.merriam-webster.com/dictionary/charisma.

61. Dale Carnegie to Donna Carnegie.

62. Dale Carnegie to Donna Carnegie.

63. Dale Carnegie to Donna Carnegie.

64. Dale Carnegie to Donna Carnegie.

65. According to Dale Carnegie & Associates.

66. Trysh Travis, phone interview by the author, Paris, January 27, 2020, digital recording.

67. Travis interview.

68. Carnegie, *How to Win Friends and Influence People*, 74.

69. Shulins, "'How to Win Friends.'"

70. Heather Long and Andrew Van Dam, "For the First Time, Most New Working-Age Hires in the U.S. Are People of Color," *Washington Post*, September 9, 2019.

71. Erin Duffin, "Gig Economy: Number of Freelancers in the U.S. 2017–2028," Statista, October 30, 2019, https://www.statista.com /statistics/921593/gig-economy-number-of-freelancers-us/.

72. Travis interview.

CHAPTER EIGHT

1. General Mills, *Our Nation's Rations* script, NBC, March 14, 1945 (courtesy of the General Mills Archive).

2. General Mills, *Betty Crocker History* (Minneapolis, MN, 1954) (courtesy of the General Mills Archive).

3. Susan Marks, *Finding Betty Crocker: The Secret Life of America's First Lady of Food* (New York: Simon & Schuster, 2005), 116.

4. General Mills, *Betty Crocker's Picture Cookbook* (New York: McGraw-Hill, 1950), 1.

5. Betty Crocker Kitchens, "The Story of Betty Crocker," General Mills, June 10, 2014, https://www.bettycrocker.com/menus-holidays-parties /mhplibrary/parties-and-get-togethers/vintage-betty/the-story-of-betty -crocker.

6. Marks, *Finding Betty Crocker*, 9–11.

7. Jean Libman Block, "The Secret Life of Betty Crocker," *Woman's Home Companion*, December 1952 (courtesy of the General Mills Archive).

8. Block, "Secret Life."

9. Block, "Secret Life."

10. Block, "Secret Life."

11. General Mills, *Betty Crocker History*.
12. Betty Crocker radio script, October 2, 1924 (courtesy of the General Mills Archive).
13. Marjorie Child Husted, Records of the Arthur and Elizabeth Schlesinger Library on the History of Women in America, 1942–2017, RG XVIII, Ser. 2.1, Box 10, Schlesinger Library on the History of Women in America, Radcliffe Institute for Advanced Study.
14. Husted, Records of the Arthur and Elizabeth Schlesinger Library.
15. Carol Pine, "The Real Betty Crocker Is One Tough Cookie," *Twin Cities*, November 1978, cited in Susan Marks, *Finding Betty Crocker: The Secret Life of America's First Lady of Food* (New York: Simon & Schuster, 2005), 126.
16. Multiple authors, letters to Betty Crocker, 1940–1950 (courtesy of the General Mills Archive).
17. Letters to Betty Crocker.
18. Letters to Betty Crocker.
19. Radio comments from listeners, 1931 (courtesy of the General Mills Archive).
20. Letters to Betty Crocker.
21. Marks, *Finding Betty Crocker*, 114.
22. General Mills, *War Work: A Daybook for the Home* (Minneapolis, MN, 1942), Schlesinger Library on the History of Women in America, Radcliffe Institute for Advanced Study (courtesy of the General Mills Archive).
23. General Mills, *War Work*.
24. General Mills, *War Work*.
25. General Mills, *War Work (The Second Year): A Daybook for the Home* (Minneapolis, MN, 1943), Schlesinger Library on the History of Women in America, Radcliffe Institute for Advanced Study (courtesy of the General Mills Archive).
26. General Mills, *War Work (The Second Year)*.
27. General Mills, *War Work (The Second Year)*.
28. Letters to Betty Crocker.
29. Letters to Betty Crocker.
30. Letters to Betty Crocker.
31. Letters to Betty Crocker.
32. Letters to Betty Crocker.
33. General Mills, *War Work (The Second Year)*.
34. General Mills, *War Work*.
35. General Mills, *Point Stretchers* (Minneapolis, MN, ca. 1940s), Schlesinger Library on the History of Women in America, Radcliffe Institute for Advanced Study (courtesy of the General Mills Archive).
36. General Mills, *Point Stretchers*.

37. General Mills, *Betty Crocker History*.

38. General Mills, *Homemakers Creed of the Home Legion*, brochure, Minneapolis, 1944, courtesy of the General Mills Archive.

39. General Mills, *Homemakers Creed of the Home Legion*.

40. Philip S. Gutis, "Marjorie Husted Dead at 94, Helped Create Betty Crocker," *New York Times*, December 28, 1986, https://www.nytimes.com/1986/12/28/obituaries/marjorie-husted-dead-at-94-helped-create-betty-crocker.html.

41. Gutis, "Marjorie Child Husted."

42. "Women & World War II," Camp Hale, Metropolitan State University of Denver, accessed February 20, 2020, https://www.msudenver.edu/camphale/thewomensarmycorps/womenwwii.

43. General Mills, *Betty Crocker Helps* script, January 21, 1946 (courtesy of the General Mills Archive).

44. David Dempsey, "Those Hidden Best Sellers," *New York Times,* December 3, 1950, cited in Marks, *Finding Betty Crocker*, 135.

45. *The New York Times,* June 12, 1952, 42, cited in Laura Shapiro, *Something from the Oven: Reinventing Dinner in 1950s America* (New York: Viking Penguin, 2004), 29.

46. General Mills, *Betty Crocker's Picture Cook Book*, 6.

47. General Mills, *Betty Crocker's Picture Cook Book*, 34.

48. General Mills, *Betty Crocker's Picture Cook Book*, 34–35.

49. General Mills, *Betty Crocker's Picture Cook Book*, 115.

50. General Mills, *Betty Crocker's Picture Cook Book*.

51. General Mills, *Betty Crocker's Picture Cook Book*, 173.

52. Claudia Goldin, *Understanding the Gender Gap: An Economic History of American Women* (New York: Oxford University Press, 1990), 119–158, cited in Susan M. Hartmann, "Women's Employment and the Domestic Ideal," in *Not June Cleaver: Women and Gender in Postwar America, 1945–1960*, ed. Joanne Meyerowitz (Philadelphia: Temple University Press, 1994), 84.

53. Susan Lynn, "Gender and Progressive Politics," in Meyerowitz, *Not June Cleaver*, 105.

54. Freda De Knight, *A Date with a Dish: A Cook Book of American Negro Recipes* (New York: Hermitage Press, 1948), xii.

55. Marion Schmidt, interview by the author, Minneapolis, MN, September 9, 2019, digital recording.

56. All details are from the Schmidt interview.

57. Schmidt interview.

58. Schmidt interview.

59. Schmidt interview.

60. Marjorie Child Husted, "Women—Their New Place in Our Economic Life" (Savings Bonds Conference, Washington, D.C., November 28, 1956) (courtesy of the General Mills Archive).
61. Betty Friedan, *The Feminine Mystique* (New York: W. W. Norton, 1963).
62. Letters to Betty Crocker.
63. Letters to Betty Crocker.
64. Letters to Betty Crocker.
65. Letters to Betty Crocker.
66. Letters to Betty Crocker.
67. General Mills, *Betty Crocker Helps* script, January 15, 1946.
68. Letters to Betty Crocker.
69. Marjorie Child Husted, "Copywriters Presentation," June 21, 1948 (courtesy of the General Mills Archive).
70. Husted, "Copywriters Presentation."
71. "Supermarket Product Choices," *Consumer Reports*, January 2014.
72. General Mills, *Market Survey* (Minneapolis, MN, 1953) (courtesy of the General Mills Archive).
73. *Betty Crocker Research Project* (Minneapolis, MN: General Mills, 1953) (courtesy of the General Mills Archive).
74. *Betty Crocker Research Project.*
75. *Betty Crocker Research Project.*
76. *Betty Crocker Research Project.*
77. *Betty Crocker Research Project.*
78. *Betty Crocker Research Project.*
79. *Betty Crocker Research Project.*
80. General Mills, *Your Responsibility as a Betty Crocker Girl* (Minneapolis, MN, ca. 1950–60) (courtesy of the General Mills Archive).
81. Block, "Secret Life."
82. Adelaide Fish Hawley Cumming Papers, 1922–1967, Schlesinger Library, Radcliffe Institute, Harvard University, Cambridge.
83. Cumming Papers.
84. Bruce Lambert, "Jean Wade Rindlaub, 87, Dies; One of First Female Ad Executives," *The New York Times*, December 22, 1991.
85. Jean Wade Rindlaub Papers, ca. 1848–1991, Schlesinger Library, Radcliffe Institute, Harvard University.
86. Rindlaub Papers.
87. Rindlaub Papers.
88. Tagline for the *Betty Crocker Magazine of the Air*.

CHAPTER NINE

1. All details are from "Dr. Reuben and His Wife: 'We Agree on Everything,'" *The New York Times*, July 13, 1971.
2. "Dr. Reuben and His Wife."
3. David Reuben, *Everything You Always Wanted to Know About Sex* (*But Were Afraid to Ask)* (New York: David McKay, 1969), viii.
4. Cheryl Lavin, "Everything You Always Wanted to Know About Dr. David Reuben," *Chicago Tribune*, February 23, 1999.
5. David B. Green, "This Day in Jewish History 1930: A Man Who Said He Knew Everything About Sex Is Born," *Haaretz*, November 29, 2016.
6. Lavin, "Everything You Always Wanted."
7. Reuben, *Everything You Always*, 3.
8. Maurice Isserman and Michael Kazin, *America Divided: The Civil War of the 1960s* (Oxford, UK: Oxford University Press, 1999).
9. Joshua Clark Davis, phone interview by the author, Paris, June 22, 2020, digital recording.
10. Reuben, *Everything You Always*, 5.
11. Reuben, *Everything You Always*, 194.
12. Judy Klemesrud, "Plain Brown Wrappers Are Out," *The New York Times*, August 15, 1970, https://www.nytimes.com/1970/08/15/archives/plain -brown-wrappers-are-out.html.
13. Richard Lingeman, "American Notebook," *The New York Times*, March 1, 1970, https://www.nytimes.com/1970/03/01/archives/american -notebook-selling-sex.html.
14. Paul Showers, "In Brief: Sex," *The New York Times*, February 1, 1970, https://www.nytimes.com/1970/02/01/archives/in-brief-sex.html.
15. Lavin, "Everything You Always Wanted."
16. Philip H. Dougherty, "Advertising: Campbell's Heats Up Soup Pot," *The New York Times*, January 20, 1971.
17. Lavin, "Everything You Always Wanted."
18. Gore Vidal, "Number One," *The New York Review of Books*, June 4, 1970.
19. Lingeman, "American Notebook."
20. Lavin, "Everything You Always Wanted."
21. Lavin, "Everything You Always Wanted."
22. David Smith Allyn, *Make Love, Not War: The Sexual Revolution, an Unfettered History* (New York: Routledge, 2000), 175.
23. Reuben, *Everything You Always Wanted*, 53.
24. Reuben, *Everything You Always Wanted*, 306.
25. Allyn, *Make Love, Not War*, 138–39.
26. Allyn, *Make Love, Not War*.
27. Reuben, *Everything You Always Wanted*, 202.

28. Reuben, *Everything You Always Wanted*.
29. Reuben, *Everything You Always Wanted*, 129.
30. Reuben, *Everything You Always Wanted*, 132.
31. Reuben, *Everything You Always Wanted*, 134.
32. Reuben, *Everything You Always Wanted*, 135.
33. Reuben, *Everything You Always Wanted*, 147.
34. Reuben, *Everything You Always Wanted*, 286.
35. Reuben, *Everything You Always Wanted*.
36. Reuben, *Everything You Always Wanted*, 287.
37. Judge Leon M. Bazile, "Indictment for Felony," court records, reproduction from microfilm, January 6, 1959, *Caroline County (Va.) Commonwealth v. Richard Perry Loving and Mildred Dolores Jeter*, 1958–1966, Caroline County (Va.) Reel 79, Local Government Records Collection, Caroline County Court Records, Library of Virginia.
38. Gretchen Livingston and Anna Brown, "Intermarriage in the U.S. 50 Years After Loving v. Virginia," Pew Research Center's Social & Demographic Trends Project, May 18, 2017.
39. Livingston and Brown, "Intermarriage."
40. Stuart Jeffries, "Joy of Sex Gets an Update," *The Guardian*, August 21, 2002.
41. Sascha Cohen, "The Book That Changed the Way We Talk About Rape," *Time*, October 7, 2015, https://time.com/4062637/against-our-will-40/.
42. Sally Koslow, "What We Lose in Losing *Ladies' Home Journal*," *The Atlantic*, May 2, 2014, https://www.theatlantic.com/business/archive/2014/05/what-we-lose-in-losing-ladies-home-journal/361520/.
43. Jill Lepore, "Fixed," *The New Yorker*, March 29, 2010.
44. Alexandra Minna Stern et al., "California's Sterilization Survivors: An Estimate and Call for Redress," *American Journal of Public Health* 107, no. 1 (2017): 50–54, https://doi.org/10.2105/AJPH.2016.303489.
45. Lepore, "Fixed."
46. Lepore, "Fixed."
47. Paul Popenoe, *Modern Marriage* (New York: Simon & Schuster, 1925), vii–viii.
48. Stefan Kühl, *The Nazi Connection: Eugenics, American Racism, and German National Socialism* (Oxford, UK: Oxford University Press, 1994), cited in Alexandra Minna Stern, *Eugenic Nation: Faults and Frontiers of Better Breeding in Modern America* (Berkeley: University of California Press, 2005).
49. Lepore, "Fixed."
50. Theodoor H. van de Velde, *Ideal Marriage: Its Physiology and Technique* (New York: Random House, 1928), preface.
51. Van de Velde, *Ideal Marriage*, 1.

52. Jane F. Gerhard, *Desiring Revolution: Second-Wave Feminism and the Rewriting of American Sexual Thought, 1920 to 1982* (New York: Columbia University Press, 2001).

53. Reuben, *Everything You Always*, 218.

54. Nancy Ordover, *American Eugenics: Race, Queer Anatomy, and the Science of Nationalism* (Minneapolis: University of Minnesota Press, 2003), 96.

55. Dr. Anna E. Ward, phone interview by the author, Paris, May 13, 2020, digital recording.

56. Eric Merkley, "Analysis: Many Americans Deeply Distrust Experts. So Will They Ignore the Warnings about Coronavirus?" *The Washington Post*, March 20, 2020.

57. Eric Merkley, "Anti-Intellectualism, Populism, and Motivated Resistance to Expert Consensus," *Public Opinion Quarterly* 84, no. 1 (Spring 2020): 24–48, https://doi.org/10.1093/poq/nfz053.

58. "Our Bodies, Ourselves: The Nine U.S. Editions," Our Bodies Ourselves, accessed June 3, 2020, https://www.ourbodiesourselves.org/publications/the-nine-u-s-editions/.

59. Beatrice Hazlehurst, "Your Slutty, Post-Woke Carrie Bradshaw," *Paper*, February 5, 2018.

60. Karley Sciortino, phone interview by the author, Paris, May 1, 2020, digital recording.

61. Dr. Anna E. Ward, "Sex and the Me Decade: Sex and Dating Advice Literature of the 1970s," *Women's Studies Quarterly* 43, nos. 3–4 (2015): 120–36.

62. David Reuben, *Everything You Always Wanted to Know About Sex* (*But Were Afraid to Ask)* (New York: David McKay, 1969), cited in Vidal, "Number One."

CHAPTER TEN

1. Micki McGee, *Self-Help Inc.: Makeover Culture in American Life* (New York: Oxford University Press, 2005), 11–12.

2. McGee, *Self-Help Inc.*

3. Stephen Covey, *The 7 Habits of Highly Effective People* (New York: Simon & Schuster, 1989), 104.

4. Louise Hay, *You Can Heal Your Life* (Carlsbad, CA: Hay House, 1984), 191.

5. Hay, *You Can Heal Your Life*, 192.

6. Mark Oppenheimer, "The Queen of the New Age," *The New York Times Magazine*, May 4, 2008.

7. Oppenheimer, "Queen of the New Age."

8. Hay, *You Can Heal Your Life*, 194.
9. Hay, *You Can Heal Your Life*, 194–96.
10. Mark S. King, phone interview by the author, Paris, May 1, 2020, digital recording.
11. King interview.
12. King interview; Colin Clews, phone interview by the author, Paris, April 30, 2020, digital recording.
13. King interview.
14. Centers for Disease Control, "20 Years of AIDS: 450,000 Americans Dead, over 1 Million Have Been Infected," National Institutes of Health, U.S. Department of Health and Human Services, May 31, 2001, https://www.cdc.gov/media/pressrel/r010601.htm.
15. King interview.
16. Oppenheimer, "Queen of the New Age."
17. Oppenheimer, "Queen of the New Age."
18. Oppenheimer, "Queen of the New Age."
19. Hay, *You Can Heal Your Life*, 79.
20. Hay, *You Can Heal Your Life*, 12.
21. Steven Sutcliffe, phone interview by the author, Paris, May 7, 2020, digital recording.
22. Wouter J. Hanegraaff, "New Age Religion and Secularization," *Numen* 47, no. 3 (2000): 289.
23. Catherine L. Albanese, *A Republic of Mind and Spirit: A Cultural History of American Metaphysical Religion* (New Haven, CT: Yale University Press, 2007).
24. Albanese, *Republic of Mind and Spirit*, 505.
25. Oppenheimer, "Queen of the New Age."
26. Gwenda Blair, "How Norman Vincent Peale Taught Donald Trump to Worship Himself," *Politico*, October 6, 2015.
27. Clayton Christensen, "My Story About Stephen Covey—Fellow Mormon, Teacher and Friend," *The Washington Post*, July 16, 2012.
28. Covey, *7 Habits of Highly Effective People*, 12.
29. Tom Peters, phone interview by the author, Paris, June 16, 2020, digital recording.
30. Covey, *7 Habits of Highly Effective People*, 12.
31. Covey, *7 Habits of Highly Effective People*, 88.
32. Lucy Kellaway, "The Highly Effective Life of Stephen Covey," *Financial Times*, July 18, 2012.
33. Sales numbers courtesy of Scott Miller, an executive vice president at FranklinCovey, May 26, 2020.
34. Scott Miller, phone interview by the author, Paris, May 26, 2020, digital recording.

35. Doug Rossinow, phone interview by the author, Paris, May 22, 2020, digital recording.

36. Jerry W. Markham, *A Financial History of Modern U.S. Corporate Scandals: From Enron to Reform* (Armonk, NY: M. E. Sharpe, 2006).

37. Benjamin Franklin, *Benjamin Franklin's Autobiography*, ed. Joyce E. Chaplin (New York: W. W. Norton, 2012), 37.

38. Robyn Meredith, "Executive Defends Downsizing," *The New York Times*, March 19, 1996.

39. Covey, *7 Habits of Highly Effective People*, 35.

40. Covey, *7 Habits of Highly Effective People*, 211.

41. Rossinow interview.

42. Rossinow interview.

43. Covey, *7 Habits of Highly Effective People*, 72.

44. Micki McGee, phone interview by the author, Paris, January 16, 2020, digital recording.

45. Leo Babauta, "Exclusive Interview: Stephen Covey on His Morning Routine, Blogs, Technology, GTD and The Secret," Zen Habits, 2008, https://zenhabits.net/exclusive-interview-stephen-covey-on-his-morning-routine-blogs-technology-gtd-and-the-secret/.

46. Babauta, "Exclusive Interview: Stephen Covey."

47. Babauta, "Exclusive Interview: Stephen Covey."

48. Babauta, "Exclusive Interview: Stephen Covey."

49. Timothy K. Smith and Ani Hadjian, "What's So Effective About Stephen Covey?," *Fortune*, December 12, 1994.

50. Covey, *7 Habits of Highly Effective People*, 241.

51. Alexis de Tocqueville, *Democracy in America* (New York: G. Dearborn, 1835–40), 144.

52. Jia Tolentino, *Trick Mirror: Reflections on Self-Delusion* (New York: Random House, 2019), 63.

EPILOGUE

1. Jonathan Cott, "The Cosmos: An Interview with Carl Sagan," *Rolling Stone*, December 25, 1980.

Selected Bibliography

Albanese, Catherine L. *A Republic of Mind and Spirit: A Cultural History of American Metaphysical Religion*. New Haven, CT: Yale University Press, 2007.

Allyn, David Smith. *Make Love, Not War: The Sexual Revolution, an Unfettered History*. New York: Routledge, 2000.

Arendt, Hannah. *On Revolution*. London: Faber & Faber, 1963.

Babauta, Leo. "Exclusive Interview: Stephen Covey on His Morning Routine, Blogs, Technology, GTD and The Secret." Zen Habits, 2008. https://zenhabits.net/exclusive-interview-stephen-covey-on-his-morning-routine-blogs-technology-gtd-and-the-secret/.

Bailey, Richard W. *Speaking American: A History of English in the United States*. Oxford, UK: Oxford University Press, 2012.

Baker, Jennifer Jordan. "Benjamin Franklin's 'Autobiography' and the Credibility of Personality." *Early American Literature* 35, no. 3 (2000): 274–93. www.jstor.org/stable/25057205.

Barker, Meg-John, Rosalind Clair Gill, and Laura Harvey. *Mediated Intimacy: Sex Advice in Media Culture*. Cambridge, UK: Polity, 2018.

Beecher, Catharine Esther. *The Duty of American Women to Their Country*. New York: Harper & Brothers, 1845.

———. *An Essay on the Education of Female Teachers*. New York: Van Nostrand & Dwight, 1835.

———. *An Essay on Slavery and Abolitionism, with Reference to the Duty of American Females*. Philadelphia: Henry Perkins, 1837.

———. "How to Redeem Woman's Profession from Dishonor." *Harper's Magazine*, November 1865.

———. *A Treatise on Domestic Economy*. New York: Harper & Brothers, 1841.

Beecher, Catharine Esther, and Harriet Beecher Stowe. *The American Woman's Home: or, Principles of Domestic Science*. New York: J. B. Ford, 1869.

Beecher, Lyman. *A Plea for the West*. Cincinnati: Truman & Smith, 1835.

Books That Shaped America. Exhibition, Library of Congress, Washington, D.C., June 25–September 29, 2012.

Bowen, Catherine Drinker. *The Most Dangerous Man in America: Scenes from the Life of Benjamin Franklin*. Boston: Little, Brown, 1974.

Bullough, Vern L. "An Early American Sex Manual, or, Aristotle Who?" *Early American Literature* 7, no. 3 (1973): 236–46. www.jstor.org/stable/25070583.

Burstyn, Joan N. "Catharine Beecher and the Education of American Women." *The New England Quarterly* 47, no. 3 (1974): 386–403. www.jstor.org/stable /364378.

Carnegie, Dale. Letter to Donna Carnegie, January 30, 1952. Courtesy of Dale Carnegie & Associates.

———. *How to Stop Worrying and Start Living*. New York: Simon & Schuster, 1948.

———. *How to Win Friends and Influence People*. New York: Simon & Schuster, 1936.

Cassedy, Tim. "'A Dictionary Which We Do Not Want': Defining America Against Noah Webster, 1783–1810." *The William and Mary Quarterly* 71, no. 2 (2014): 229–54.

Child, Lydia Maria. *The American Frugal Housewife*. Boston: Marsh & Capen; Carter & Hendee, 1829.

Christensen, Clayton. "My Story About Stephen Covey—Fellow Mormon, Teacher and Friend." *The Washington Post*, July 16, 2012. https://www.wash ingtonpost.com/national/on-leadership/my-story-about-stephen-covey— fellow-mormon-teacher-and-friend/2012/07/16/gJQAR2QPpW_story.html.

Claridge, Laura. *Emily Post: Daughter of the Gilded Age, Mistress of American Manners*. New York: Random House, 2008.

Cott, Nancy F. *The Bonds of Womanhood: "Woman's Sphere" in New England, 1780–1835*. New Haven, CT: Yale University Press, 1977.

Covey, Stephen. *The 7 Habits of Highly Effective People*. New York: Simon & Schuster, 1989.

Cumming, Adelaide Fish Hawley. Papers, 1922–67. Schlesinger Library, Radcliffe Institute, Harvard University, Cambridge, MA.

Curtis, William. "Some Recent Books." *Town & Country*, September 1, 1922. Courtesy of the Emily Post Institute.

Denker, David. "American Almanacs in the Eighteenth Century." *The Journal of the Rutgers University Libraries* (1954): 12–25. https://ejbe.libraries.rutgers .edu/index.php/jrul/article/viewFile/1328/2765.

Douglass, Frederick. *Narrative of the Life of Frederick Douglass, an American Slave.* Boston: Anti-Slavery Office, 1845.

"Dr. McGuffey, the Man Behind the Readers." *The New York Times*, April 29, 1923. https://timesmachine.nytimes.com/timesmachine/1923/04/29/105860653.

"Dr. Reuben and His Wife: 'We Agree on Everything.'" *The New York Times*, July 13, 1971. https://www.nytimes.com/1971/07/13/archives/dr-reuben-and-his -wife-we-agree-on-everything.html.

Dunbar-Ortiz, Roxanne. *An Indigenous Peoples' History of the United States.* Boston: Beacon Press, 2014.

Ehrenreich, Barbara. *Bright-Sided: How the Relentless Promotion of Positive Thinking Has Undermined America.* New York: Henry Holt, 2009.

Ellison, Ralph. "The Golden Age of Jazz: Time Past." *Esquire*, January 1959.

Etter, Sarah. "Probing Question: How Did Regional Accents Originate?" *Penn State News*, August 2005. https://news.psu.edu/story/141216/2005/08/29/re search/probing-question-how-did-regional-accents-originate.

Evans, William B. "John Adams' Opinion of Benjamin Franklin." *The Pennsylvania Magazine of History and Biography* 92, no. 2 (1968): 220–38. www.jstor.org /stable/20090161.

Frank, Jenifer. "Hartford's Nook Farm." Connecticut History: A CTHumanities Project, June 5, 2014. https://connecticuthistory.org/hartfords-nook-farm/.

Franklin, Benjamin. *Benjamin Franklin's Autobiography: An Authoritative Text, Backgrounds, Criticism.* Edited by J. A. Leo Lemay and P. M. Zall. New York: W. W. Norton, 1986.

———. *Benjamin Franklin's Autobiography.* Edited by Joyce E. Chaplin. New York: W. W. Norton, 2012.

———. *Fart Proudly: Writings of Benjamin Franklin You Never Read in School.* Edited by Carl Japikse. New York: Penguin Random House, 2003.

———. Letter to Mary Stevenson, November 28, 1768. Papers of Benjamin Franklin, 1706–1790, Yale University Library. New Haven, CT. https:// franklinpapers.yale.edu/.

———. Letter to Mary Stevenson, September 14, 1767. Papers of Benjamin Franklin, 1706–1790. Yale University Library, New Haven, CT. https:// franklinpapers.yale.edu/.

———. Letter to Sarah Franklin Bache, June 3, 1779. Papers of Benjamin Franklin, 1706–1790. Yale University Library, New Haven, CT. https://franklinpa pers.yale.edu/.

———. *Poor Richard's Almanack.* Philadelphia: Benjamin Franklin New Printing Office, 1732.

———. Positions to be Examined, April 4, 1769. Papers of Benjamin Franklin, 1706–1790. Yale University Library, New Haven, CT. https://franklinpapers .yale.edu/.

Fraser, James W. *Between Church and State: Religion and Public Education in Multicultural America*. Baltimore, MD: Johns Hopkins University Press, 1999.

Friedan, Betty. *The Feminine Mystique*. New York: W. W. Norton, 1963.

Garfinkel, Susan. "Finding Franklin: A Resource Guide." Library of Congress, Washington, D.C., 2016. https://www.loc.gov/rr/program/bib/franklin/autobiography.html.

Gates, Paul W. "Problems of Agricultural History, 1790–1840." *Agricultural History* 46, no. 1 (1972): 33–58. www.jstor.org/stable/3741556.

General Mills. *Betty Crocker's Picture Cookbook*. New York: McGraw-Hill, 1950.

———. *Betty Crocker History*. Pamphlet. Minneapolis, MN, 1954. Courtesy of the General Mills Archive.

———. *Betty Crocker Research Project*. Minneapolis, MN: General Mills, 1953. Courtesy of the General Mills Archive.

———. Betty Crocker Letters, 1940–1950. Courtesy of the General Mills Archive.

———. *Homemakers Creed of the Home Legion*. Brochure. Minneapolis, MN, 1944. Courtesy of the General Mills Archive.

———. *Market Survey*. Minneapolis, MN, 1953. Courtesy of the General Mills Archive.

———. *Our Nation's Rations*. Script. NBC, March 14, 1945. Courtesy of the General Mills Archive.

———. *Our Nation's Rations*. Script. NBC, January 1946. Courtesy of the General Mills Archive.

———. *Point Stretchers*. Pamphlet. Minneapolis, MN, ca. 1940s. Schlesinger Library on the History of Women in America, Radcliffe Institute for Advanced Study. Courtesy of the General Mills Archive.

———. *War Work: A Daybook for the Home*. Brochure. Minneapolis, MN, 1942. Schlesinger Library on the History of Women in America, Radcliffe Institute for Advanced Study. Courtesy of the General Mills Archive.

———. *War Work (The Second Year): A Daybook for the Home*. Brochure. Minneapolis, MN, 1943. Schlesinger Library on the History of Women in America, Radcliffe Institute for Advanced Study. Courtesy of the General Mills Archive.

———. *Your Responsibility as a Betty Crocker Girl*. Pamphlet. Minneapolis, MN, ca. 1950–60. Courtesy of the General Mills Archive.

Gerhard, Jane F. *Desiring Revolution: Second-Wave Feminism and the Rewriting of American Sexual Thought, 1920 to 1982*. New York: Columbia University Press, 2001.

Goffman, Erving. *The Presentation of the Self in Everyday Life*. New York: Doubleday, 1956.

Goldin, Claudia, *Understanding the Gender Gap: An Economic History of American Women*, cited in Susan M. Hartmann, "Women's Employment and the Domestic Ideal." In *Not June Cleaver: Women and Gender in Postwar America*,

1945–1960, edited by Joanne Meyerowitz, 84–100. Philadelphia: Temple University Press, 1994.

Goldston, Robert C. *The Great Depression: The United States in the Thirties.* Indianapolis, IN: Bobbs-Merrill, 1968.

Griffith, John. "Franklin's Sanity and the Man Behind the Masks." In *The Oldest Revolutionary: Essays on Benjamin Franklin*, edited by J. A. Leo Lemay. Philadelphia: University of Pennsylvania Press. 1976.

Gutis, Philip S. "Marjorie Husted Dead at 94, Helped Create Betty Crocker." *New York Times*, December 28, 1986. https://www.nytimes.com/1986/12/28/obituaries/marjorie-husted-dead-at-94-helped-create-betty-crocker.html.

Hackett, Alice Payne, and James Henry Burke. *80 Years of Best Sellers (1895–1975).* New York: R. R. Bowker, 1977.

Hagedorn, Thomas. *Founding Zealots: How Evangelicals Created America's First Public Schools 1783–1865.* Maitland, FL: Xulon Press, 2013.

Haitch, Richard. "Follow Up on the News; McGuffey Revival." *New York Times*, April 3, 1983. https://www.nytimes.com/1983/04/03/nyregion/follow-up-on-the-news-mcguffey-revival.html.

Hale, Judson D. *The Best of the Old Farmer's Almanac: The First 200 Years.* New York: Random House, 1991.

Hanegraaff, Wouter J. "New Age Religion and Secularization." *Numen* 47, no. 3 (2000).

Harriman, Margaret Case. "He Sells Hope." *Saturday Evening Post*, August 14, 1937.

Hay, Louise. *You Can Heal Your Life.* Carlsbad, CA: Hay House, 1984.

"History of *The Old Farmer's Almanac*." *Old Farmer's Almanac*, August 4, 2016. https://www.almanac.com/content/history-old-farmers-almanac.

"History of Yankee Publishing." Yankee Publishing, July 5, 2019. https://ypi.com/history

Hofstadter, Richard. *The Age of Reform.* New York: Vintage Books, 1955.

———. *Anti-Intellectualism in American Life.* New York: Vintage Books, 1962.

———. "The Myth of the Happy Yeoman." *American Heritage*, April 1956.

Hoover, J. Edgar. Letter to Betty Crocker, April 16, 1945. Courtesy of the General Mills Archive.

Husted, Marjorie Child. Records of the Arthur and Elizabeth Schlesinger Library on the History of Women in America, 1942–2017, RG XVIII, Ser. 2.1, Box 10. Schlesinger Library on the History of Women in America, Radcliffe Institute for Advanced Study.

"Introduction to Yankee Magazine First Issue in 1935." New England Today. *Yankee*, November 9, 2018. https://newengland.com/yankee-magazine/living/new-england-history/introducing-yankee/.

Isaacson, Walter. *Benjamin Franklin: An American Life.* New York: Simon & Schuster, 2003.

Jefferson, Thomas. *Notes on the State of Virginia*. Boston: Lilly and Wait, 1832. Pdf. https://www.loc.gov/item/03004902/.

———. Letter to John Jay, Paris, France, August 23, 1785, housed at the Library of Congress Manuscript Division, Washington, DC.

Johar, Marzuki Jamil Baki Bin Haji Mohamed. "Benjamin Franklin and His Critics: John Adams, Mark Twain, and David Herbert Lawrence." Master's thesis, Eastern Illinois University, 1997.

Kellaway, Lucy. "The Highly Effective Life of Stephen Covey." *Financial Times*, July 18, 2012.

Kendall, Joshua. *The Forgotten Founding Father: Noah Webster's Obsession and the Creation of an American Culture*. New York: G. P. Putnam's Sons, 2010.

———. "Redefining Webster's." *Johns Hopkins Magazine*, February 28, 2011.

Kittredge, George. *The Old Farmer and His Almanack*. Cambridge, MA: Harvard University Press, 1904.

Lavin, Cheryl. "Everything You Always Wanted to Know About Dr. David Reuben." *Chicago Tribune*, February 23, 1999.

Lawrence, D. H. *Studies in Classic American Literature*. New York: Thomas Seltzer, 1923.

Leavitt, Sarah. *From Catharine Beecher to Martha Stewart: A Cultural History of Domestic Advice*. Chapel Hill: University of North Carolina Press, 2002.

Lemay, J. A. Leo. "Franklin and the Autobiography: An Essay on Recent Scholarship." *Eighteenth-Century Studies* 1, no. 2 (1967): 185–211.

Lepore, Jill. "Fixed." *The New Yorker*, March 29, 2010.

———. "Noah's Mark." *The New Yorker*, October 30, 2006.

———. *These Truths*. New York: W. W. Norton, 2018.

Letters to Betty Crocker, 1940–1950, General Mills Archives.

Libman Block, Jean. "The Secret Life of Betty Crocker." *Woman's Home Companion*, December 1952.

Loewen, James W. *Lies My Teacher Told Me*. New York: Touchstone, 1995.

Marks, Susan. *Finding Betty Crocker: The Secret Life of America's First Lady of Food*. New York: Simon & Schuster, 2005.

Martin, Peter. *The Dictionary Wars: The American Fight over the English Language*. Princeton, NJ: Princeton University Press, 2019.

Matthews, Glenna. *"Just a Housewife": The Rise and Fall of Domesticity in America*. New York: Oxford University Press, 1987.

McCulloch, Gretchen. *Because Internet: Understanding the Rules of Language*. New York: Riverhead Books, 2019.

McGee, Micki. *Self-Help Inc.: Makeover Culture in American Life*. New York: Oxford University Press, 2005.

McGuffey, Alexander. *McGuffey's Rhetorical Guide or Fifth Reader*. Cincinnati, OH: Truman & Smith, 1844.

McGuffey, William Holmes. *The Eclectic Readers*. Cincinnati, OH: Truman & Smith, 1836–37.

McIntosh, Elaine. *American Food Habits in Historical Perspective*. Westport, CT: Praeger, 1995.

McParland, Robert. *Bestseller: A Century of America's Favorite Books*. London: Rowman & Littlefield, 2019.

Melville, Herman. *Israel Potter*. New York: G. P. Putnam, 1855.

Minnich, Harvey. *William Holmes McGuffey and His Readers*. New York: American Book Company, 1936.

Mugglestone, Lynda. *Dictionaries: A Very Short Introduction*. Oxford, UK: Oxford University Press, 2011.

Mulford, Carla. "Figuring Benjamin Franklin in American Cultural Memory." *The New England Quarterly* 72, no. 3 (1999): 415–43. https://doi.org/10.2307/366890.

Neem, Johann N. *Democracy's Schools: The Rise of Public Education in America*. Baltimore, MD: Johns Hopkins University Press, 2017.

———. "The Strange Afterlife of William McGuffey and His Readers." *The Hedgehog Review*, Summer 2018.

Oppenheimer, Mark. "The Queen of the New Age." *The New York Times Magazine*, May 4, 2008. https://www.nytimes.com/2008/05/04/magazine/04Hay-t.html.

Ostler, Rosemarie. *Founding Grammars: How Early America's War over Words Shaped Today's Language*. New York: St. Martin's Press, 2015.

———. "Trial by Stagecoach." *American History* 52, no. 5 (December 2017): 44–51.

Paul, Heike. "Pilgrims and Puritans and the Myth of the Promised Land." In *The Myths That Made America: An Introduction to American Studies*. Transcript Verlag, 2014, 137–96.

Perkins, Jeanne. "Close Up: Emily Post." *Life*, May 6, 1946. Courtesy of the Emily Post Institute.

Popenoe, Paul. *Modern Marriage*. New York: Simon & Schuster, 1925.

Porter, Katherine Anne. "Etiquette in Action." *New-York Tribune*, December 26, 1925. Courtesy of the Emily Post Institute.

Post, Edwin. *Truly Emily Post*. New York: Funk & Wagnalls, 1961.

Post, Emily. *By Motor to the Golden Gate*. New York: Appleton, 1916.

———. *Etiquette in Society, in Business, in Politics and at Home*. New York: Funk & Wagnalls, 1922.

———. Family photo album, 1895. Courtesy of the Emily Post Institute.

———. *The Flight of a Moth*. New York: Dodd, Mead, 1904.

———. "Mrs. Post's Own Story About Herself." *The Bell Syndicate*, n.d. Courtesy of the Emily Post Institute.

———. Scrapbooks, 1895–1960. Courtesy of the Emily Post Institute.

Rawson, Hugh. "Slang." *American Heritage*, October 2003.

Raymond, Allan R. "To Reach Men's Minds: Almanacs and the American Revolution, 1760–1777." *The New England Quarterly* 51, no. 3 (1978): 370–95.

Reuben, David. *Everything You Always Wanted to Know About Sex* (*But Were Afraid to Ask)*. New York: David McKay, 1969.

Rindlaub, Jean Wade. Papers, ca. 1848–1991. Schlesinger Library, Radcliffe Institute, Harvard University, Cambridge, MA.

Robbins, L. H. "Counselor & Friend." *The New York Times*, March 9, 1947, sec. SM, 18. https://www.nytimes.com/1947/03/09/archives/counselor-friend-the-farmers-almanac-has-offered-wisdom-wit-and.html.

Rothenberg, Winifred B. "The Market and Massachusetts Farmers, 1750–1855." *The Journal of Economic History* 41, no. 2 (1981): 283–314.

Sagendorph, Robb. *America and Her Almanacs*. Dublin, NH: Yankee, 1970.

Saunders, Judith P. "The Autobiography of Benjamin Franklin: The Story of a Successful Social Animal." In *American Classics: Evolutionary Perspectives*, 1–22. Boston: Academic Studies Press, 2018. https://www.jstor.org/stable/j.ctv4v3226.6.

Schlesinger, Arthur. *Learning How to Behave: A Historical Study of American Etiquette Books*. New York: Macmillan, 1946.

Scudder, Horace E. *American Men of Letters: Noah Webster*. Cambridge, MA: Riverside Press, 1881.

———. "Franklin, Washington, Lincoln." *The Atlantic*, November 1889.

Seavey, Ormond. *Becoming Benjamin Franklin: The Autobiography and the Life*. University Park: Pennsylvania State University Press, 1988.

Shapiro, Laura. *Something from the Oven: Reinventing Dinner in 1950s America*. New York: Viking Penguin, 2004.

Sheidlower, Jesse. "The Closing of a Great American Dialect Project." *The New Yorker*, September 22, 2017. https://www.newyorker.com/culture/cultural-comment/the-closing-of-a-great-american-dialect-project.

Shenker-Osorio, Anat. "Why Americans All Believe They Are 'Middle Class.'" *The Atlantic*, August 1, 2013.

Shumsky, Neil Larry. "Noah Webster and the Invention of Immigration." *The New England Quarterly* 81, no. 1 (2008): 126–35. www.jstor.org/stable/20474606.

Silverman, David J. *This Land Is Their Land: The Wampanoag Indians, Plymouth Colony, and the Troubled History of Thanksgiving*. New York: Bloomsbury, 2019.

Skinner, David. *The Story of Ain't: America, Its Language, and the Most Controversial Dictionary Ever Published*. New York: HarperCollins, 2012.

Sklar, Kathryn Kish. *Catharine Beecher: A Study in American Domesticity*. New York: Norton, 1976.

Skrabec, Quentin. *The Ohio Presidents: Eight Men and a Binding Political Philosophy in the White House, 1841–1923*. Jefferson, NC: McFarland, 2018.

———. *William McGuffey: Mentor to American Industry*. Sanford, NC: Algora, 2009.

Smith, Helena Huntington. "Lady Chesterfield." *The New Yorker*, August 16, 1930.

Smith, Henry Nash. *Virgin Land: The American West as Symbol and Myth*. Cambridge, MA: Harvard University Press, 1950.

Smith, Timothy K., and Ani Hadjian. "What's So Effective About Stephen Covey?." *Fortune*, December 12, 1994.

Society for the Diffusion of Useful Knowledge. *British Almanac*. London: Baldwin and Cradock, published annually, 1828–88.

"Soft Answers." *The New York Times*, February 14, 1937. https://timesmachine .nytimes.com/timesmachine/1937/02/14/issue.html.

Stavely, Keith. "What America's First Cookbook Says About Our Country and Its Cuisine." *Smithsonian*, January 12, 2018. https://www.smithsonianmag .com/history/what-americas-first-cookbook-says-about-our-country-its -cuisine.

St. John de Crèvecoeur, J. Hector. *Letters from an American Farmer: Describing Certain Provincial Situations, Manners, and Customs, Not Generally Known*. Dublin, Ireland: John Exshaw, 1782.

Strazdes, Diana. "Catharine Beecher and the American Woman's Puritan Home." *The New England Quarterly* 82, no. 3 (2009): 452–89.

Sullivan, Dolores P. *William Holmes McGuffey: Schoolmaster to the Nation*. Rutherford, NJ: Fairleigh Dickinson University Press, 1994.

"Talking the Tawk." *The New Yorker*, November 2005. https://www.newyorker .com/magazine/2005/11/14/talking-the-tawk.

Thomas, Robert B. *The Old Farmer's Almanac*. Boston: Jenks and Palmer, published annually, 1792–.

Thomas, Tracy A. *Elizabeth Cady Stanton and the Feminist Foundations of Family Law*. New York: New York University Press, 2016.

Tipton-Martin, Toni. *The Jemima Code: Two Centuries of African American Cookbooks*. Austin: Texas University Press, 2015.

Tocqueville, Alexis de. *Democracy in America*. New York: G. Dearborn, 1835–1840

Travis, Trysh. "Self-Help in America: A Project for Moral Perfection." *The American Historian*, 2017. https://www.oah.org/tah/issues/2017/august/self -help-in-america-a-project-for-moral-perfection/.

Twain, Mark. "The Late Benjamin Franklin." *The Galaxy*, July 1870.

Unger, Harlow G. *Noah Webster: The Life and Times of an American Patriot*. New York: John Wiley & Sons, 1998.

Vail, Henry H. *A History of the McGuffey Readers*. Cleveland, OH: Burrows Brothers, 1911.

Van de Velde, Theodoor H. *Ideal Marriage: Its Physiology and Technique*. New York: Random House, 1928.

Van Doren, Carl. *Benjamin Franklin*. New York: Viking, 1938.

Vergennes, Charles Gravier, and Benjamin Franklin. "Contrat entre le Roi et les Treize Etats-Unis de l'Amérique Septentrionale." Paris, July 16, 1782. Papers of Benjamin Franklin, 1706–1790. Yale University Library, New Haven, CT. https://franklinpapers.yale.edu/.

Vester, Katharina. *A Taste of Power: Food and American Identities*. Berkeley: University of California Press, 2015.

Ward, Anna E. "Sex and the Me Decade: Sex and Dating Advice Literature of the 1970s." *Women's Studies Quarterly* 43, nos. 3–4 (2015): 120–36. www.jstor.org/stable/43958555.

Wardrop, Daneen. "'While I Am Writing': Webster's 1825 Spelling Book, the Ell, and Frederick Douglass's Positioning of Language." *African American Review* 32, no. 4 (1998): 649–60. https://doi.org/10.2307/2901243.

Warfel, Harry R. *Noah Webster: Schoolmaster to America*. New York: Macmillan, 1936.

Watts, Steven. *The People's Tycoon: Henry Ford and the American Century*. New York: Random House, 2005.

———. *Self-Help Messiah: Dale Carnegie and Success in Modern America*. New York: Other Press, 2013.

Webster, Noah. *An American Dictionary of the English Language*. New York: S. Converse, 1828.

———. *The American Spelling Book, Containing an Easy Standard of Pronunciation: Being the First Part of a Grammatical Institute of the English Language*. Boston: Thomas and Andrews, 1783.

———. *A Compendious Dictionary of the English Language*. Hartford, CT: Hudson and Goodwin, 1806.

———. *Dissertations on the English Language*. Boston: Isaiah Thomas, 1789.

———. Letter to Alexander McGuffey, March 3, 1837. McGuffey Collection, Walter Havighurst Special Collections, Miami University, Oxford, OH. https://digital.lib.miamioh.edu/digital/collection/mcguffey.

———. "On the Education of Youth in America." *American Magazine*, December 1787.

———. *Plan of Policy for Improving the Advantages and Perpetuating the Union of the American States*. Hartford, CT: Hudson & Goodwin, 1785.

Weisberg, Jessica. *Asking for a Friend*. New York: Bold Type Books, 2018.

White, Barbara A. *The Beecher Sisters*. New Haven, CT: Yale University Press, 2003.

Winthrop, John. Letter to Nathaniel Rich, May 22, 1634. Gilder Lehrman Institute of American History. https://www.gilderlehrman.org/collection/glc01105.

Wood, Gordon S. *The Americanization of Benjamin Franklin*. New York: Penguin Books, 2005.

Worrall, Simon. "Ben Franklin Slept Here." *Smithsonian*, March 2006. https://www.smithsonianmag.com/travel/ben-franklin-slept-here-112338695/.

Wyllie, Irvin G. *The Self-Made Man in America*. New York: Free Press, 1954.

Zaloom, Caitlin. "Does the U.S. Still Have a 'Middle Class'?" *The Atlantic*, November 4, 2018. https://www.theatlantic.com/ideas/archive/2018/11/what-does-middle-class-really-mean/574534/.

Zuckerman, Michael. "Franklin's Masks." In *Benjamin Franklin's Intellectual World*, edited by Paul E. Kerry and Matthew S. Holland. Lanham, MD: Rowman & Littlefield, 2012.

Index

Adams, John, 62, 104

AIDS, 323–24

Albanese, Catherine L., 329

Alcoholics Anonymous, 241

almanacs: competition among, 19–20; early, 28; folklore traditions of, 13–14; functions of, 29–30; political consciousness of, 30–31; popularity of, 19; religious tones in, 32–33; and rural nostalgia, 41; superstitions in, 22. See also *The Old Farmer's Almanac*

The American Frugal Housewife (Child), 160–61

The American Minerva (newspaper), 61–62

American Spelling Book (Webster): and American identity, 50–52, 54, 55–56, 131; and book tour, 52; and Christian homeschoolers, 71; critics of, 64; and Douglass, 58–59; and McGuffey Readers, 133–34; and McGuffey's education, 117; nationalist tone of, 50–51; sales/success of, 53; standardizing

influence of, 53–54; and Washington, 56; Webster's motives for writing, 46–50; writing of, 46

The American Woman's Home (Beecher and Stowe), 169–74; anti-suffrage sentiments in, 148; influence of, 148; on moral roles of women, 148, 175; social/political context of, 147–48

Ames, Nathaniel, 30, 31

Anthony, Carolyn, 295

Anthony, Susan B., 163, 170

anti-Semitism, 128, 133, 140

Aresty, Esther B., 211

Autobiography of Benjamin Franklin: and American identity, 86–87; on appearance of success, 91; candor and self-deprecation in, 92; and Carnegie, 245–46; and Covey's *7 Habits*, 333; critics of, 108–9, 111–12; deceptive aspects of, 95–96, 97; editions and reprints of, 86, 87; on financial philosophy of Franklin, 92–94; influence of, 112–13; legacy of, 106, 107; and middle class, 110;

"Can This Marriage Be Saved?"
(Popenoe), 302–5
Carlton, Osgood, 18
Carnagey, Amanda Harbison, 244–45
Carnegie, Andrew, 111, 113
Carnegie, Dale, 218–51 ; on attitude as
key to success, 238; celebrity of, 238;
and charisma, 242–44; on dogs,
237; and Franklin's *Autobiography*,
245–46; group-based approach of,
241–42; influence of, 231; legacy of,
248; mother's influence on, 244–45;
name change of, 225; and national
story of America, 5; positivity
emphasized by, 226, 231, 232–33,
236, 250; public speaking career/
classes of, 222, 223–26, 233–34,
238, 241–42, 249; resilience of, 236,
251; royalty check of, 240; shame
and anxiety of, 221–23, 225–26,
237; social awkwardness of, 237;
youth of, 218–21
Carnegie, Dorothy, 248
Cassidy, Frederic G., 76–77
Catholics and Catholicism, 122–23,
125, 128, 131, 140, 158
Cawdrey, Robert, 80
celebrity, 237–38, 243
charisma, 242–44
Child, Julia, 206
Child, Lydia Maria, 160–61, 175–76
Chinese immigrants, 136
citizenship: and Beecher/Stowe's
American Woman's Home, 174; and
Beecher's *Treatise*, 155–56; and
Betty Crocker's guidance, 262; and
domestic manuals, 160–62; and
etiquette, 208; farmers as
embodiment of, 26; and Franklin's
Autobiography, 109; and McGuffey
Readers, 125, 129; and *Old
Farmer's Almanac*, 14–15, 20, 21,
26; and Popenoe's eugenics plan,
304; and Republican motherhood,

156; and Thomas, 33; and women's
domestic manuals, 160–62
Civil War, American, 31, 137, 147–48,
167–69, 173
Claridge, Laura, 189
Clark, Tim, 11–12, 13, 22, 23, 42
Clinton, Bill, 340
Clinton, Hillary, 44, 78
Columbus, Christopher, 28, 50
Comfort, Alex, 302, 309
commercial culture, emergence of,
37–38
conformity: and *Betty Crocker's Picture
Cook Book*, 254; and domestic
manuals, 175; and Franklin's
Autobiography, 112; and Post's
Etiquette, 195, 201; and Reuben's
*Everything You Always Wanted to
Know*, 289; and social mobility, 99.
See also uniformity
Constitution of the United States, 2,
6, 7, 31
Conway, Kellyanne, 43
corporate America, 247–48
Cott, Nancy F., 164
Covey, Stephen: with Clinton at Camp
David, 340; efficiency emphasis of,
344–45; influence of, 318, 336, and
leadership training, 335–36;
Mormon background of, 332;
public speaking career of, 331–32;
research on success literature, 333;
success of, 318. See also *The 7
Habits of Highly Effective People*
COVID-19 pandemic, 81–82,
175, 250
Crocker, Betty: cooking school of,
258–59; and emotional struggles of
housewives, 279–81; friendship
sentiments inspired by, 258–59,
260, 262–64, 279–80, 284, 286; on
happiness, 280–81; and Home
Legion campaign, 265–66;
Husted's role in crafting image of,

257–58, 265; on importance of
women's work, 256–57; influence
of, 253–54, 259, 271, 283, 285–86;
invention of, 255, 284; letters
exchanged with, 253, 255, 258–60,
261, 262–64, 265, 279–80; as
marketing fiction, 253; name
recognition of, 282, 283; pamphlets
of, 261–62, 265; popularity of, 260;
portraits of, 275; on postwar
transition to homemaking, 267–68;
products of, 276–77; radio
programs of, 255–56, 258, 260,
265; relatability of, 283–84; success
of, 256, 282; women taken
seriously by, 264; and World War
II era, 252–53, 260–67. See also
Betty Crocker's Picture Cook Book
Crockett, Davy, 88
Crom, J. Oliver, 248
cult of domesticity: Beecher's
advocacy of, 156, 164, 165, 169,
172, 176; and *Betty Crocker's Picture
Cook Book*, 254; emergence of, 149;
and Emily Post, 183; General
Mills's revival of, 281–82, 285; and
reality of antebellum America,
162. *See also* Crocker, Betty;
domestic manuals and literature
culture of America: and debates on
schoolbooks, 138; determinants of,
134; and immigrant population,
136–37; and national myths,
134–35; sense of loss of, 142; and
Webster, 2, 45
Cumming, Adelaide Hawley, 284
Cushing, William, 101

Darwin, Charles, 141
A Date with a Dish (De Knight), 273
Davis, Donald D., 261
Davis, Joshua Clark, 293
Declaration of Independence, US, 7, 15

Delvey, Anna, 113
de Tocqueville, Alexis, 206–7, 345
dialects, 48, 56–57, 61, 68, 76–77
dictionaries: and Dictionary Wars, 72;
functions of, 80–81; and
nonstandard/slang language,
80–81; and vernacular English,
76–77. See also *Merriam-Webster's
Dictionary*; *Webster's Dictionary*
*Dictionary of American Regional
English (DARE)*, 77
Didion, Joan, 204
Dilworth, Thomas, 48
diversity in authors, lack of, 6
domestic manuals and literature:
expansion of formats, 165–66;
goals of, 150; and home-as-haven
sentiment, 174–75; influence of,
175–76, 177; of nineteenth century,
159–62; popularity of, 149; and
Post's *Etiquette*, 183; and slavery,
166–67, 173; and women's place in
the American project, 160–62. See
also *The American Woman's Home*;
Betty Crocker's Picture Cook Book; *A
Treatise on Domestic Economy*
Douglass, Frederick, 58–59
Du Bois, W. E. B., 40
Dunbar-Ortiz, Roxanne, 27
Dyer, Wayne, 325, 331

education and public schools: in
American South, 61; Beecher's
advocacy for women as students/
educators, 150–51, 152–53,
154–56, 158–59, 163–64, 176–77;
and Bible Wars, 131–32, 142;
common school movement, 123,
129–31, 142, 164; and debates on
schoolbooks, 138–39, 143;
dictionaries' function in, 75, 80–81;
and home economics movement,
176–77; and homeschoolers, 71,

About the Author

Jess McHugh is a writer and researcher whose work has appeared in a variety of national and international publications, including *The New York Times, The Wall Street Journal, The Washington Post, The Nation, Time, The Paris Review, The Guardian, The New Republic, New York Magazine's The Cut, Fortune, The Village Voice, The Believer,* and *Lapham's Quarterly,* among others. She has reported stories from four continents on a range of cultural and historical topics, from present-day Liverpool punks to the history of 1960s activists in Greenwich Village.